A FEW THOUSAND DOLLARS

A FEW THOUSAND DOLLARS

SPARKING PROSPERITY FOR EVERYONE

Robert E. Friedman

THE NEW PRESS

NEW YORK
LONDON

Published in the United States by The New Press, New York, 2018
Distributed by Two Rivers Distribution

ISBN 978-1-62097-404-9 (ebook)

LIBRARY OF CONGRESS CATALOGING-IN-PUBLICATION DATA
Names: Friedman, Robert (Robert E.), author.
Title: A few thousand dollars : sparking prosperity for everyone / Robert E. Friedman.
Description: New York : New Press, [2018] | Includes bibliographical references and index.
Identifiers: LCCN 2018017794 | ISBN 9781620974032 (hardcover : alk. paper)
Subjects: LCSH: Poverty--United States. | Capitalism--United States. | Entrepreneurship--United States. | Economic assistance, Domestic--United States. | Economic development--United States.
Classification: LCC HC110.P6 F75 2018 | DDC 339.20973--dc23 LC record available at https://lccn.loc.gov/2018017794

The New Press publishes books that promote and enrich public discussion and understanding of the issues vital to our democracy and to a more equitable world. These books are made possible by the enthusiasm of our readers; the support of a committed group of donors, large and small; the collaboration of our many partners in the independent media and the not-for-profit sector; booksellers, who often hand-sell New Press books; librarians; and above all by our authors.

www.thenewpress.com

Book design and composition by Bookbright Media
This book was set in Janson Text and Gill Sans

Printed in the United States of America

10 9 8 7 6 5 4 3 2 1

Contents

Prosperity Stories and Illustrations

Prosperity Stories

Illustrations

To the women on the bus,
And the millions like them,
Who ought to have the chance
To live their dreams and
Realize the promise of America

I

Wealth

Real wealth is the confidence, competence, connections, and capital to make choices, meet responsibilities to others, pursue dreams, and make mistakes knowing it is possible to recover, learn, and try again. The enduring source of real wealth is people.

All people, including people who are often overlooked, have a stake in wealth creation. Some measure of liquid financial assets is the prerequisite for participating in the economy. Opening the mainstream economy to those who are systematically excluded from participating in it is perhaps the most transformative and effective way of growing the economy from the bottom up.

In 1971, on a bus from Decatur to downtown Atlanta, I learned something valuable about economic participation. Midafternoon, African American maids filled the bus. There were about thirty or so, mostly napping between jobs. These women appeared to me tired, proud, brave, wise, strong. As I got off the bus, three of the women preceded me, each unique, their hard-earned character etched on their faces. As luck would have it, they were going to the bank, as I was. I lined up behind them in the teller line and watched as one after the other presented a wrinkled envelope filled with change and a few stray bills to the teller. When I got to the front, I asked, "What was that?"

"It's our Christmas Club," the teller informed me. "We're helping them save for presents for their kids at Christmas."

"That's cool," I said. "What interest rate do you pay?"

"Oh, we don't pay interest. This is a free service we provide to help."

I was outraged. How could a financial system value the dollar of a poor person less than that of the wealthy? Should not a financial system serve low-income people as well as their better-off counterparts?

When I look back on my work since that point, I realize that all of it has aimed to honor, recognize, and liberate those women on that bus, and millions like them, who work and sacrifice, dream and hope, but are never really given a chance.

I have learned to believe in the unique power of markets and capitalism to attract and deploy capital, to innovate, add value, create and build great enterprises, stimulate competition to reduce costs and increase returns, and at their best embrace the talents of people and increase the general welfare. I have believed enough in markets to raise suspicion on the left. I also believe in government, nonprofits, and households as necessary and crucial partners in creating and sustaining a resilient and vibrant economy. Government is necessary to curb market excesses, but even more to create the infrastructure, regulation, institutions, laws, and common investments that make markets fair and inclusive—that make them work. I have witnessed how government builds markets through interventions as ingenious and valuable as the GI Bill, funding the creation of the internet, combating predatory lending, and extending competent financial services to all. That belief has raised suspicion of me on the right. But I remain convinced that this path advances core values of right and left alike.

It is often a long distance between governments, markets, and households, so the connections, innovations, and services of the independent sector are essential. Too often we think of economic progress as dependent solely on the business and financial sector, but what would our economy and society look like without schools, health care, and Social Security? Social innovation has spawned a huge share of progress.[1] "In the long story of human history," notes Michael Sherraden, "*massive social innovations have created conditions that make technological and economic advancements possible.* It is not the other way around."[2] Last, too often overlooked, but crucial are individuals and families themselves, the great means and ends to economic progress.

Prosperity Now, founded in 1979 as the Corporation for Enterprise Development (CFED), became the vehicle for me to work to unleash economic potential. CFED dug into its mission of working with real families and real communities to increase economic opportunity. Our work eventually resulted in our theory and practice of change: find strategies that might move millions of families toward economic independence by virtue of their own ideas and energy; develop and test those strategies on the ground in partnership with community practitioners backed by appropriate applied research; and, when we knew that they worked, determine how best to move them to scale through public policy development and advocacy. The ultimate goal was to expand the private marketplace with new energy and new ideas by moving people previously on the margins into the mainstream economy as producers creating wealth.

From the beginning, the organization, like this book, has been focused on solutions. Prosperity Now's strategy is a triangle of community practice, public policy, and private

Robert E. Friedman

The day I was born, I was worth more than my father—a former Navy Seabee who became an architect and who was lured from New York by the California dream. The money came from my mom's side of the family, from selling pants, leading Levi Strauss & Co. from a small dry goods supplier to gold rush miners to one of the largest clothing suppliers in the world. My grandmother instructed my mom, "You have money. Don't brag about it. *[You didn't earn it.]* Don't be ashamed of it. *[It was earned honestly.]* Use it well."

The economic legacy from my family meant that I was expected to go to college; indeed, I went to Harvard College and Yale Law School, and graduated debt free. It meant that I didn't have to work just to support myself, and could ask instead what was worth doing. It meant I could buy a house and afford to found the nonprofit Corporation for Enterprise Development (which became Prosperity Now), even when I knew little about what building a nonprofit required. It meant that I could to devote my life to creating for others some measure of the opportunities I was given.

Even more valuable than the financial assets my family passed on to me were the family values. One of the most important values was putting people at the center of wealth creation. Levi Strauss & Co. was at one point the largest and most admired apparel brand in the world. Not just because it was financially successful, but because it was a model of doing well by doing good. During the Great Depression, unneeded sewing machine operators were kept on at full pay polishing the floors in the Valencia Street factory. In the 1950s, as the company built manufacturing plants in the Jim Crow South, the company would only consider communities that would agree to integrated plants. In the 1980s, when even folks in San Francisco thought AIDS could be transferred by shaking hands, the company began its work to combat discrimination and advance prevention and treatment for HIV. In more recent years, Levi Strauss & Co. was one of the first to develop supplier terms of engagement to ensure responsibility and implement worker and family protection practices throughout the supply chain. I got to serve on the board of directors at a heady and then vexing time in the 1990s. The company was a $6 billion firm aspiring to grow to a $10 billion firm; it promised every employee one year's salary if it made the goal. It never did. Confronted by new competition from above (Gucci, Diesel), below (Gap and Old Navy), the sides (vertically integrated stores such as H&M), and overseas, the company-owned U.S. plants, long a comparative advantage, were eliminated, and Levi Strauss & Co. shrank back to a $4 billion company. This change was not because of our values but because we fell asleep as the world transformed. Today, two decades later, Levi Strauss & Co. is rising again, expanding from its core, changing the world, a testament to the renewing power of resilience and enduring values.

My family has shared our good fortune with the San Francisco community. My forebears helped create the civic Bay Area we know today: Levi Strauss & Co., Wells Fargo Bank, Stern Grove, Chrissy Field, the San Francisco Foundation, the AIDS Memorial Grove, the Council for Civic Unity, Temple Emanuel, the ballet, the symphony, and many other Jewish and civic institutions and progressive causes in San Francisco and beyond. They helped support the Hebrew Free Loan Fund, which was established in 1897 to provide college, business, and home loans to Jews at a time when mainstream lenders refused to do so.

Why this sense of responsibility to the larger community? It goes back generations—to days when my Jewish forebears banded together to support one another against the increasing anti-Semitism of Bavaria and Latvia—and extends forward to future generations. My maternal grandfather, Daniel E. Koshland Sr., and my great-uncle Walter A. Haas Sr. took a failing firm—their first exercise, in fact, was to do the accounting to figure out that the company was losing money on each pair of bib overalls it sold—and transformed the company. Uncle Walter was, for most of his adult life, the CEO and the numbers guy, the hard business mind who, well into his eighties, could look at a spreadsheet and recall every number on the page. My grandfather preferred the backseat, serving as vice president and number two, giving anonymously, overseeing human resources and community relations. When he was seventy years old and I toured the Levi Strauss factory on Valencia Street with him, he could still recall the name of every sewing machine operator and often the names of their husbands and children. He not only oversaw Levi Strauss & Co.'s labor policy but also for years served on the California Labor Relations Board. Lew Butler, a community leader who considered my grandfather his mentor, recalls a trip they made together to Sacramento riding a commercial bus late at night: "Dan was so excited to be with the people on that bus that he exclaimed, louder than he thought, 'Look at the people here. They're the real people!' At which point a voice from the back of the bus rang out: 'Will you please shut up and let the real people sleep?'" My grandfather would retell that story with pleasure—for him, having a sense of humor was vital, and being able to laugh at yourself was its essence. He loved paying taxes, even though he lived in the era of 70–90 percent marginal tax rates. He figured that if he was paying a lot, he was probably doing pretty well. He also figured that his ability to do well was a function of the larger community, and so giving back was only fair.

I have been the accidental inheritor of privilege: White privilege. Male privilege. Wealth privilege. Family privilege. I was born into a rare extended family, who afforded me every opportunity to develop whatever skills and pursue whatever interests I desired, with love and encouragement and security. Whenever I failed, I had the opportunity to harvest the lessons of that failure without major tribulation, and move on. I could and did take advantage of unpaid internships, even an unpaid enterprise. I had access to an unparalleled social network, one so deep in the San Francisco Bay Area that I had to escape to Atlanta to find myself, and then networks at Harvard and Yale Law School and Washington, DC. Always I had much more than a few thousand dollars to pursue my dreams. How to be responsible to privilege? Where privilege is a zero-sum game, and someone must lose for another to gain, there must be limits to the privilege of the lucky few like me. Internships must be paid if they are to truly embody equal employment and career opportunity. Confronting and ending race and gender and age discrimination must be a continuing battle. There are many realms, however, where privilege is a positive-sum game, where more is more, and we should seek to spread privilege. Democratizing asset subsidies may take some from the very richest, but nothing that makes a fundamental difference in their lives, while it opens lifelong opportunities for all and expands the economy. We can use technologies and community groups to expand connections to all. The easiest frontier to expand is to spread essential privileges to all. And of all such fundamental privileges, is the privilege of capital, of an essential nest egg.

markets, driven by ideas and strategy and disciplined by applied research and evaluation. The basic architecture of policy demonstration proved to be the essential DNA of Prosperity Now and the projects we generated: the Self-Employment Investment Demonstration during the 1980s; the American Dream Demonstration during the 1990s; the Saving for Education, Entrepreneurship, and Downpayment Initiative to develop child savings accounts of the 2000s; and Innovations in Manufactured Homes, also during the new millennium.

This methodology led us to realize some fundamental truths of development, including a practical epistemology, an appreciation of human potential, and the importance of community. Perhaps most important, it led us to recognize that development is something people do, not something that is done to them.

None of the development strategies we explored—self-employment, asset-building, Individual Development Accounts, Child Development Accounts, manufactured housing—would have gone anywhere without the ideas, energy, work, and co-investment of low-income people themselves. Whenever we have invested in the capability of low-income and even very poor people over the last forty years, we have never been disappointed. While there may be bad people and bad investments, even fraud and frailty, when projects invest in people and offer them respect, they overwhelmingly respond positively, often ingeniously. People want to do the right thing; they want to provide for their families; they want to give back; they want to do things for their kids they will not do for themselves. What they need are options to move forward.

Each of CFED's and later Prosperity Now's policy demonstrations included applied research and evaluation along with community practice and public policy. The research element expanded as the demonstration design grew to encompass many evaluation and research inquiries, including randomized controlled experiments, case studies, interviews, surveys, and data collection on participants, practice assessments, and more.[3]

Policy development and advocacy and effective practice development were, of necessity, iterative and continuing. Ultimately, the stories, behaviors, experiences, and lessons of asset-builders themselves shape the direction of the field. Their voices are the most persuasive, and the value and magic of asset-building is in their hands and minds. Paying respect and attention to these prime movers is key. Impact evaluation will always have difficulty accounting for the multiplicity of inputs and outputs, contexts and perceptions, and institutional and market constraints involved in entrepreneurship, education, homeownership, saving, and investing.

The founding of CFED marked a fundamental departure from the development of the welfare state during the twentieth century. The mainstream liberal focus of combating poverty was the provision of means-tested benefits and social services to address the perceived deficits in food, housing, employment, education, and capacities of low-income and economically marginalized people. Through these systems, people who would otherwise be hungry, homeless, and hopeless received a basic level of food, income, housing, training, and employment support. This support, however, was premised on the incapacity and deficits of low-income people, and the support was phased out as people's lives and material conditions improved. Learn, work, earn, save, invest—welfare recipients who did any and all of the things one needs to do to move forward economically would lose benefits, often precipitously. If earnings increased, welfare benefits decreased. If savings exceeded a few thousand dollars, one became ineligible for benefits. What was needed, and what CFED and later Prosperity Now focused on, was an alternative, if complementary, approach that recognized, rewarded, invested in, and built upon the capacities, energies, strengths, and accomplishments of low-income people moving forward.

In 1987, Jack Litzenberg, a legendary program officer of the Charles Stewart Mott Foundation, asked us to find out what worked in economic development.[4] We hired a very talented young researcher, Alan Okagaki, who interviewed more than two hundred program directors, welfare mothers, counselors, and unemployed teens over two years in inner-city neighborhoods in Boston, Chicago, San Antonio, Minneapolis, and Oakland. His conclusion? All the strategies and programs that worked had three characteristics in common: they built efficacy, learning, and linkage.[5]

William Nothdurft later alliterated these three critical elements into the four C's of development: confidence, competence, connections, and capital.[6] The growth and vitality of the individual, family, community, and nation arise from the confidence, competence, connections, and capital of individuals. These four interacting and reinforcing capacities unleash and drive development of productive capacity and entrepreneurship.

Development is a process for social change. Development builds fields—starting with the wealth-creating acts and personal development of common people, the nonprofit and community initiatives that liberate their efforts, then connecting with policy makers, funders, and finally the marketplace. What works in real lives and real communities attracts support across the political, economic, and social spectrum and provides the evidentiary, constituency, and advocacy base for policy change, which in turn can generate market inclusion and growth.

One major expression of this approach was the Self-Employment Investment Demonstration (SEID), which focused on the self-employment efforts of welfare recipients

Warren Hellman

Warren Hellman, the legendary investor and community leader, in many ways exemplified the successful entrepreneur. His many ventures, each impressive in its own right, together demonstrate enormous range and extraordinary depth: Lehman Brothers (president, youngest partner at twenty-eight), Hellman & Friedman (founder), San Francisco Foundation (chair), San Francisco Free Clinic (lead supporter), San Francisco Committee on Jobs (chair), Bay Citizen (founder), Hardly Strictly Bluegrass (founder and endower), The Wronglers (banjo player). He was a very successful venture capitalist and investment banker, who took Levi Strauss & Co. private, but he preferred to talk about his failures, and did so with characteristic modesty and humor. As chair of the board at Mills College, he led the board to declare that the financially challenged but distinguished women's college would go coed to address its woes, setting off fierce rebellion among students and alumni, who famously unfurled a banner that read "Warren: Go to Hell, Man," and rallied to the school's support. Two weeks after the board changed course, Warren proudly unfurled another banner: "Mills. For Women. Again." But it was the original banner he kept and treasured.

In later life, Warren enjoyed his civic and philanthropic ventures as much or more than his for-profit ones. He led efforts to reform San Francisco's troubled pension system, to the admiration of both labor and business, and the effort to build a garage in Golden Gate Park, through which he ran in the early morning most days. He was a competitive athlete for years, but after age compromised his ability to win at hundred-plus-mile Ride and Tie events and skiing, he took up the banjo. Perhaps his proudest accomplishment was the creation of Hardly Strictly Bluegrass, a three-day free bluegrass festival in Golden Gate Park, which continues to this day.

He was aware of the role of privilege and inheritance in his life. Even though his own father had not done that well, he was the nephew of Isaias Hellman, founder of Wells Fargo Bank, and grew up with some privilege. He would say, "I can't take myself too seriously. I realize that a huge percentage of everything is luck." And he was fond of saying, "Money is a lot like manure: Hoarded in one place, it stinks. Spread it around and good things grow."

and gave rise to the microenterprise field in the United States. Behind this expression was a more far-reaching theory and ambition: to convert an income maintenance system into an investment system. A decade of work and thought culminated in the publication of *The Safety Net as Ladder: Transfer and Economic Development* by the Council of State Planning

Agencies in 1989.[7] In that book, I argued that income maintenance funds could serve double duty, not only providing a floor and safety net but also acting as an investment in self-sufficiency and economic advancement. Welfare payments essentially could become investments.

Over time, however, I became convinced that a tattered safety net transformed becomes a rickety ladder. Other sources of investment are necessary. The United States needs a system to invest in the education, employment, entrepreneurial, and housing pursuits of Americans. And it has one, in the form of the asset subsidies and incentives contained in the tax system.

Low-income and economically marginalized people are not simply beneficiaries, trainees, and potentially employees. They are also entrepreneurs, homeowners, savers, investors, and creators of wealth. Creating a universal progressive investment system could unlock and unleash their productive capacity, confounding traditional political and economic lines.

For the past four decades, CFED (now called Prosperity Now) has been experimenting with these systems. On one hand, we embraced traditional liberal values—concern with the poor and working class and the provision of support for their well-being. On the other hand, we embraced conservative values of enterprise, work, character, self-reliance, freedom, and unequal, earned outcomes. This meant that sometimes our work was well received across the political spectrum, and at other times it was not. Our conferences and work were supported by institutions ranging from the American Enterprise Institute and the Heritage Foundation to the Service Employees International Union and Citizens for Tax Justice; politicians ranging from Jack Kemp, Orrin Hatch, and Rick Santorum to Chuck Schumer, Bill Clinton, and Barack Obama; and by governors both Republican and Democratic.

CFED and its successor Prosperity Now have championed

democratic capitalism. Recognizing and celebrating the innovation, wealth creation, vitality, and competition of capitalism, Prosperity Now believes that drawing on the abilities of people pursuing their own economic gain is a way to power national growth. Common people have the capabilities and potential to drive their own and more general development, if provided with a modicum of resources and respect—a basic portion of capital.

I founded CFED to build paths to opportunity for economically marginalized people whose capacity exceeded their opportunity in this supposed land of opportunity. In 1981, we compiled some of the most innovative ideas for stimulating inclusive economic development in *Expanding the Opportunity to Produce.*[8] Over the ensuing three and a half decades, Prosperity Now and our hundreds of partners across the country took a powerful idea—that our people themselves are our primary source of wealth, and that common people, including the poor and excluded, are college material, can start and grow businesses, can buy and keep homes, and can save and create wealth—and used it to nurture community practice and to shape public policy and private markets so that they are more inclusive and vital. These efforts were backed up with appropriate applied research.

I led CFED through its first decade, during which my managerial limitations became increasingly clear. Three succeeding presidents of CFED continued its growth. Doug Ross, who had been secretary of commerce of the state of Michigan and the vanguard of a set of economic development policy leaders that David Osborne celebrated in his *Laboratories of Democracy*, brought us into league with pioneering states and governors. Brian Dabson, fresh from leading our British counterpart, saved the organization from financial crisis, cultivated the talents of a growing staff, and built the organization over the ensuing

PENALIZING THE POOR MISSING THE MID
GOVERNMENT SUBSIDIES
INCOME
UNDER
CONSTRUCTION
BRIDGE TO
OPPORTUNITY

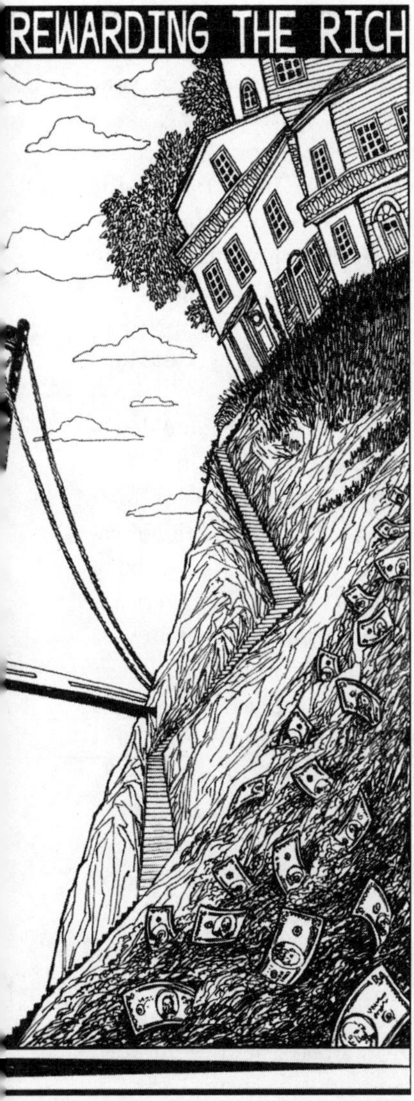

thirteen years. Development finance pioneer and teacher Andrea Levere, Brian's first hire, took the lead when Brian moved on in 2003, and has led the organization and the fields it has pioneered to new levels of performance and impact. Andrea marries financial prudence and excellence, human resource development, diversity, and innovation in both management and economic development. Understanding that no single organization, however big and well-performing, can create the change we envision, Andrea and an expanding, diverse, and talented staff have created nationwide partnerships and networks that bring together tens of thousands of individual and organizational partners, synthesizing community practice, public policy, private markets, and applied research into a platform for systemic change and real economic opportunity for all. In 2017, recognizing that being able to communicate was critical to our ability to create the change we sought, Andrea consummated the multiyear rebranding effort that remade CFED into Prosperity Now, because everyone deserves the opportunity to prosper.

While most discussions of economic opportunity center around money, at base time is really all we have: time to use our eyes, ears, minds, bodies; time to do and learn; time to unfurl our dreams, our ventures, our energy, our vision to make the world different, maybe even better. And the use of time is filtered and channeled by money. From that perspective, there are three kinds of money: PresentMoney, PastMoney, and FutureMoney.

Mostly, people understand money as current income designated to cover current consumption and expenses. This is PresentMoney. In truth, though, PresentMoney flows to cover last month's and last year's expenses—incurred debt and the interest, fees, and fines of those past expenditures. Recognizing PastMoney and reconciling with the fact that most Americans are in debt or one $400 accident or illness away from it provide a sobering perspective on money.[9]

Less obvious, if more profound, are the psychological and future implications of PastMoney. Someone who is in debt is not someone who feels good about himself and is generally not looking ahead with expectation, planning, and optimism. Shame, stress, anxiety, depression, and maybe anger and self-loathing are the more common handmaidens of PastMoney. Moreover, the cost of accumulated debt grows inexorably, a slow and ever more insistent pull down and backward.

FutureMoney is the portion of current income, savings, reserves, or inheritance available to make investments in the future. Most people view FutureMoney as a luxury afforded only the wealthy. I view it as a universal necessity—indeed, the prerequisite for a future better than the present, the key to a better tomorrow. If individuals are to move forward economically, they will have to be able take advantage of opportunities to multiply their money with interest and returns that exceed current value. The ability to make such investments is a precursor to imagining they are even possible, an essential foundation for confidence, hope, and planning. FutureMoney is not just a luxury reserved for the lucky few; it is a necessity for all if individuals are to be able to move forward as savers, entrepreneurs, students, homeowners, and citizens. People need an economic place to stand, a nest egg, a starting block, from which to take off forward.

Most Americans lack FutureMoney, including supermajorities of people of color, women, people with disabilities, the young, the old, and immigrants. A national economy cannot move forward confidently and consistently if most of its people are locked in debt and beholden to the past. To move ahead, people need an economic place to stand. A few thousand dollars each year helps people see that the future is possible.

The basic thesis of *A Few Thousand Dollars*, based on Prosperity Now's forty years of research and experience, is that common people, regardless of race, ethnicity, gender, income, and circumstance, can and will start businesses, create jobs, buy and keep houses, go to college, save, invest, and build family, community, and national wealth. However, they can do this only if they have at least a few thousand dollars of investable capital. Many call this few thousand dollars a nest egg.

This capital foundation is a buffer to absorb the unanticipated costs of emergencies, accidents, illnesses, and other exigencies that destabilize and demoralize otherwise determined people, diverting them from their economic pursuits. Beyond stability, however, a reserve of discretionary capital provides a reason to imagine a future better than the present, a reason to dream and plan and prepare, and ultimately the ability to invest in oneself and one's children.

There is a price of entry to the economic system, to the marketplace, and especially to the paths offering substantial economic gains—education, entrepreneurship, homeownership, saving, and investing. Wealth, common wealth, is that price of entry, the key to achieving financial well-being and prosperity.[10] A basic measure of wealth is not just "what rich people have," but the few thousand dollars it takes to play in today's economy.

Most Americans today lack the few thousand dollars that is a key to the American dream. One-fifth of the nation is un- or underbanked, mired in debt, trapped by yesterday, facing an average $2,400 a year in interest, fines, and fees. Much of the country lacks the savings necessary to survive a temporary misfortune, let alone a nest egg that would allow them an excuse to dream about the future.

For more than ten years, Prosperity Now has been tracking liquid asset poverty in a Prosperity Scorecard. Liquid asset poverty is a measure first suggested by Thomas Shapiro and Melvin Oliver in their classic *Black Wealth/White Wealth*.[11] It assesses whether a family has enough liquid reserves to survive three months at the poverty line if their basic source of income were disrupted. Even by this minimal measure, between 33 and 44 percent of Americans—and three-fifths of people of color—register as liquid asset poor.[12] At best, however, having this amount of liquid assets is only the threshold of real opportunity. Some minimal cache of savings above this survival base is necessary to underwrite, legitimate, and invigorate asset-building and economic progress—a minimal down payment on business, home, and education.

In other words, having money saved above the level of liquid asset poverty is the first step; having a few thousand dollars of investable capital above this is the next step. How much basic wealth is necessary? It is difficult to pinpoint an exact dollar amount. More is better, but some is essential. The past four decades of experimentation with microenterprise loans, IDA matched savings, Child Development Accounts, and housing down payment support suggest that as little as a few thousand dollars can be transforming.[13]

What portion of U.S. households have even $5,000 above basic stability to invest in their own futures? The answers are horrifying. Two-thirds (66.9 percent) of Latino families lack such a nest egg, and 63 percent of black families do not have this investable capital. A third of white and Asian families lack this essential nest egg.[14] An analysis by the Institute for Assets and Social Policy at Brandeis University in 2009 found that fewer than half of American households then had the $12,000 in savings needed to make a down payment on a house, business, or college education, and less than 20 percent—one out of five—people of color did.[15]

An opportunity economy needs an opportunity structure. Fortunately, the United States has the makings of one. Each year the U.S. federal government invests in the productive capacity of American households to the tune of $709 billion in 2017 in the form of housing, retirement, investment, and education tax incentives. This would amount to about $2,200 for every man, woman, and child in the country every year if it were distributed equally. Unfortunately, it isn't. Instead, this national investment in family economic security and opportunity goes almost wholly to the wealthiest tenth of Americans. They do not need the subsidy provided by these tax incentives, nor would they fail to invest otherwise. Moreover, this investment misses the vast middle and bottom of the income spectrum. The wealthiest one-tenth of 1 percent get an average annual benefit of $160,190 just from these subsidies, while the vast majority of Americans get 1/700th that amount ($226).[16]

If even half of the current expenditure were redirected in ways great and small into the savings of common Americans, the result would be the generation of literally millions of new nest eggs supporting businesses, jobs, homeowners, and skilled workers. It would offer, in Abraham Lincoln's words, "an equal start, a fair chance in the race of life," and it would be a boon to the national economy.

A Few Thousand Dollars explains how the United States can change the contours of this basic landscape of economic opportunity.

A FEW THOUSAND DOLLARS
AN AMERICAN DREAM
CONNECTIONS
CAPITAL
COMPETENCE
CAPITAL
CONFIDENCE
COMPETENCE
CONFIDENCE
CONNECTIONS
CAPITAL

2

Saving

People need an economic place to stand if they are to move forward. They need enough money to buffer them from the pressures of everyday and unexpected expenses and to suggest that there might be the possibility of a brighter economic future, a reason to dream and plan and prepare. Eventually, people need a nest egg so that they can invest in their new life path. A nest egg is equity owned by an individual. It is completely within one's control, and discretionary in its use. It is money earmarked for high-return investments in oneself and one's family.

A nest egg is a few thousand dollars. A few thousand dollars can be transformative. A few thousand dollars opens the door to entrepreneurship, education, homes, futures, self-determination, imagination. A few thousand dollars is a minimum—more is usually better. For children, a few hundred dollars can be liberating. For everyone, a nest egg is a crucial beginning.

Assets—that is, wealth—are a central determinant of economic and social behavior, attitude and success, the bedrock. Economic futures are built on savings. As Michael Sherraden explained in his seminal book, *Assets and the Poor,* "Assets are the key to economic development. Individual and family development is not built on receiving and spending a certain amount of monthly income. Rather, development is built on planning for the future, accumulating savings, investing, using financial assets to support life goals, and passing along assets to offspring."[1]

Assets are psychological as well as financial and behavioral. Sherraden realized that "income may feed people's stomachs, but assets change their heads. . . . Assets are hope in concrete form." He identified nine primary effects of assets:

1. Improve household stability
2. Create an orientation to the future
3. Stimulate development of other assets
4. Enable focus and specialization
5. Provide a foundation for risk-taking
6. Increase personal efficacy
7. Increase social influence
8. Increase political participation
9. Enhance welfare of offspring[2]

Sherraden presented abundant evidence of each of these effects in his 1991 book; since then, the evidence has only mounted.[3]

Most Americans lack an economic place to stand. That absence stymies not only their prospects but also the country's future. Declining wages and increasing debt—mortgage debt, credit card debt, student debt—over the past three decades have hollowed out American savings and relegated the majority of Americans to the economic margins of despair.[4] Today, an increasing majority of households—and fully two-thirds to four-fifths of people of color—lack a nest egg. Without an economic place to stand, people have no economic future.

ASSET EFFECTS AND ECONOMIC MOBILITY
BANK
SCHOOL
BUSINESS
HOUSING
RETIREMENT
ASSET
ASSET
ASSET
ASSET
A
SOCIAL INFLUENCE
WELFARE OF OFFSPRING
FOCUS SPECIALIZATION
POLITICAL PARTICIPATION
RISK TAKING
HOUSING STABILITY
FUTURE ORIENTATION
OTHER ASSETS
PERSONAL EFFICACY

$5000 NEST EGG OR NOT
LATINO HOUSEHOLDS
33.3 %
% 66.6
BLACK HOUSEHOLDS
37 %
% 63
NATIVE AMERICAN AND OTHER HOUSEHOLDS
% 59.9
ALL HOUSEHOLDS
57.5 %
% 42.5
ASIAN HOUSEHOLDS
63.4 %
% 36.6
WHITE HOUSEHOLDS
65.9 %
% 34.1
THE UNITED
FEDERAL RESERVE
5000

Wealth inequality dwarfs income inequality, not only in magnitude—one in six Americans is income poor, while at least twice that many are liquid asset poor—but also in dynamics.[5] Yet wealth inequality gets little attention, especially given that the bottom 90 percent of Americans have been losing wealth since the 1980s.[6] Wealth has become so concentrated that most people don't even understand wealth as a concept that might apply to them. They see it as a luxury afforded the rich, not as a necessity and prerequisite for economic citizenship.

If assets are the bedrock of family economic functioning, wealth inequality is the topography upon which the nation struggles. If most families have little or nothing, if gaps are huge, the economy built on top is unstable, overleveraged, and top-heavy. When it comes to race, America's wealth topography emerges particularly starkly—dwarfing income inequality and employment, education and housing disparity—with African Americans, Latinos, Native Americans, and many Asian Americans possessing a few cents for each dollar white males have. A third of American households are liquid asset poor, lacking the $6,000 needed to survive above the poverty line for three months if current income fails. The proportion rises to more than three-fifths in communities of color. In fact, most families are in debt, which tends to mount, and the fifth of the population that is un- or underbanked accumulates fines, fees, and interest averaging $2,400 each year. Most frighteningly, most Americans lack a basic nest egg to invest and believe in their own future, with up to four-fifths of people of color lacking such a starting block.

Wealth is dispersed unequally, and its dispersal reflects the U.S. racial structure. White Americans own $10 to $13 in wealth for every $1 owned by African Americans and Latino Americans. Native Americans do worse; Asian Americans do better on average. There are other asset fissures, each with different dynamics confronting women, foster kids, people with disabilities, the young, ex-offenders, and immigrants also face significant asset disparities. In 2016, white Americans had a median net worth of $127,200; Hispanic Americans had $12,550, African Americans $9,250, Native Americans $8,000, foster kids nothing, and others—Asian Americans, people with disabilities—somewhere in between.[7] If this were life's marathon, a 26.2-mile race, and dollars were feet, white Americans would be starting the race less than two miles from the end of the race, armed with assets sufficient to traverse the bumps along the way: the cost of a home, educational enrichment, child care, transportation, college tuition (without borrowing), et cetera. Meanwhile, people of color would be clustered within the first few miles of the race—Native Americans and African Americans within two miles of the start, Hispanic Americans at about the two-and-a-half-mile mark. And foster kids would be still be at the starting line. Bedrock eco-

nomic and social inequality in America today undergirds all manner of differential consequences, including those associated with education, health, occupation, income, and housing.

The racial wealth divide is the product of different histories, most centuries old. It lives today as, in Tom Shapiro's and Melvin Oliver's memorable phrase, "the sedimentation of past discrimination." How much will the path out of these canyons have to differ by racial group and history? How will the paths of recovery differ?

Ronald Reagan popularized a caricature of the diamond-brooch-wearing welfare queen. Grace Capitello and Regina Blackmon, whose stories are included in this chapter, provide a much more accurate and representative picture of poor people in the United States. Poor people confront large demands and limited resources, and they face multiple penalties if they do all the right things to get ahead—learn, earn, save, invest. Lack of opportunity, not lack of capacity, is what limits most poor people. One can argue about what percentage of the poor are like Grace Capitello and Regina Blackmon, but penalizing them for trying to move forward is counterproductive and wrong.

How can a poor person in the United States build savings, economic independence, and financial security? The simple basic building block of an inclusive economy is the Individual Development Account (IDA). IDAs are the central recommendation of the book *Assets and the Poor: Toward A New American Welfare Policy*.[8] Sherraden explained, "IDAs would be optional, earnings-bearing, tax-benefited accounts in the name of each individual, initiated as early as birth, and restricted to designated purposes."[9] Or, as one welfare mother explained, "Oh, I see. You mean 401(k)'s . . . except for us."[10]

The American Dream Demonstration (ADD) was a five-year policy demonstration project, running from 1997 to 2002, to explore the efficacy of IDAs. Started with contributions from

Grace Capitello

Grace Capitello, a thirty-six-year-old single mother, lived on $440 a month in welfare benefits plus $60 in food stamps. Just surviving on this modest stipend took enormous discipline and resourcefulness, but Grace, like thousands of other welfare mothers, wanted more for herself and her daughter. She saved on clothing by shopping at thrift stores, and stocked up on 67¢ boxes of saltines and 39¢ cans of chicken soup. She pieced together presents for her daughter from Goodwill. Over a number of years, she managed to save $3,000. She hoped to use those savings to buy a washing machine and to send her daughter Michelle to college.

Many observers might find in Grace Capitello's story the seeds of hope, renewal, resourcefulness, and determination to create a better future. The Milwaukee County Department of Social Services saw it differently: it charged her with welfare fraud and took her to court, demanding she pay back all the money she had saved, plus penalties. Judge Charles B. Schudson, who heard her case, was skeptical: "I don't know how much more powerfully we could say it to the poor in our society: Don't try to save." Noting that President George H. W. Bush had just advanced his plan for Family Savings Accounts, Judge Schudson commented, "Apparently, that's an incentive that the country would only give to the rich."[11]

Michael Sherraden

Michael Sherraden had never had much savings. He had worked his way through college and graduate school with some scholarships, but never had any extra at the end of the month. When he became an assistant professor of social work at Washington University in St. Louis, he began to receive quarterly statements from TIAA-CREF showing that the retirement account that came with his employment now amounted to a few thousand dollars. He didn't know very much about the account, so when he saw a poster announcing a 5:00 p.m. session in Room 100 on the accounts, he decided to go find out more. He didn't expect that many others would show up—after all, it was not easy to get faculty to show up at any meetings, even faculty meetings. But when he got to Room 100, he found it packed with faculty. Why? Asset-holding, he would reflect, has a way of grabbing people's attention. They, like he, had been given an asset of growing value, which now demanded attention, learning, and management. It did not escape Michael's attention that these accounts, although called "private," were in fact created by public policy, with substantial public subsidies through tax benefits.

During this same period, Sherraden's research involved interviewing welfare recipients about what was wrong with welfare and what would improve their lives. They disliked welfare. It provided meager assistance, and insult came with the support—the silent accusation that they could not or would not work to support themselves and their children. They were not afforded any assistance in saving for the future; indeed, if they saved even $1,000, they would lose welfare benefits immediately.

Michael reflected on the duality of these policies—some people were encouraged and subsidized in building assets, while others were discouraged and penalized. He considered the precepts, structures, and institutions that undergirded the dual policies. And then he designed and tested potential solutions, devoting much of his career to the simple idea of bringing everyone fairly and firmly into asset-building policies.

a dozen national foundations, ADD became a $16 million, fourteen-site demonstration organized by CFED and Michael Sherraden's new Center for Social Development.[12] Fourteen community partners—community action programs, credit unions, youth employment programs, the Cherokee Nation, community development corporations and banks, and women's self-employment programs, spanning the country from New York to California, Vermont to Texas—created unprecedented IDA programs customized to their communities under general guidelines: $2,000 per account holder with basic and asset-specific financial education and support.[13] ADD was thoroughly and rigorously evaluated using multiple methods, including an experimental test of randomly assigned treatment and control groups in Tulsa, Oklahoma. The 2,378 participants in ADD were overwhelmingly poor women of color.[14]

In short, ADD proved that the poor can save a few hundred dollars a year—rates that, proportionally speaking, exceed those of higher-income families—if that saving is structured and made easy and rewarded.[15] ADD yielded several fundamental lessons:

1. **Poor people can and will save, both for long-term goals and for short-term needs.** Over half of participants in ADD saved in the accounts, accumulating more than $1.12 million in savings.[16] Forty-six percent of savers had incomes below the poverty line, and more than one-fifth had annual incomes less than half of poverty level, proving beyond the shadow of a doubt that the poor can save. The median average monthly deposit was $23 and the mean was $33.[17] Families at half the poverty line—$9,000 at the time for a family of four—saved 8 percent of their income, about the same absolute level but four times the rate of families making 150 percent of poverty-line income.[18]

ADD account holders actually made gross deposits of $2.2 million in their accounts but ended up taking out half this amount in unmatched withdrawals to cover emergencies and short-term needs.[19] IDAs acted not only as a means of long-term savings but also as a reservoir for shorter-term needs. Since each dollar withdrawn sacrificed two in potential match, the opportunity cost of withdrawals was high; it stands to reason that the short-term need was insistent.[20] Long-term and short-term savings are better seen as complementary rather than at odds.

ADD also yielded lessons on how people save and

how to facilitate savings. ADD participants reduced consumption—coffee, alcohol, cigarettes, dining out—and increased income by working more.[21] Minimum and maximum monthly savings limits came to be viewed as targets. ADD also established that match rates of 1:1 to 3:1 increased savings frequency and levels; match rates above 3:1 increased skepticism, not savings. Higher match rates, however, do enable a more rapid and greater accumulation of assets, still tied to individual savings and striving behavior.[22]

2. **Aided by matched savings, low-income and even very poor people will pursue higher education, start businesses, buy and repair homes, save for retirement, and otherwise build long-term assets.** Within two years of starting their IDAs, one-third of ADD participants had purchased assets: a third for small businesses, a quarter for homes, a fifth for home repair, and a fifth for education.[23] The other two-thirds of ADD savers planned to make purchases as well. Ten years later, the impact evaluation showed that account holders were much more likely to be homeowners and to have retirement savings and liquid assets.[24]

3. **Financial education increases savings and their impact.** Each hour of basic financial education up to six hours increased average monthly savings by $1.20; each additional hour up to twelve resulted in an additional 56¢ of savings.[25] Each hour of asset-specific financial training up to six hours increased average monthly savings by $2.50.[26] Thus the average account holder who completed twelve hours of basic financial education and six of asset-specific training deposited $25 more per month and $300 more per year.[27]

4. **Assets "change people's heads."** Because of their IDA, 84 percent of account holders felt more economically

Regina Blackmon

Attending a parent orientiation for her preschool-age daughter, Regina Blackmon, low-income mother of three girls, saw a flyer for the pilot Individual Development Account (IDA) program in Kansas City, Kansas. "Wait a minute, matched funds?" she thought. "Ooh, I put in $100, they give me $300—this is unbelievable." It came at a good time: her husband was leaving her and she knew she couldn't hang on to the house she and her daughters were living in without more income. Here was a way out. She persuaded her sisters, a niece, and a work colleague to join her.

The program required her to save $30 a month, which would be matched 2:1 for home purchase or repair, business, or education. She went initially for home repair. She knew she could save the $30 a month: "I spent that eating out with my girlfriends each month." She figured she could skip that.

Indeed, the IDA program enabled her to keep the house, but it turned out to offer much more. The program was a path to a business, a new job, and college for her youngest; it offered a chance to discover she was smart, to connect across the community, to forge a brighter future for herself and her daughters.

Regina had been working at the same minimum-wage, "mentally abusive" job as a receptionist for seventeen years; it was mind-numbing but stable, allowing her health coverage and the flexibility to tend to her daughter with sickle-cell anemia when needed, but it did nothing to affirm her self-esteem and potential.

At one of the required monthly financial education classes for the IDA program, the instructor suggested she think of starting a business; this idea had never occurred to her. For several years she had been decorating and filling candy jars as gifts for friends and family. Spurred by the instuctor's suggestion, she decided to turn her hobby into a business: Ooh! That's So Cute! candy jars. She enrolled in entrepreneurial training classes, made up brochures and business cards, paid her sister-in-law to pass out flyers, and began to focus on key holidays and events—Valentine's Day, Christmas, graduations. She kept her day job, working at the business at night and on the weekend. It was a seasonal and risky business: one Valentine's Day she made $2,400, but the next she made nothing because her source for the doll heads ran out of supplies. Still, the business enabled her to buy her first reliable car. It gave her the confidence to leave her job as a receptionist and get a better-paying and more satisfying job. Her fortieth birthday coincided with her middle daughter's eighteenth birthday. She started saving for her youngest daughter's college education, buoyed by her newfound resources and confidence.[28]

secure, 93 percent were more confident about the future, and 85 percent felt more in control of their lives; 60 percent said they had made educational plans for themselves or their kids.[29]

The opportunity to acquire a few thousand dollars through savings matches is enough to ignite economic transformation. The ultimate finding of ADD is best found not in data but in the trajectory of economic success. Consider these headline summaries of some ADD participants:

- Homeless Man Becomes Chef
- Day Care Center Worker Goes to Law School
- Husband and Wife Team Up to Sell Their Artwork
- Salon Employee Becomes Salon Entrepreneur
- Bank Teller Saves 5 Percent of $22,000 Salary, Buys Home
- Waitress Saves $10 per Month, Goes to College, Becomes Accountant

Beyond changing the lives of hundreds of participants and yielding powerful research results, ADD built a field and impelled policy change across the country. Inspired and supported by ADD publications, conferences, and examples, four hundred community IDA programs with 10,000 account holders were operating by the end of the ADD program in 2001. Thirty-one states and the District of Columbia had passed IDA-related legislation by that point, and an additional eight used administrative reforms and rulemaking to reduce asset penalties and promote asset-building. In 1998 Congress passed and President Clinton signed the Assets for Independence Act (AFIA), which

Mauricio Lim Miller

Mauricio Lim Miller, the son of a poor but heroic single mother, spent twenty years as the recognized leader of Asian Neighborhood Design, trying to bring social services, training, and support to low-income women and men, before concluding that people develop by building on their strengths, not remedying their weaknesses. Challenged by Oakland mayor Jerry Brown (who had previously been California's governor and would go on to be governor again) to reimagine our approach to combating poverty, Mauricio envisioned what has become the Family Independence Initiative.

One of his first conceptual exercises was to plot government support by income level. The steep J-shaped graph illustrated how we provide maximum supports to the very poorest and the very wealthiest Americans, missing the broad aspiring middle. We have illustrated it here as Penalizing the Poor, Missing the Middle, Rewarding the Rich.[30]

The poorest Americans draw the most support from means-tested income maintenance and social service programs, including welfare (Temporary Assistance to Needy Families), food stamps, Medicaid, and housing assistance. But as their earned income or assets increase, benefits plunge, zeroing out just short of the poverty line at $20,000. Tax incentives for education, business, savings, and homeownership don't pick up until families reach $80,000 or more in income—the wealthiest quintile. In the forgotten middle, the majority of Americans labor without support in an increasingly hostile labor market of disappearing jobs and declining wages.

Over the last decade, Mauricio and his colleagues at the Family Independence Initiative (FII) modeled a new approach to fighting poverty—respecting, chronicling, celebrating, and investing in the capacities, efforts, and strategies of low-income families to move forward based on their own dreams and talents.

The achievements of 3,400 families—nearly 14,000 men, women, and children—who stepped forward to embrace their futures are nothing short of astounding.[31] In about two years, income rose 23 percent and welfare receipt declined 60 percent; savings increased tenfold and liquid assets increased more than seven times, from an average of $371 to $2,740; and children's grades increased 60–80 percent.[32] How did FII achieve these impacts, and many others? Not through a program, not through service delivery, not by suggesting to the families what they should do (in fact, any staffer who suggested to families what they might do was summarily fired). The families—whole families—step forward to climb, and they recruit other families similarly poor and motivated as peers to work with on their common journey.

FII gives each family a computer, but no instructions on how to use it; families (usually led by their children) must teach themselves how to use the computers. FII asks families to report monthly (using the computers) on their progress on income, balance sheet, education, health, housing, community networking, engagement and leadership. For each report FII pays them about $100 to $200, for a total of about $2,400 per family per year.[33] FII verifies the data provided quarterly, reviewing check stubs and the like. Families can see their reports in real time and check their progress against that of other families. FII has added other supports, including UpTogether, a networking site that allows families to learn from what their peers are doing, and a resource bank where families can get their savings matched or other initiatives they take rewarded. Families approach the resource bank to (from most common to least common) match youth and education efforts, pay for family events, support health and fitness initiatives, start a business, cover car repair and purchase costs, buy a home and make home improvements, reduce debt and repair credit, help others, acquire job skills and training, acquire technology, and deal with an emergency—but always and only after families take the initiative and pursue their paths.[34]

The whole process embodies respect—respect for the integrity, potential, creativity and collaboration of people. Mauricio cites Daniel Pink's recognition of the "deep human need to direct our own lives, to learn and create new things, and to do better by ourselves and our world."[35] "We have . . . learned," Mauricio writes, that the "biggest 'reward' is the personal satisfaction families get by creating, being in control of the change, of directing their own progress, and making things better for themselves and others."[36] He summarizes the FII approach and vision going forward:

> Let people rise to whatever level they choose without pre-judgement. Create a vacuum of leadership so they can step up for themselves. Let their creativity and resourcefulness come out and be rewarded. Only then can we imagine the millions of solutions, the millions of tipping points, and the fundamental change in how we would view one another across class, race, religion or region.[37]

And he concludes:

> Our country, and the world, needs to have the hard conversation that distinguishes between efforts that primarily help make poverty tolerable, and efforts that lead to sustained upward

mobility. If we want to address income, wealth, and social stratification, we have to invest in what people are already doing to get above the poverty line and help them to work together and grow that initiative.[38]

If we want most people's lives to improve, then we must invest in the ordinary folks like us. They don't need large investments.[39]

authorized a five-year, $125 million IDA demonstration program that would continue for twenty years.[40]

Hundreds of thousands of low-income Americans have used IDAs, more than 111,000 in the Assets for Independence Act program alone. More than half of those IDA participants purchased assets: if the pattern holds, that's more than 26,000 new homeowners, 10,000 new entrepreneurs, 13,000 new students and skilled employees, and 50,000 families with raised economic horizons.[41] A randomized, control group evaluation of AFIA IDAs found that after one year in the program, IDA participants had increased their liquid savings nearly three times more—by 293 percent, to be specific—than the control group, to $881.[42] Account holders were 34 percent less likely to have difficulty paying for utilities, housing, or health care, 39 percent were less likely to resort to non-bank check-cashing services, and 10 percent were more confident of their ability to meet monthly living expenses.[43]

Two other large federal initiatives supported the creation of another 100,000 IDAs. The Office of Refugee Resettlement of the U.S. Department of Health and Human Services ran and funded an IDA program from 1999 to 2008, in which 21,512 refugees saved more than $30 million, earning a roughly equal match, which in turn leveraged 7.5 times that amount in lending to purchase some $358 million in assets. Almost four out of five savers made at least one asset purchase—60 percent for vehicles, 13 percent for homes, 8 percent for education, 8 percent for business, 2 percent for home remodeling.[44] The Family Self-Sufficiency (FSS) Program at the Department of Housing and Urban Development, which froze rents at 30 percent income and reserved income above that as savings, opened more than 75,000 accounts over the first decade of its existence. Approximately half (48 percent) of participants earned an average balance of $2,400.[45] Together these large-scale initiatives pointed the way to IDAs for all struggling Americans.[46]

There is an understandable confusion between saving, which is the act and behavior of reserving money for another day, and savings, which is the amount of money reserves. Both are important, and arguably they are more important for lower-income people, who need the reserve even more and for whom it is most difficult to achieve. The behaviors, understandings, attitudes, and effects associated with consciously adding revenue, cutting expenses, and storing money for future use are important, and many asset-building organizations focus on cultivating this behavior.[47] Of equal concern is the amount of savings from whatever source. Though the effects of small amounts of saving are profound, size matters, and the amount low-income and very poor people can save is limited. Interestingly, most people do not distinguish where savings come from; owners of 401(k) accounts claim the full balance of accounts as their own, despite the fact that the total includes generous employer matches and government tax incentives.

In 2017, Congress ended funding for the Assets for Independence Act. On one hand, the act did not deserve this fate: it was one of the few government initiatives that really and effectively aimed at opening economic opportunity for low-income and asset-poor communities. On the other hand, it was wholly unsuited to reap the promise it sowed: 10,000 time-limited IDAs, controlled by restrictions included in legislation developed before there was any operating IDA program and built on the delivery capacity of nonprofit organizations and community largesse, are simply inadequate in a country where 200 million people or more lack an economic place to stand. IDAs ought to be not just a temporary program but an ongoing fact of life and support for initiative. The program ought to be universal, accessible, simple, automatic, progressive, and race positive.[48]

So how can the United States move from these successful demonstration projects and a growing field to a universal savings system? Kriss Deiglemeier, creator of the Stanford Center for Social Innovation, argues that major social innovations follow an arc of fifty years or more.[49] Having studied ten major social innovations, she outlines the five stages of social innovation: definition of the problem and opportunity, idea generation, piloting and prototyping, diffusion, and scale. If so, now is the golden age of innovation around family economic inclusion and inspiration. The IDA field is well into that fourth stage. But she notes that almost all the social innovations studied, unlike for-profit innovations, become stymied at the point of growing to scale as a result of lack of growth capital, fragmentation of the social sector, and lack of leadership. IDAs, through no fault of their own, have been caught in what she calls the "stagnation chasm."

The field—tens of thousands of organizations and individuals all across the nation, devoted to financial capability, inclusion, and asset-building—is growing on all sides, tackling the key challenges facing the ambitious budding movement and the nation. Artificial barriers that delineated and divided the field early in its development are falling to proof of need and effectiveness. The early trinity of uses—business, college, home—has expanded to a range of assets that also includes a rainy-day emergency savings cushion, longer-term and retirement savings, automobiles, citizenship, assistive technology, and more. In fact, studies of the use of Earned Income Tax Credit refunds and families in the Family Independence Initiative make a strong case that the funds will in the vast majority of cases be used for goals most beneficial to each particular family.[50]

The field has also recognized and expanded the Household Security Framework, which acknowledges that achieving economic security and opportunity requires earning, learning, saving, investing, protecting, and navigating the system.[51] Even the definition of what we are aiming for has broadened to "financial well-being," which, as defined by the Consumer Financial Protection Bureau, means more than just paying one's bills and having liquid savings sufficient to buffer unexpected expenses—it also includes the ability to invest in lifetime goals.[52]

Financial empowerment is relevant to great swaths of humanity, and particularly to people of color, people with disabilities, foster kids, the old, the young, women, the middle class, displaced workers, immigrants, and returning citizens. Even infants can benefit from accounts and financial inclusion; in fact, as they grow into adulthood they will need it to navigate productive and resilient lives.

Barriers are falling across the life span. Different assets become more salient at different times, and in turn they build the base for later investment. Early in life, a central investment is education, followed by business, home, and retirement savings. Human capital translates into higher earnings and savings, which can capitalize a business or buy a house, which in turn provides a retirement nest egg and a potential inheritance to start the next generation. Retirement savings at the workplace—expanding with Secure Choice programs, which extend access to all employees, including those in smaller firms currently without pension plans—not only can occur across the life span but will be augmented by earlier saving. While retirement savings advocates worry about "leakage" of retirement savings by allowing early withdrawals—even if structured as loans requiring repayment—for education, home, or emergency, current law allows for these uses, and there is little evidence that ultimate savings are reduced by these options. The last three decades of savings experimentation suggest that people, especially poor families, save for more immediate and tangible goals—for savings to weather emergencies and accidents first, and then for needs and opportunities before retirement, including education, business, and home. As Gene Steuerle and the Urban Institute have argued, saving and asset-building should be seen as a lifelong process; the savings of each decade build on top of the previously accumulated base. Wealth-building, including for retirement, is a lifelong process extending even beyond retirement and death, for it also involves future generations.

No longer is the field of asset development focused on one product, the Individual Development Account; now it encompasses a range of products and services, from credit-building savings groups to financial coaching. Nor is the field based on freestanding, privately supported nonprofits. Financial inclusion practices and policies are being integrated into education, social service agencies, housing services, and even the tax system. As Jonathan Mintz, founder of Cities for Financial Empowerment, noted, financial inclusion is the "supervitamin of development," enhancing all social services.

Innovations in asset development are happening in multiple locations. The prime delivery agent and platform for retirement savings, large employers, may be joined by their smaller brethren in offering automatic deductions funneled to accounts held by others. New software has the ability to attach matching incentives and financial coaching prompts to all manner of accounts, while the internet and blockchain technology surmount geographic and market divides. Behavioral economics and human-centered design are building customer insights and behavior into all of these interfaces.

The greatest barrier to universal IDAs is funding. A few thousand dollars for a million Americans is billions. A few thousand dollars for hundreds of millions of Americans is hundreds of billions. In fact, the United States is already spending hundreds of billions of dollars annually to encourage families to save, build businesses, buy homes, go to college, save for retirement, and otherwise build their family's balance sheet. This is done in the form of tax incentives, which totaled $709 billion in 2017 alone, an average of $2,000 per person per year. But these tax subsidies go almost entirely to the wealthiest 10 percent of Americans, who need it least. The people current tax policy misses are the asset-poor majority who would use these incentives to build wealth.

It is time for change.

It is time to make saving and wealth-building universal and equitable in the United States. It is time to take the proven principles, lessons, and results of matched savings, IDAs, and other wealth-building tools to scale.

Debt has been piling up for the last three decades, with consumer, mortgage, and student debt reaching historic highs. Nearly 60 percent of American families spend more than they take in each month, adding "thousands of dollars to their debt load each year." Many are "headed irreversibly toward default."[53] Indeed, the futures of two upcoming generations have been mortgaged to student debt. To lift this yoke from people's necks, the United States must not only reduce or write off some of this debt and cut interest rates on the rest but also create new ways to generate common wealth.

For 80 percent of the population, incomes have been

stagnating or declining for most of the past five decades. Technology threatens to decimate whole classes of jobs. Drivers, for example, are the largest employment class in twenty-nine states; the advent of driverless cars and trucks may well wipe out this whole category of workers in a couple of decades. Noting these trends, a growing chorus of leaders as diverse as former Service Employees International Union president Andy Stern, sociologist Amitai Etzioni, consumer advocate Ralph Nader, venture capitalist Vinod Khosla, tech leader Elon Musk, former labor secretary Robert Reich, Facebook co-founder Chris Hughes, and others have begun calling for a Universal Basic Income (UBI). Calling it "a twenty-first-century solution to a twenty-first-century problem," Andy Stern describes UBI as granting "an income to every US citizen without any obligation to work or perform a socially mandated task."[54]

While there are many variations to the proposal, the Roosevelt Institute suggests five features of a "full" Universal Basic Income: the funds are distributed unconditionally, there is no means test, the UBI is long-term, the sums are adequate to cover basic living expenses, and the cash is distributed to everyone within a set region.[55] In some ways, it is an idea whose time has come, an obvious response to stagnating incomes and disappearing jobs, which is attracting increasing attention. There is abundant evidence that people make good decisions about how to use income, so unrestricted grants make sense.

But UBI raises a host of issues. If indeed it is to be adequate to cover basic living expenses, it is hugely expensive. Where will the money come from? Proponents suggest eliminating all 126 welfare programs and means-tested benefits programs, eliminating all $1.2 trillion in tax expenditures, levying a value-added tax of 5–10 percent, implementing a financial transaction tax or wealth tax, or other budget cuts.[56] Some have suggested devoting all foundation giving to this purpose. Recognizing that a full basic income may be too expensive to install overnight, some proponents suggest introducing support at lesser levels. However, without progressive features, and depending on how it is funded, UBI may do little to level the playing field and may in fact increase inequality. The political and social viability of UBI is also in question. Both critics and recipients of cash welfare have questioned the concept of payments without desert, as David Ellwood suggested in his provocatively titled book *Poor Support*.[57]

Whatever form UBI takes, even in its most robust versions, it is unlikely to address or significantly reduce wealth inequality or the racial wealth divide. It will not generate asset effects or invigorate the economy except through consumption increases. It is not likely to generate new businesses and jobs. And it treats people as consumers, not producers. At its worst, UBI insults most recipients by supporting them without respecting, demanding, or investing in their productive energy—the quid pro quo and investment multiplier that lies at the center of matched saving and asset-building programs.

To maximize savings and savings behavior, new systems should:

- Open accounts automatically, with the opportunity to opt out
- Allow automatic deposits, such as via payroll deduction
- Enable short- and medium-term modest savings goals—rainy-day funds, vehicles, business savings
- Provide regular feedback on accounts, savings, matches earned, and capital appreciation; reinforcing regular savings, including reports on peers' savings
- Restrict withdrawals to asset-building purposes
- Be simple—in account types, matching rules, and investment options

The United States spends more than $100 billion a year rewarding capital investment in property, stock, savings, and investments. This huge annual subsidy comes in the form of preferential tax rates on realized capital gains, dividends, and carried interest. The preferential tax rate on capital gains and dividends of 20 percent that was enacted in 2003 is half the rate paid by taxpayers in the top income bracket—the bracket where most owners of capital find themselves.

Reduced tax rates on capital gains and dividend income overwhelmingly benefit the wealthiest Americans, who own the lion's share of stocks and property. The wealthiest quintile of Americans own more than 90 percent of all such investments.[58] Millionaires get an average annual tax break from these preferential rates averaging $138,280 per year, more than 13,000 times the $10 working families get.[59]

Is it fair or wise to tax income from investments at a lesser rate than wages, which is where most Americans derive their income? Proponents of the preferential rates argue that taxes on capital gains and dividend income constitute double taxation, since corporations have already paid corporate income tax. They also cite the importance of capital investment to the expansion of the marketplace, and the need for reduced rates to induce investors to assume the risk of equity investments and the time it takes for any gains to accrue or dividends to pay. Corporate tax (greatly reduced in the Tax Cuts and Jobs Act of 2017) is a separate issue, and the risk and patience of equity investing is more than repaid in outsized returns. These tax benefits accrue on top of the underlying capital appreciation and dividends that are ample reward for the investments made. Especially at a time when wealth inequality is skyrocketing while wage income stagnates or declines, preferential tax rates on capital gains, dividends, and carried interest seem neither prudent nor fair.

A majority of Americans are effectively locked out of the mainstream economy because they do not have a few thousand dollars. A key element is a universal system of savings with a significant federal refundable tax incentive. This system needs to be anchored by accessible, low-cost, quality accounts with positive investment options backed by financial services, new and old. All Americans need and deserve universal savings accounts (USAs).

USAs are savings-based and savings-triggered: no savings, no match. Matches are earned by saving and asset-building behavior, not bestowed. Universal means that all ages, incomes, races, ethnicities, and genders are included. It should also mean universally accessible, exploiting the reach of online as well as bricks-and-mortar access and services. These accounts provide a real equity base for every American. USAs call forth a new foundation for American capitalism, in which all people can participate. These accounts can be funded by taxing investment income at the same rates as earned income, as we did fifteen years ago.

A refundable, sliding-scale tax credit matches up to $500 saved each year. For the quarter of the population with the lowest amount of net wealth,[60] the tax credit would match savings at a 4:1 rate; for each dollar a person saved, the government would deposit four dollars. The next wealthiest quarter could be matched at a 3:1 rate while the third quartile could be matched 2:1 and the top quartile 1:1. This would result in annual accumulations of a few thousand a year—$2,500 $2,000, $1,500 and $1,000 respectively for the U.S. population. This universal savings account tax credit would transform a windfall to the rich into an opportunity for every American to build wealth and receive non-labor income.

Since supermajorities of people of color are asset poor, they would disproportionately benefit from the higher match rates;

over time, USAs would help close the racial wealth gap, binding us together even while growing our economy and commonwealth by tapping the productive capacity of all Americans.

Matched withdrawals from USAs generally would be limited to investments in business, homes, education, retirement savings, assistive technology, and citizenship.[61] Such restrictions actually promote savings and direct capital to areas that enhance economy-wide growth.

Recognizing the volatility of household balance sheets, however, either in addition to the USA or integrated into it should be a provision for matched emergency savings modeled on the bipartisan Rainy Day Earned Income Tax Credit savings proposal and the Side-Car Savings proposal to supplement and protect retirement savings accounts.[62] The Rainy Day EITC would provide a 50 percent match for up to $500 of the Earned Income Tax Credit deferred for six months to help low-income families deal with increased volatility and unexpected expenses that would otherwise block economic progress.

All amounts in USAs would be exempt from asset limits contained in any income maintenance or social service program.

While some may regard the matches as unduly generous, they are earned. Account holders need to save in order to earn a match, and they must use their matched accounts in ways that require them to apply their talents and efforts to enlarging not only their wealth but also the country's. Education, business, and homeownership all add value and generate outsized and enduring returns, but they are not self-executing; they require matching investments of work and wisdom.

Saving $500 or $1,000 will be difficult for poor people. States that follow the federal tax structure with preferential capital gains and dividend rates should consider reducing these tax breaks, which overwhelmingly favor wealthier individuals, in favor of matching the savings of lower-wealth savers. Local

UNIVERSAL SAVINGS ACCOUNTS
Prosperity
$500
$500
PROPERTY
ANNUAL ACCUMULATIONS
$2500
$2000
$1500
$1000
POOREST
MIDDLE
WEALTHIEST
$220 BILLION
WORKING FAMILIES
$10
$138 280
1%
STATE AND LOCAL TAX DEDUCTIONS
20% TAX RATES ON CAPITAL GAINS AND DIVIDENDS
Adversity

governments, community groups, foundations, and employers could consider similar matches. These actions could help lift up poor people, maximize federal matches for which they're eligible, and otherwise allow them to participate fully in the economy.

Of course, there will need to be accounts in which to save money and accrue the matches. We can build on existing accounts—including 401(k) and 403(b) retirement plans, IRAs, 529 college savings accounts, and the Federal Thrift Savings Plan—but we need to recognize that a fifth or more of Americans lack the savings accounts and financial institution relationships that allow savings to grow. All employers, including small employers, should allow workers to set up retirement accounts and direct that a portion of their wages go into these accounts. States including California, Illinois, and Oregon have been experimenting with Secure Choice plans, which expand enrollment to small employers. However, the federal government, after authorizing states to set up such plans under the Obama administration, reversed course in 2017. We should encourage the spread of such plans, considering it to be the price of a revitalized and democratic capitalism. The existence of savings vehicles that are widely publicized and easily accessible would make saving more common. We should build on our existing systems of retirement accounts while allowing the funds to be used before retirement on things such as education and business, since an adequate retirement depends on asset-building along life's course.[63]

Special attention should be paid to expanding the options for appreciating and protected savings vehicles. Just as the federal government guaranteed deposits by individuals into banks and offered banks access to the discount window after the Great Depression in exchange for banks providing banking services to all, the federal government should guarantee

USAs in regulated financial institutions, including community development financial institutions (CDFIs), whose investment objectives reinforce those of USAs; perhaps the government should even subsidize and guarantee returns. Financial institutions that don't offer quality savings accounts at reasonable rates to small savers should not receive federal deposit guarantees or Community Reinvestment Act credit.

Savings is a structure more than it is an individual behavior. We need a universal savings system with accounts opened for all automatically. Analogizing this structure to the emerging infrastructure for self-driving cars, Michael Sherraden notes: "People are not good savers any more than they are good drivers. With new technologies, we can create a savings system that does the saving for us, just like it will do our driving for us—more safely and efficiently than we ever could."

Basic and asset-specific financial education and coaching should be offered by employers and integrated into social service, housing, employment, and education programs, as well as the universal savings structure recommended above.

At its best, capitalism excels at allowing new ideas and ventures and wealth to arise and grow. America today can justly boast about innovation, wealth, and productivity, but in truth, American capitalism is presently resting on a very narrow base, as only a minority of Americans have the minimal capital necessary to participate fully in the economy today. Every American deserves to add the full measure of her or his creativity, energy, talent, and labor to our country and harvest the just rewards of that contribution.

There is a price of entry to the American economy today—the cost of a buffer from economic shock, the down payment required on a home, the money needed to start a business, the cost of a college education. Most Amercans today, including the vast majority of Americans of color, lack this ticket to the table.[64] We have capitalism without capital for too many people. It is like playing Monopoly without the initial bankroll: the likely outcome is bankruptcy.

With USAs, for the first time in our history, everyone would have a chance to bring their talent, vision, and energy to the economy, and build capital—human, financial, social. This is capitalism where everyone can play, and the American economy as a whole will be the winner.

3

Education

Child Development Accounts (CDAs), or Generation Accounts, are "hope in concrete form."[1] They are lifetime savings and investment accounts established as early as birth in the name of the child, earmarked for lifelong and life-changing opportunities for postsecondary education first, and later business, homeownership, retirement, and bequests to the next generation. They are generally "seeded" with initial endowments, after which children, parents, and the community are encouraged to contribute additional funds, often incentivized by savings matches or benchmark deposits marking key achievements such as school graduation. They become vehicles for financial education and a financial backbone for lifelong planning and development.

CDAs provide a foundation for education outcomes, lifelong learning, and positive economic and social outcomes. Experimentation with child saving accounts across the country and around the world demonstrates the effectiveness of these accounts in improving educational outcomes for all, but particularly for children of color and children born to families that live in poverty. A universal system of accounts for every child in the country would be a way to begin closing the racial wealth gap and provide a base for lifelong asset-building and democracy for succeeding generations.

Why are child savings accounts important? Obviously, there are many competing needs for child welfare, especially in the earliest and most formative years. In a 2006 national poll, seven out of ten Republican and Democratic participants and more than three-quarters of parents supported federal deposits and savings matches to child savings accounts, even to the degree of preferring a candidate who espoused them on top of other traditionally partisan stands. Yet they were hard-pressed to explain exactly why.[2]

People support child savings accounts because they recognize that the American promise is that all children have an equal opportunity to build a meaningful life and that economic inequality is one of the greatest challenges to realizing this promise.

Wealth inequality in the United States is greater than in any other industrialized country, greater even than in Russia and Iran. It hasn't been this great since the end of the Gilded Age of the 1920s, just before the Great Depression—and this era is just as full of portent as that was. Today the wealthiest 1 percent own more than the half the wealth in the country. More problematic, the net worth of a majority of American households fell between 2000 and 2011, the wealth gap between whites and blacks doubled, and the gap between whites and Hispanics widened. Meanwhile, the share of wealth held by the richest 10 percent increased 250 percent. This huge and growing disparity will inevitably imprint itself on the unequal inheritances of emerging generations. When we recognize the importance of wealth as a foundation for generations to come, we see that the very last thing we need to do is to continue to subsidize and invest in inequality.

Juliet Garcia

When Juliet Garcia's father, Romeo Villarreal, was about eight years old, his family fled their home country to escape the turmoil and danger of the Mexican revolution. Pancho Villa's soldiers had taken over their home to use as stables, dragged all their furniture outside and burned it, and confined the family to a single room. Juliet's grandfather knelt, pleading that the family be allowed to live and leave. The family of six, their stature in the community and foundations crushed, traveled through the town of Camargo and across the Rio Grande to Rio Grande City, on the U.S. side of the border.

Juliet remembers seeing a photo of the six many years later: "I remember . . . how sad and exiled they all looked." Juliet's grandfather tried to rebuild the family's life, selling kerosene and lamps, buying small properties around his new home, but he was wiped out again by the Depression, and never recovered. "I think he died brokenhearted."

Juliet's mother, Paulita Lozano, was born in the United States, a member of a pioneer family in deep south Texas. Her father owned Lozano & Sons, "the first mercantile store in downtown Harlingen." While the family worked downtown and owned a business there, they had to live on the "Mexican" side of town, where the housing was run-down and services were lacking. Mexican kids could only swim in the public pool one day a year, the day before the pool was drained and cleaned for the next year.

Juliet's parents came of age during the Great Depression, a time when a college education was out of reach for most. Although both of them had excelled while in high school—Paulita was salutatorian of her graduating class—neither was able to attend college. Romeo Villarreal prized the value of education and the quality of life it produced, particularly because he and his generation would never have the benefit of it. Romeo's and Paulita's unfulfilled dreams for a college education fueled their desire to make sure that Juliet and her brothers got to attend.

"Every month, my parents placed $5 into savings accounts designated for one purpose—to fund our college education. It wasn't because my family had a lot of money; quite the contrary." A small man physically—"I don't think my father weighed more than 100 pounds"—Romeo worked the night shift at one of the refineries in town, and then began a career at Pan American Airways as a janitor, working his way up to manage the same office where he had once emptied trash cans.

Paulita died of cancer at the age of forty. Juliet remembers that her father, "now alone, had to work even harder to raise my brothers and me. I recall him sitting down at my mother's sewing machine one evening after she had died and asking me to help him thread the needle so that he could mend something. Jobs in our home had no gender after our mother's death." Expectations for doing well in school were also without regard to gender. "Son or daughter, it didn't matter to my parents; we were all expected to do well in school," Juliet says. "Growing up, I remember that we always seemed to be trying to get my father to use that money from the college savings account. Our house had only two small bedrooms and one bathroom. I would beg our father for another bathroom and suggest that he use some of our college savings to build it. He would respond, '*Ese dinero no se toca*'—that money cannot be touched.

"My brothers would ask him to buy a new car with that money; our cars were always five, six, or seven years old by the time we got them. But he wouldn't hear of it. His response was always the same: '*Ese dinero no se toca.*'

"We never knew how much was actually in our savings accounts, nor did we know how much it cost to actually go to college. But what we did know was that our parents had saved hard-earned money every month so that we might fulfill the dream for ourselves that had been out of reach for both of them.

"We also knew that is was our job to take the more

rigorous courses to prepare to do well in college. And most importantly, we knew college was in our future because our parents had saved money for us to go.

"At some point, my older brother, tired of school and of being under the ever-vigilant eye of my father, announced to us that he was leaving home and school to make his own way in the world. Defiantly, he asked my father for his portion of the college money that had been saved.

"Without hesitation or apology, my father responded with, 'That money is for college; if you don't use it to go to college yourself, then I will use it to go to college.' My brother decided to stay home and return to school.

"The savings account that my father faithfully contributed to, despite his modest income, did not ever amount to the cost of sending three children to college, but it represented a sacred promise in our family."

Juliet and her brothers did graduate from college, supplementing the family savings with work, grants, and loans to complete their educations. Her father lived to see Juliet named president of the community college in her hometown. Her older brother became a registered nurse and now owns a hospice center and has helped hundreds of people through the difficult passage of the last days of their lives. Her younger brother became a civil engineer who, to this day, travels worldwide helping companies design new technology-based processes. Most of her cousins also graduated from college. In just one generation, education transformed a family that now includes lawyers, physicians, engineers, and teachers.

"My father also lived long enough to get to know my children. My children have both graduated from college and have five children between them. My father would have adored his great-grandchildren. . . . But I'm convinced that even if his great-grandchildren had asked him for money from those college savings accounts, he would have said the same thing to them: '*Ese dinero no se toca.*'"

Juliet graduated at the top of her class from Brownsville High School; she earned her BA in English and speech communication at the University of Texas in Houston in 1970, her master's in classical rhetoric in 1972, and her PhD in communications from UT Austin in 1976. On each of those diplomas, her name appears as Juliet Villarreal Garcia. "It is customary in Spanish-speaking countries to carry your maiden name as well as your married name. But most importantly, my father wanted to see his name on my diplomas."

She married and had two children while in college. She started working as a teacher's assistant while in graduate school and then at Texas Southmost College (so named because it literally bordered the

Rio Grande). Juliet served as academic dean of Texas Southmost for five years and as president for six. In her second year at Southmost, in 1987, "as a baby president," the school decided to establish an endowment to fund scholarships for poor seventh-graders in the region if they took rigorous courses and earned A's or B's. They applied for a $2 million challenge grant from the Department of Education to establish the endowment; they would receive the money only if they could raise $1 million in eighteen months. Every member of the school became a fund-raiser, and they solicited every member of the community. They solicited the Elks Club and the Lions Club—"all the animal clubs, as I call them." They reached out to garden clubs, businesses, carpenters, lawyers, doctors, and plumbers, waiters. The students at one elementary school went for three days without eating lunch so they could fill a big mayonnaise jar with nickels and dimes for the endowment. They held bake sales and pancake breakfasts and car washes, and even shadowed bingo winners for contributions. In a final push during the last week of the campaign, a woman came up to the door of Juliet's house with a baby in her arms and one in a stroller. Juliet went out to meet her. "I saw her fumbling to take something out of her pocket—a crinkled $5 bill, which she proceeded to iron in her free hand. I could tell that she needed the money more than we did. When I urged her to keep it, she said, 'Please, it is the only hope I have for my kids.'"

Texas Southmost College raised the $1 million, and collected the $2 million match from the federal government. In the thirty years since, that endowment has funded 13,000 scholarships and grown to $8 million.

On January 1, 1991, Juliet Garcia and other community leaders convinced the University of Texas system that the Rio Grande region deserved a four-year university with a graduate program. The University of Brownsville was born, and Juliet became the first Mexican American woman appointed president of a college or university in the United States. She held that position for the next twenty-two years.

In 2013 UT Brownsville and UT Panamerica merged to become the University of Texas Rio Grande Valley (UT RGV), the second largest Hispanic-serving university in the United States. Juliet became its president and led it until she retired. The school headquarters is in an old cavalry fort established to block Mexican expansion. "The border crossed us," Juliet likes to joke. The Rio Grande Valley is in fact a binational area, with permeable borders. Everyone is bilingual, and most families have relatives on both sides. UT RGV is the melting pot and launching pad for the region.

"When I first became a community college president, I had no idea of what a community college president did," she acknowledges now. She identified and then visited five community college presidents who were acclaimed as the best. Her most memorable meeting was with Bob McCabe, president of Miami-Dade Community College. When she asked what the most important part of the job of a community college president was, she expected him to name facilities, or building the faculty, or fund-raising. He replied, "Preserving the democracy of the United States." When she reacted with surprise, he explained, "My job is to prepare the next wave of Floridians and immigrants—to welcome them to higher education and make sure they succeed. If we do our job, they'll be invested in the American dream and be successful, and they'll nurture, defend, and sustain this democracy." Juliet found her own purpose then: "To build the next generation of American citizens to preserve, nurture and sustain our democracy."

Juliet has a dream. She will not rest until every kid in the Rio Grande Valley has a college savings account, a dream and a nest egg that no one can take away. "We can build the greatest libraries and laboratories and classrooms, and even a new medical school, but if the kids don't have the money to aspire and attend, all is for naught." The Rio Grande Valley's population of 1.3 million is younger than most of Texas, and growing with young families. "We will grow even if all migration from Mexico and other areas of the U.S. stopped. We can grow dumb, unprepared, and uneducated, or we can endow all our children with dreams and the means to realize those dreams. If we can do it here, we prove it can be done anywhere.

"For more than twenty-eight years I have had the great privilege of leading the expansion of higher education opportunities in the border region that welcomed my father's family. I have seen the difference a college education has made in individual families, as well as the social impact it has made on our region.

"If in a democracy, the public—not merely the wealthy or the elite, but the public—does not have access to high-quality public higher education, there will be no sustained democracy. But if there is, we fling open the doors of a college education to produce a new generation of voters, of Americans, of people proud of their destiny here in the United States.

"And if we do that really well, they'll be vested in our country, they will nurture it, and they will protect, defend, and sustain it. I cannot imagine any more important work to be involved in than sustaining the democracy of our country."

Evidence mounted during the 1990s that wealth was much more unequally distributed than income; a small number of people held the majority of the assets (money held in short- or long-term investments). The attitudinal and behavioral effects of assets are profound, and different from those associated with income. Often, income is used to cover basic life expenses; assets provide the money for dreams and ambitions. The effects of asset-holding and, perhaps more important, of asset poverty (having few or no assets) are even more profound for children. Asset poverty thwarts dreams before they can even be formed. Moreover, asset poverty is even more prevalent among children, and particularly children of color.

Evidence has accumulated that the presence or absence of durable assets is highly predictive of a wide range of educational, economic, health, occupational, and social outcomes. Controlling for other significant factors, family savings are associated with years of schooling, high school graduation, college enrollment, and college graduation rates.[3] Only 10 percent of children who grow up in families with incomes in the bottom 20 percent will complete college.[4] A boy or girl born in the bottom 20 percent by income/assets has a 67 percent chance of ending up in the bottom 40 percent of income earners as an adult. By contrast, the child of parents in the top 20 percent of income earners is six times more likely to become wealthy than the child of a poor family, and eight times more likely than the poor child to get a bachelor's degree before the age of twenty-four.[5] White students are twice as likely to get help from their parents for college as are African American students. For African American children, the money more often than not flows the opposite way, with children sending their parents funds.[6] Rigorous experimental evidence demonstrates significant psychosocial effects from a lack of assets even in the first few years of life. Students from asset-poor families are less likely to expect to go to college, less likely to graduate, more likely to take on more debt, and more likely to suffer from that debt—earning less, acquiring fewer assets over the course of their lifetimes.[7] We are not a meritocracy, and will not become one without deliberate and bold change.

Universal child savings accounts make financial education

and learning relevant and more effective, and a fair subject for school study and discussion. Savings for college, in particular, proved to be a major predictor of college expectations, attendance, and completion—a prerequisite for forming a "college-going identity." As data on the gaping racial disparities in child and family assets mounted, it became clear that universal progressive child accounts are one of a very few politically popular ways of closing the racial wealth gap. And last, but not least, it has become increasingly clear that universal child accounts are one of the few ways to provide a stable platform across generations for full participation in the society and economy—something that is foundational to the exercise of popular democracy.[8]

Education is not the leveler it is often seen to be. A black college graduate today will command less income than the average white high school graduate. Students of color will earn more with more education, but their wage gains are less, and their ability to translate those wage gains into wealth are less.[9] Each additional $1 in income translates to 69¢ in assets for African Americans, while it adds more than $5 for whites.[10] Between 2007 and 2013, college-educated whites gained $31,000 in wealth, while college-educated blacks lost nearly $20,000.[11] In fact, in the twenty-five years from 1992 to 2013, college-educated whites increased their wealth by 86 percent, while college-educated blacks lost 55 percent of their wealth.[12] Changing these outcomes will require change outside the educational system; we need changes in the structure of economic and financial opportunity in this country.

In spite of these statistics, in the United States college is the likeliest route to a job with a living wage. A college degree brings an average dividend of an additional $1 million in lifetime income.[13] An associate's degree can be expected to raise lifetime income by half a million dollars. Kids with a college savings account in their own name are three times more likely to go to college and four times more likely to graduate, even with less than $500 in their accounts.[14] While savings are financially important—especially in the wake of whole generations of young people being strangled by debt—they may be even more psychologically important, ingraining a college-going identity, acting as "hope in concrete form."[15]

The student debt crisis, which surpassed the mortgage debt crisis several years ago, has become the new yoke around the necks of generations coming of age, and it disproportionately affects students of color. Part of this growing indebtedness was triggered by the 26 percent reduction in state public support of higher education over the last few decades, and it will not abate until those investment levels recover. But predatory and discriminatory policies and practices play a role as well. Fewer than 5 percent of colleges are affordable to low-asset people.[16] The value of need-based aid has declined, with Pell Grants losing half their purchasing power since 1990. Student debt for whites averages $28,000, which is bad enough, but debt for black students is almost double that, at $52,726.[17]

"Defining the solution as 'free college' presumes that what ails the withering American Dream is just lack of money to pay for tuition, when in reality the problem goes much deeper, starts much earlier, and lasts much longer," write William Elliott and Melinda Kay Lewis.[18] Cruelest, perhaps, is the debt load of low-income students whose financial fragility was so great they had to drop out of school before securing a degree or the benefits of a degree. Eliminating the first $50,000 of student debt entirely would shrink the racial wealth gap by a little more than a third. Excusing student debt up to $25,000 would shrink the racial wealth divide by a whopping 50 percent.[19] A more complete solution, however, must start earlier, replacing debt with equity in the form of pre-college savings. After all, each dollar of pre-college savings removes the need for $2 to $4 in post-college debt.

Saving money for education early makes time an ally. Endow a child at birth, invest those assets well, and that investment can double or triple by the age of majority. Investing in babies or young children, before their outcomes can be attributed to merit or lack thereof, is also an easier political sell. Clearly, all children are—or should be—created equal. The question for society is whether it endows them with equal chances of realizing their potential from there. Starting early and being proactive makes it possible to generate a more equitable racial and gender landscape going forward, with greater opportunities for all to contribute to a more prosperous, resilient, and productive future. Child Development Accounts are the foundation of a truly universal, inclusive, progressive, and productive foundation for building equity—wealth, ownership, and fairness.

How could the United States make CDAs a reality for all children born here? Proposals for universal child accounts are as old as the American republic. In 1795, Thomas Paine, in his essay on agrarian justice, proposed "to create a national fund, out of which there shall be paid to every person, when arrived at the age of twenty-one years, the sum of fifteen pounds sterling, as a compensation, in part for the loss of his or her natural inheritance, by the introduction of the system of landed property."[20] The fifteen-pound endowment was intended to get people started in an occupation or economic endeavor. "Would it not, even as a matter of economy, be far better to adopt means to prevent their becoming poor?"[21] He continued, "A plan upon this principle would . . . multiply the national resource; for property, like vegetation, increases by offsets."[22]

In 1968, James Tobin called for universal child accounts, saying memorably, "After high school, every youth in the nation—whatever the economic means of his parents or his earlier education—should have the opportunity to develop his capacity to earn income and to contribute to the society."[23] Economists Robert Haveman and Lester Thurow called for universal child accounts in 1988 and 1992, respectively, and Bruce Ackerman and Anne Alstott called for them in their 1999 book *The Stakeholder Society*.[24] In 2004, Sherraden and Ray Boshara called for universal progressive child accounts in a *New York Times* opinion piece.[25]

By the turn of the new millennium, it became clear to advocates in the field that to implement the idea of universal progressive child accounts in the United States, they would have to start with real experience—real kids with accounts, real programs, real evidence of their effectiveness. The Saving for Education, Enterprise and Downpayments (SEED) Policy Initiative became the first systematic test of the efficacy of Child Development Accounts, with more than 2,700 children participating from birth through age eighteen.[26] Led by the Ford and Charles Schwab Foundations, a dozen national foundations underwrote the $30 million cost.[27] SEED unfolded in fourteen sites: twelve community partners distributed over eleven states; a quasi-experimental site, the Oakland-Livingston Human Services Agency, in Michigan, with 419 kids in Head Start programs; and SEED for Oklahoma's Kids (SEED OK), a fully randomized statewide experiment in Oklahoma. Each of these components of the program contributed different insights and lessons, revealed by a range of different research studies and methods.

Each SEED community partner served about seventy-five kids. The partners used a common framework, but each was customized by the responsible agency to the community and target group. Each offered initial deposits, savings matches, benchmark payments (based on the achievement of specified objectives), age-appropriate financial education, and connection to the financial system. Within that foundation, each design varied. For example, while each program was offered $2,000 in account incentives per participant, each partner decided how to apportion that sum among initial deposits, benchmark deposits, and savings matches. Community partners operated in communities as different as New York City, rural Arkansas, St. Louis, Denver, Philadelphia, Puerto Rico, San Francisco, and Austin, Texas. Partners included the Harlem Children's Zone, United Way, a Boys and Girls Club, a religious charter school, nonprofit youth development programs, and the Cherokee Nation.

By separating SEED participants into four age cohorts—preschool, elementary school, middle school, and high school—SEED compressed an eighteen-year development cycle into five years and demonstrated that accounts could propel kids and families forward throughout the first two decades of life. The community partner and quasi-experimental portions of SEED yielded seven important lessons:[28]

1. Child Development Accounts appeal broadly to Americans across political and geographic lines, especially to parents.
2. Outreach and recruitment are challenging when participation is not universal and enrollment is not automatic. Distrust of financial and governmental institutions, reluctance to share information, embarrassment about financial knowledge and circumstances, and fear of reduction in benefits all discouraged participation. Nevertheless, children of all ages, disproportionately low-income children and children of color, participated. Half of SEED participants were from families living below the poverty line, and most participants were children of color.

3. Families at all income levels and across racial lines saved and built assets. Savings averaged $10 a month over three years, enabling total accumulations ranging from $885 to $2,626 with an average accumulation of $1,500. Overall, 57 percent of families saved in the accounts; at some partners more than 90 percent did. Families used innovative strategies for saving, including eating out less often, spending less on recreation, and encouraging relatives to contribute, but it was not easy: tight family budgets, high costs of food and energy, multiple children, short-term needs, predatory lenders and excessive borrowing, and complicated or inaccessible financial products all mitigated against saving. Thus the savings performance was remarkable even though modest. Even with all these barriers, the fact is that after three years families had acquired enough to cover two years at a community college if the accumulated funds earned modest returns over the ensuing years.
4. Restrictions that made SEED funds inaccessible and savings automatic, such as withdrawal restrictions, direct deposit, account matches and incentives, facilitated the saving process and were appreciated by participants. Match caps—the upper limit on matches—often became targets.
5. SEED accounts had positive attitudinal and behavioral effects. Youth participants reported increased financial prudence (the ability to distinguish between wants and needs), improved self-esteem and self-efficacy, enhanced future-orientation, an increased sense of security, and increased financial knowledge. Parents reported increases in self-esteem, self-efficacy, hope for the future, future-orientation, sense of security, fiscal prudence, and interaction with children about finances

and college. Parents, including Head Start parents, reported seeing college as a more viable option and placed greater value on education.[29]

6. Community partner programs were relatively expensive to administer, with personnel costs often exceeding the amount of savings achieved by participants. If financial education is to be delivered efficiently, it should probably be delivered by schools and integrated into the curriculum.
7. Available account structures were often inaccessible, expensive, and unsustainable, and investment options did not allow attractive returns. Reporting responsibilities devolved to the nonprofit programs, which used account-monitoring software that was developed for SEED, but overall those responsibilities were not a good match with the core competencies of nonprofit agencies.

Despite challenges, CDAs seem to be a promising social policy to provide children with a head start in life and increase expectations that children will attend college.

SEED for Oklahoma Kids, rolled out four years after the community partner demonstrations, is a rigorous experimental test of a large-scale, state-administered program. Designed by the Center for Social Development and administered by the State of Oklahoma, SEED OK assigned 1,358 children born in 2007 and their primary parents to the treatment group and 1,346 to the control group. Treatment group members automatically received an Oklahoma 529 plan account with a $1,000 initial deposit. They were sent educational materials and encouraged to open an optional individual Oklahoma 529 account with a $100 account-opening incentive. Deposits into the individual accounts of low-income children earned 100 percent matches, and those made to the accounts of moderate-income children earned 50 percent matches.[30] SEED OK added significant, rigorous findings to those of the community partners:

- It is possible to put in place a system of child accounts that reaches *all* children. Because of automatic account opening and initial deposits, all children in the SEED OK treatment group, regardless of income, race, and other indicators of socioeconomic status, have dedicated college savings. Without automatic account opening, very few children have college accounts and college savings, and those who do tend to be socioeconomically advantaged.[31]
- A 529 plan with inclusive features provides the kind of capital appreciation, investment options, centralized administration, and reporting features that local programs and financial institutions alone cannot.[32] The SEED OK initial deposits appreciated by more than 60 percent from 2007 to 2016, despite a large drop in value during the 2008 recession.[33]
- Sixteen percent of treatment families opened individual Oklahoma 529 accounts, and 8 percent contributed savings to them. These figures were higher than those for the control families in SEED OK, but far lower than in the community partners.[34]
- Even after only three years, the SEED OK CDA seems to have positive nonfinanical effects on both parents and children. Mothers have more hope for their children's future and are more likely to "see their children as college-bound."[35] The mothers themselves are less likely to experience depression, especially those with low educational levels or low incomes. SEED OK kids score better on measures of social-emotional

development. In fact, the effect of the SEED OK CDA on early social-emotional development is similar to the effect of Head Start programs.[36]

- Even if parents don't add their own contributions to the initial funding provided by the project, the children still show improvements in nonfinancial outcomes. Said differently, the behavior of saving may be less important than the presence of some amount of savings

SEED raised the issue of what is most important about child accounts, saving (building savings behavior and offering financial education on top of asset subsidies) or savings (merely offering asset subsidies and financial connection). Indeed, there are different views in the field today about the value of inculcating savings behavior and knowledge compared to the value of providing nest eggs. The answer from SEED is that all these things matter, and CDAs can have significant impacts in all these areas. Initial or seed deposits are the best and easiest way to build account balances, which have significant nonfinancial effects on outlook even in the earliest years and have shown potential for raising expectations about going to college. At the same time we found that savings deposits and matches (especially match limits, which set expectations), along with the support of teachers, parents, and programs, could achieve high rates of savings participation across the income spectrum of low-income families. Still, the effort that goes into facilitating high rates of participation may not be worth it, and while poor families save, it will never be easy or even feasible for them to save a lot (more than \$120–\$240 per year).

In the mid-1990s, when the experimentation with IDAs and asset-building was young, the emergent field decided that the key question was "Can the poor save?" And it began to use the word "savings" as a substitute for the descriptive but hard-to-understand "assets." The American Dream Demonstration answered that question emphatically. So perhaps it was understandable that as SEED unfolded, and with it the realization that the major impacts of child accounts could only really be measured ten, twenty, fifty, or a hundred years hence, savings behavior—the number of families who saved and the amounts they saved—became the measure of the efficacy of accounts. In retrospect, it was the wrong question and measure. The real question in ADD and SEED was "What can low-income people, both adults and kids, do with some input of capital?" The issue was savings, not saving.

SEED OK demonstrated that the source of the savings—the saver or others—was largely irrelevant. Consider retirement accounts, such as 401(k)s or IRAs. They are highly subsidized by employers and the government, and they grow through tax-preferred appreciation. Yet there is no question that when one asks account holders whose money it is, they proudly declare, "It's my money." Savings proves to be a function not of individual attitudes and behavior but of institutional arrangements. People save when it is made easy for them: most of us save in Social Security, 401(k)s, or 403(b)s, where we make a decision once (or, perhaps, just decide not to opt out), and thereafter contributions to retirement accounts are made for us, without active or conscious participation on our part. Nevertheless, it is important how people receive the money; the sense that it is earned, by saving, learning, and working, is essential to feeling ownership and empowerment.

The same is true for low-income and poor people and families: savings is a function of institutional arrangements. In this light, perhaps the most important lesson of SEED and especially SEED OK is the definition of the institutional structure for child savings.[37] Ten elements are crucial:

1. Universal eligibility[38]
2. Automatic, opt-out enrollment
3. Automatic initial deposit[39]
4. Automatic progressive subsidies
5. At-birth start (so accounts have time to grow)
6. Centralized saving plan (with low costs, limited investment options, regular reporting, high fiduciary standards)
7. Targeted investment options (with limited choice)[40]
8. Potential for investment growth
9. Restricted withdrawals
10. State public benefit exclusions[41]

As the SEED community partner initiatives wound down in 2008 and SEED OK unfolded, the seeds SEED planted were germinating at both the local and state levels, in noticeably different ways. (Social innovation does not yield annual harvests.) Besides smaller community initiatives around the county, large-scale, universal progressive child account initiatives were sprouting. San Francisco's Kindergarten to College program spawned a line of local initiatives around the country, while at the state level, CDAs using 529 plans were introduced in Rhode Island and Maine, with Maine leading the way. Both the similarities and the differences between these parallel lines of development are instructive. The most notable similarities: the new child account initiatives were large in scale (thousands of accounts), universal across the jurisdiction, and progressive, with higher deposits, match rates, and supports to poorer children.

Local initiatives tended to begin in kindergarten, while state programs started at birth. Local programs used smaller incentives, provided more education through the schools, devoted more effort to cultivating savings behavior, and used retail banks more. At the local level it was possible to integrate different services across public and private agencies to build community and financial capability, college-going culture, and savings behavior. The infrastructure needed to efficiently and competently roll out large systems of child accounts—account administration, accounting, investing, reporting, et cetera—is better done at the state level, building on the 529 base.[42] Indeed, most local programs, like most SEED community partners after SEED ended, rolled their accounts into 529 plans.

Congress added Section 529 Qualified Tuition Plans to the Internal Revenue Code in 1996 and expanded it over the years. The program authorized states and educational institutions to set up plans with tax incentives (and potentially other incentives) to "make it easier to save for college and other post-secondary training for a designated beneficiary, such as a child or grandchild." Plans have now spread to every state and command more than $200 billion in savings, spurred by the federal government's allowing contributions to grow and be withdrawn tax-free. Thirty-four states also exempt contributions to accounts. Federal 529 tax expenditures are actually a small proportion of federal on- and off-budget spending to promote higher education, but like the rest of the $30 billion in annual federal higher education tax incentives, 529 incentives are really useful primarily to the wealthiest taxpayers, who itemize their deductions and can prepay college expenses.[43] Only about 3 percent of America's children have 529 accounts, and they are overwhelmingly from upper-income families who would have been able to afford college anyway.[44] Financial institutions operate the programs under direction from the states.

These 529 plans were not born or necessarily designed to be the ideal infrastructure for universal child savings accounts. The tax incentives associated with 529s are highly regressive, and the design and administration of state programs sometimes have elements that discourage participation, especially of low-income families. For example, low-income families may be intimidated by the account-opening process, which typically requires them to select an investment from a long list of options. And some 529 plans have high minimum deposit requirements. Some of the 529 plans are not even interested in managing large numbers of small accounts, let alone marketing them. But in the 529 plan structure and core competencies lie the bedrock of an efficient, inclusive, productive system. Indeed, a number of 529 plans have inclusive features, such as no minimum deposit requirements and a "quasi-default investment" to streamline the investment choice and simplify account opening.[45]

Two of the first to recognize the potential of 529 plans were Michael Sherraden and former investment adviser Margaret Clancy. Despite the plans' regressive features, Sherraden and Clancy recognized that 529s were an "underutilized public good waiting to be designed to serve all families in America."[46] The design principles for universal child accounts developed by Michael and Margaret for SEED OK had been developed and tested for years through work with innovative state treasurers and 529 college savings programs to make them more universal and progressive. Led by enlightened state officials and a daring philanthropist, Maine has developed its 529 plan into a universal, progressive, automatic, efficient, and effective model of a truly inclusive system of child accounts.[47]

Nevada and Rhode Island have also adopted automatic universal progressive CDAs using 529 plans, and other states continue to develop their own. More philanthropists are stepping forward, including New York's Gray Foundation, which is underwriting the development of universal 529 plan accounts in New York City.

The other line of development has been city and regional programs, stimulated by San Francisco's pioneering Kindergarten

Maine's Harold Alfond Challenge

Alfond never went to college. He came from a family too poor to send him to school. Instead he went on to build a fortune as an entrepreneur. Perhaps he developed even more reverence for college and postsecondary training because he had been denied the opportunity himself. Whatever the cause, toward the end of his life, while he was chair of the Harold Alfond Foundation, he viewed higher education as both a right and responsibility of citizenship and worried that too few of Maine's children completed college, especially poorer children. He long dreamed of making college education accessible to every child in Maine, both for their sake and because he saw education as the key to Maine's future. He admired the Maine NextGen 529 plan, demanding engagement by students and families in saving, investing, and preparing for college. Harold Alfond died before seeing the launch of the Harold Alfond Challenge in 2008–9, which offered a $500 initial deposit into the account of every Maine child in her first year of life. For the first five years of the challenge, families had to apply for the grant by opening a NextGen account, based on Harold Alfond's belief that all families should have skin in the game.[48] By 2013, only 40 percent of Maine's newborns participated in the Alfond Challenge. Unhappy with this outcome, the Harold Alfond Education Foundation solicited Sherraden and Clancy's recommendations for increasing the utilization of the program.[49] Among other streamlining recommendations, Sherraden and Clancy recommended automatic account opening.[50] The board agreed. "We've come to realize that providing the opportunity to receive the [College Challenge] grant isn't enough. We need to make sure that all Maine babies actually receive the grant," Gregory Powell, chair of the foundation, admitted in 2014.[51] As a result, almost all of the 12,500 children born in Maine each year now get accounts. Automatic enrollment enabled the foundation to shift its operating budget dramatically, with the percentage devoted to enrollment declining from 85 percent to 15 percent, while families' saving increased fifteenfold to 45 percent and funding for education efforts increased fourfold. To date, the Harold Alfond College Challenge has enrolled 80,000 kids and invested more than $40 million in their futures.

to College initiative. Unlike the SEED expenditure of $2,000 per account for incentives, subsequent child account programs built expectations, skills, and significant balances with smaller incentives. San Francisco treasurer José Cisneros, creator of the program with the encouragement of then mayor Gavin Newsom, was frustrated at not having the funding to afford $500 accounts, and he had the temerity to ask whether $50 accounts might work. As of this writing, 31,000 San Francisco elementary school children from kindergarten through seventh grade have accounts and $3.8 million in savings, with three-quarters of that amount from families themselves (matched by $1 million in community incentives). About one-fifth of families have saved, with poor families eligible for food stamps saving in the same proportions as other families.[52] San Francisco's Kindergarten to College program inspired initiatives in cities across the country, from St. Louis to New York, Detroit to Jackson, Mississippi.

How can the United States adopt universal education accounts for all children? In 2005, Senators Jon Corzine (D-NJ) and Rick Santorum (R-PA) stood on a Philadelphia elementary school stage surrounded by kids to recognize the early results of the SEED Initiative and announce the introduction of the ASPIRE (America Saving for Personal Investment, Retirement and Education) Act, which would create accounts for every child at birth, seeded with $500 along with an annual $500 saving match. Their co-sponsors on the legislation were from across the political spectrum, including Chuck Schumer (D-NY) and Jim DeMint (then R-SC, now president of the Heritage Foundation). Though the bill generated growing interest for several years, efforts to pass it faded with the press of other business. But the idea and architecture of a system of child accounts remains, waiting for the right moment.

On a stage with former president Bill Clinton in June 2015, child savings account grassroots leaders announced the Campaign for Every Kid's Future with the goal of empowering and inspiring 1.4 million kids in five years, and every kid in America in ten. Ambitious, to be sure, but built on a foundation of experience, evidence, practice, policy and market development, and momentum from dozens of state and local initiatives. As of 2018, there are fifty-four state and community initiatives and 381,000 child accounts open in thirty-two states and the District of Columbia; there are good prospects for model systems with 1 million kids in all fifty states by

Educational Opportunities for Children in Foster Care

Twenty-five thousand of the half million children in the U.S. foster system age out of the system each year at age eighteen.[53] Some have had no family; others have had too many families and none has stuck. They generally have no financial resources and few social resources. Most have been held back a grade, suspended, or expelled. At age seventeen, they read, on average, at a seventh-grade level.[54] They face dismal prospects: one-fifth of them will be homeless, only 58 percent will graduate from high school (29 percentage points less than the national average), and one-quarter of them will be incarcerated within two years. Only 3 percent will graduate from college by age twenty-five.[55]

The Jim Casey Youth Opportunities Initiative (JCYOI), a partnership of the Annie E. Casey Foundation and Casey Family Services, works with agencies in eighteen states and localities to change the system. Ultimately JCYOI offered 3,000 of these foster kids an Opportunity Passport—an IDA, a bank account, financial education, and opportunities for leadership and engagement. That is, they were offered respect and opportunity. The futures of those foster kids, who would otherwise cost the system $300,000 to support, has been changed.

LC's story illustrates the challenges foster children face, and the resilience and potential they possess if only they are provided a base on which to build.

LC

LC never knew her father. Born in 1984, she lived her first seven years with her drug-addicted mother in the St. Thomas and Desire public housing projects in New Orleans. She remembers the Desire housing project as being cut off on all sides by water, railroad tracks, and an industrial zone. The projects consisted of block after block of three- and four-story public housing, and they were beset by violence, drugs, and gangs. Today she says, "I'm sure there were good things, but I don't remember any."

The only time LC left New Orleans was in the summer, when she and her two brothers went to visit her *nanan* or godmother, Miss Ruby.[56] Miss Ruby lived on a sugar plantation in a two-room wood shack where generations of family members had lived and died. LC remembers summers there on the bayou as peaceful times in her life, with particularly fond thoughts of sucking sugarcane on the porch in the evenings. LC cleaned, cooked (usually in the early morning), and did other odd jobs to earn her keep. And though Miss Ruby and her husband worked their whole lives for the family who owned the plantation, they never owned anything—not the truck they drove, not the shack they lived in. "I think they weren't even aware a larger world existed," LC mused.

LC's family lived on public assistance and the bits of cash her brother, who dropped out of school at the age of eleven, earned washing cars at the gas station. When LC was seven, her brother got into an altercation with another kid. As LC watched, a man snuck up on her and stabbed her in the neck with a broken bottle. At the time, her mom was living with a man who abused LC and her brothers and beat her mother. When LC's mother had had enough and was ready to leave, they waited until the man was out, ran to the Greyhound station, and, with money lent by her aunt, bought tickets to Denver, where they had relatives.

LC, her mother, and her brothers arrived in Denver in the midst of a snowstorm; it was the first time LC had ever seen snow. "It was a cold welcome," LC recalled. In Denver, the family lived with LC's aunt. To make ends meet, the aunt took in a number of kids and worked two jobs at the King Sooper and another grocery store, barely managing to keep food on the table. LC's mom soon disappeared; she was using drugs again. A few months after their arrival, Colorado's Department of Social Services, much more organized than Louisiana's, found out about her mother's disappearance and informed Child

Protective Services. Child Protective Services removed LC and her brothers from their aunt's home, concluding that the home environment was not supportive enough. That was the last time LC lived with her brothers. Over the next eleven years, LC lived in eighteen different foster placements spread all over the Denver metropolitan area, never for much longer than a year, and usually for just a few months, sometimes being sent to respite homes when no foster homes were available. "I never knew why I had to move; I never expected to stay. I was defiant and independent."

LC was never at the same school for very long, but she knew she had to go to school, and began to regard it as her real home. She excelled in school, almost always earning A's. She had learned to read early and well. "I loved to read. This was my escape. I remember reading the entire Boxcar Children series, and all the Choose Your Own Adventure books. I always looked up words I didn't know. Reading felt so different from everyday life; it felt like a vacation." LC recalls, "I didn't make friends; I read books. I walked down the sidewalk reading books." In spite of liking school and doing well there, she never really went to high school because she moved around to "so many homes, so many homes." She took and passed the exam to get her GED at age seventeen. She did not find out until after she took the two-day test that GED prep courses were available. "I didn't know it wasn't supposed to be easy. I thought it was just protocol."

When she was fourteen, she made a close friend, and her friend ultimately convinced her parents to adopt LC. She lived with her adoptive family for a year and a half—the longest period she spent in any one place. Her adoptive family's home was a shock to her: "They lived on a farm. I had seen dogs and cats, but never before goats and chickens and cattle." However, it became clear pretty quickly that the arrangement wasn't working. "None of us knew how to integrate me into the family. Sometimes my new mom would do laundry for the whole family. It seemed weird to me. I was working, earning my own money. I was used to buying what I needed—laundry detergent, hangers. I didn't want to owe anybody anything. I wanted to own my own stuff so that I could take it with me when I left. They wanted me to be a fourth child; I didn't know how to be a child." Within a year and a half, the adoptive parents' marriage ended, and they decided not to keep her. "It wasn't their fault. They should not have adopted me. I wasn't easy.

"I wanted to emancipate myself then, at age sixteen. I was denied. I tried again at seventeen; I demanded a hearing. I had been at dozens of hearings over my lifetime: when my mom was charged (she was incarcerated more often than she was free), when her parental rights were terminated with different placements, et cetera. But this was the first time I spoke. I had had a guardian ad litem for ten years, but only saw him twice during that time. He was a good guy, but didn't really know me. He showed up at that hearing and though he hadn't seen me in two years, testified that I wasn't ready, and my petition was denied.

"I think I was about nine when I realized that no one else was going to raise me. I needed to do it myself. I think it was then that I first thought I needed to go to college, but it wasn't until I was fifteen that I decided I actually would go to college." By then, LC had found her way into an independent living program. The program took her and other kids to Washington, DC, where she remembers hearing Victoria Rowe, the actress who played a doctor on *Diagnosis: Murder* and who was herself a foster care alum, tell the group, "You didn't get a childhood and you won't get one now. If you're going to do anything, you'll need to do it yourself." LC thought, "This was the last straw. I was pissed at the injustice of my life, but I realized that if I was going to get anywhere I really would have to do it myself." LC loved the larger world of Washington, DC, and vowed she would return there to live.

"The Independent Living Program was wonderful and rare—as good as my life up to then had been bad. It was the one of the few times the system got it right. Everything I needed was in place. Granted, I hustled hard, but the system worked hard for me too." They rented her an apartment for $225 per month, paid for by stipends the Independent Living Program provided. She met with a social worker on-site regularly, and with the whole team monthly. She worked at Taco Bell (she had begun working as a babysitter at age twelve, and when she turned sixteen she began a series of jobs at Dairy Queen and other fast-food restaurants and at Ross stores). She enrolled in Colorado Community College while in the program. "I was finally on my own," she says. LC earned so many scholarships during this time—from the Orphan Federation of America, Pell Grants, Governor's Opportunity Scholarship, and more—that she had to return some of the money.

While she was in the Independent Living Program, LC encountered the Jim Casey Youth Opportunity Initiative and the Mile High United Way IDA program. Through that program, she received leadership training, a spending stipend, and an Individual Development Account. "I thought it was too good to be true at first. This was the first time in my life that people invested in me and my individual goals. It was a literal investment . . . in cold hard cash. I could save and watch it grow. I had had lots of programs, even some training in financial education, but this was the first time anyone put actual money that I could use for my future. If I saved, they would match my savings $2 to $1. I was in work-study; I didn't earn much, but I put money into my account monthly, sometimes only a few pennies, most often $15 a month. I saved $1,500 over two years."

In 2008, LC graduated from Metropolitan State University of Denver with a 3.74 GPA and double bachelor's degrees in psychology and health care administration. "I thought I would open my own practice." She cashed in her IDA to move to Washington, DC. She worked at Every Child Matters, where she had interned while in school, consulting on child welfare policy. LC seemed to have started a successful life in the world after foster care. Yet there were new challenges. What had seemed like an adequate salary when she was still living in Denver turned out not to be sufficient in the District of Columbia. LC decided she needed another path.

She had always done well in school, and law seemed like a good fit with her affinity for advocacy and telehealth interests. She applied to several law schools; Catholic University Law School was the only school to offer her scholarships, though not enough to cover the very high tuition. "I expected law to be like social work," she says now, but law school proved to be very different from her college experience. She was not happy. "I had no family support; I didn't know anyone; there was no support system; I was often the only black person in the class." She struggled with classes and the Socratic approach often used to teach law, a learning approach that seemed to her to be too conflictual; she had to work full-time to be able to live, which made studying even harder. In order to concentrate on her studies, she stopped work for a couple of semesters, relying on loans. Within two years she accumulated $170,000 in loans. "It made me sick to my stomach. I didn't want to spend another day taking out loans to do a job I did not want to do. I didn't want to let people down." LC made the hard decision to drop out of law school a few months short of graduation. She continues to pay $2,500 a month on her student debt and says she feels as though she'll never get out from under that debt. "I was a wreck at the time," she acknowledges now, "but once I made the decision, I never regretted it."

Today, LC is married to a fine artist and working as a skilled nanny for newborns. Her career as a nanny began unexpectedly when an acquaintance asked her to take care of her kids when LC was between jobs. It has grown into a profession. She works for two families and has taken courses and developed a particular expertise in working with newborns, especially newborns who begin their lives in the newborn intensive care unit, or NICU. "It's crazy—I'm close to making a six-figure income; I never thought that was possible." She is helping put families together with what she has learned over her lifetime, and she says, "I'm helping to build the kind of loving families I never had."

Minh Tranh

Minh Tranh, the eleventh of twelve kids born to a family in Lagi, Vietnam, saw no need to study, no need to earn more than his customary C's and D's in school. His family, like everyone in Lagi, were rice farmers, as their families had been for generations. But then the seasonal rains flooded Lagi three years in a row. Minh saw no future there. His oldest brother and sister, who had emigrated to the United States some years earlier, offered him a plane ticket if he wanted to try to make it in the United States. He didn't really see a choice.

Minh arrived in the San Francisco Bay Area at age fifteen, speaking no English. "I would nod my head like I understood, but didn't." While he had thought schooling was irrelevant in Vietnam, he quickly realized that there was no path forward in the United States without schooling. He enrolled in the local public high school and vowed to follow his siblings' path to college. He completed San Mateo High, spent two years at the College of San Mateo, a community college, then completed his bachelor's degree in electrical engineering at the University of Texas at Dallas. He managed to get through with a single one-year loan his first year so he could concentrate on his studies; otherwise he lived with his siblings and worked his way through school as a teaching assistant during the school year and by repairing air conditioners in the summers. While he was working as a teaching assistant, a friend told him about an IDA program offered by EARN, a national nonprofit founded in 2001 that works to empower low-income people by helping them take charge of their finances. Getting a thousand-dollar match to his savings at first seemed impossible, but it was also irresistible. He had saved almost the full amount when his secondhand laptop gave up just as he was coming up on his final college project and semester. He used his IDA to purchase a new computer, which allowed him to finish.

Minh Tranh is now an electrical engineer specializing in power systems with YEI Engineering. "There are really just two career choices if you graduate in electrical engineering: high-tech and power. Competition in Silicon Valley for high-tech positions is fierce and the pay is low. I chose power."

Minh is working toward his professional engineer's license. He sends money home monthly to his mother in Vietnam.

2020.[57] Though bipartisanship is failing in Washington, there is now a two-decade record of bipartisan support for child savings accounts at the local, state, and federal levels. Here is the locomotive to scale.

Building on this extensive intellectual, experimental, political, economic, and social history of child accounts, we propose

The Oakland Promise

The community that is demonstrating the power of universal child accounts to transform the future lies just across the Bay Bridge. On January 28, 2016, Oakland, California, came together to make the Oakland Promise: "We as a community will ensure every child in Oakland graduates high school with the expectations, resources and skills to complete college and be successful in the career of his or her choice." This in a community where as of 2015 fewer than 10 percent of Oakland's kids were completing college. Led by Mayor Libby Schaaf and Superintendent Antwan Wilson and backed by a unanimous city council and school board, one hundred community partners, twenty-two colleges, and seventy private donors, the entire community of Oakland came together around the future of their kids—all their kids.[58] Oakland Promise is committed to providing college savings accounts to every child and combines that with mentoring. Says Mayor Schaaf: "I have never felt so aligned by a shared vision for an equitable Oakland where everyone thrives."

The waves from Oakland Promise are spreading. Darius Aikens, whose abusive mother has been diagnosed with bipolar disorder and has only a ninth-grade education and whose father died when he was nine, commented, "I think the Oakland Promise will create a new conversation amongst families and parents at their kitchen tables and within their living rooms that is currently absent: college and its importance. . . . So this is a promise from me to my five siblings also that they will not only have the opportunity to go to college, but most importantly to complete college." Caheri Gutierrez, another student, had survived being shot in the head while riding in a car just before graduation. At the announcement of the program, Gutierrez said, "Instead of looking at Oakland's young people as at-risk youth, after today we are going to be looking at our young people as at-promise youth."

Today Oakland Promise consists of five elements supporting kids from cradle to career: (1) Brilliant Baby, for Head Start infants; (2) a new preschool initiative to ensure full- or half-day preschool for all; (3) Kindergarten to College, modeled on San Francisco's initiative; (4) Future Centers in all middle and high schools, to provide college and career awareness and advice plus application and scholarship support to all 24,000 Oakland middle and high school students; and (5) the East Bay College Fund, to provide scholarships and mentors to all college-going graduates. Progress is tracked and measured through the achievement of eight outcomes: college as an expectation in the family, kindergarten readiness, third-grade literacy, eighth-grade algebra, high school graduation, college enrollment, college graduation, and career success.

The test of Oakland Promise's ambition is implementation. Thus far Oakland has raised $31 million of the $35 million it needs for the first four pilot years and has rolled out all elements of the initiative with the exception of the recently added preschool initiative. Moreover, the city has developed a strategy to sustain the initiative for twenty years and 100,000 students based on the development of a $50 million Generation Fund and a Children's Initiative that will go before voters in 2018.

The backbone of Oakland Promise is a system of universal individual accounts and real investments from birth through college—a countable index of inclusion and progress on which to anchor a changed culture. Lieutenant Governor Gavin Newsom, creator of San Francisco's Kindergarten to College program, introduced a bill to create a California system of college savings accounts. At the inauguration of Oakland Promise, he said:

> There is something that happened in Death Valley, the driest place on earth, in 2004–5 that defines

this moment and this program. In the fall of 2004 about seven inches of rain fell overnight, which was remarkable in itself, until the spring of 2005, when the entire valley was carpeted by wildflowers. It turns out that Death Valley wasn't dead after all. It was just dormant. The seeds of possibility had been planted years and years before, waiting for the right conditions to come along. When the right conditions come along, success becomes irresistible. Isn't that what Oakland Promise is about? Success is synergistic with environment. You've changed the environment of Oakland much better. Congratulations, Oakland. The best is yet to come.

Libby Schaaf radiates joy—joy in her job as mayor of her native Oakland, joy in her central initiative, Oakland Promise. The joy of the first three hundred college scholarship recipients, the joy of all kindergartners, the joy of parents and teachers and the growing ranks of Oakland kids and adults—indeed, the joy of an entire community that has found its heart and future, and is aligned and supported by a growing web of connections and expectations. The greatest worry as they build the complex infrastructure of a simple idea is the sustainability of the system. And their hope is that state and federal governments will learn from what Oakland has achieved.

A peculiar alignment of forces allowed Oakland Promise to achieve culture change, but now that

Oakland has proved it possible, the path for other communities is much less steep. Indeed, the College Promise Campaign already boasts 150 state and local Promise programs in thirty-seven states that provide free community college and often college savings accounts. Today Oakland, tomorrow the nation.

the creation of Generation Accounts, to level and raise the educational and life prospects of new generations of Americans for centuries to come.[59]

Generation Accounts are a progressive endowment and savings match for every kid born each year. They are designed to provide every child with a nest egg to invest in themselves, their education, and their future. Generation Accounts are the kind of initial investment that breeds long-term returns: the unfolding of human potential. Generation Accounts are not just an investment in our children but the gift of an equitable and stable foundation on which everyone can reach her full potential, a foundation for generations to pull us together and forward. This is what parents do for their children and grandchildren. It is what our generation can bequeath to future generations: equity, not debt.

How can we fund these accounts? By restoring inheritance taxes, just as the United States did in other eras to combat growing inequality, such as the post–World War II years, when the country halved wealth inequality. Throughout history, Americans have eschewed hereditary aristocracies in favor of a meritocratic democracy; it is time to reassert this core value. Instead of growing the fortunes of the wealthy few, seed the promising future for all with Generation Accounts.

Specifically, we should reverse the 2013 and 2017 reductions in the estate tax and eliminate the exclusion of inherited investments, each costing the federal treasury about $25 billion a year, for a current total of nearly $50 billion a year in 2018.[60] These are just two of the big tax incentives to encourage inheritance, both delivering almost all of their benefits to the large estates of the wealthiest American families.[61]

If we believe in equal opportunity, we must address the gaping inequities in the ways we promote inheritance in this country. One-third of American households received family financial transfers between generations, with white households four and a half times more likely to benefit from these than African American households.[62] Between 1984 and 2011, almost half (46 percent) of white households received an inheritance, with a median of $83,692, while only 10 percent of African Americans received an inheritance, with a median of $52,240—some $30,000 less.[63] Inheritance accounts for 31 percent of net wealth.[64] This was particularly the case for major wealth-building transfers for homeownership and college. Two-thirds of college-educated whites received parental help, with the average being $73,500, while only a third (34 percent) of African Americans received such help, with an average of $16,000.[65]

In 2013, Congress raised the minimum estate subject to the estate tax to $5.34 million per person ($10.68 million per couple), cutting estate tax revenues to the government by two-thirds, from $37.7 billion to $14.2 billion—a decline of $23.5 billion. As a result, only two out of 10,000 estates had to pay tax each year. This means that several thousand wealthy heirs share the bounty. The Tax Cuts and Jobs Act of 2017 doubled the estate tax thresholds to an inflation-adjusted $11 million and $22 million for single and joint filers, further shrinking this important intergenerational tax.

The confusingly named "stepped-up basis of capital gains at death," also referred to with the equally illuminating term "exclusion of inherited investments," pertains to the policy of revaluing property at death so that no inheritance tax is owed on any and all capital appreciation accrued since the asset was acquired. Thus, stock in Apple purchased for $25 a share that is trading at $500 a share at the time its owner's "estate matures," in the euphemism of tax attorneys, occasions no tax. Here again the current tax code subsidizes inherited wealth. This exemption of capital gains at death confers another $25 billion annual windfall to heirs, with the lion's share going to wealthy heirs.[66]

Critics of the estate tax decry what they call the "death tax." But who better to tax than the dead? They can't really use the money. They can't complain or vote. And they face it only because life and the system rewarded them richly for whatever brilliance, work, and luck they displayed. Their heirs have more reason for complaint, but again, when the minimum inheritance to even be subject to some tax is a few million dollars, that is already a significant boost in life. Instead of lavishing bounty in addition to that enjoyed in life, we should use the proceeds of a revitalized estate and capital gains tax to provide a start to future generations.

Closing these two loopholes would provide a healthy financial foundation for a robust system of universal progressive system of Generation Accounts capable of closing the racial wealth divide and the economic opportunity divide without increasing government spending or deficits.

Generation Accounts could help close the racial wealth

GENERATION ACCOUNTS THREE CHILDREN
$50000
$20000
$8750
18 TODAY
18 TODAY
18
$25000
$10000
$4375
5 TODAY
5 TODAY
5 TODAY
$ 2500
$ 1000
$ 250
AT BIRTH
AT BIRTH
AT BIRTH
BOTTOM FIFTH
MIDDLE FIFTH
TOP FIFTH

divide. Imagine the America that might grow from that. According to projections computed by Tom Shapiro and his associates at the Institute for Assets and Social Policy at Brandeis University and the Annie E. Casey Foundation, accounts like Generation Accounts could help eliminate the racial wealth divide by as much as 40 to 80 percent, and they are arguably one of the few politically, socially, and economically acceptable solutions that could.

Even in a time of division and dimmed hopes, it is possible to envision a generation of children born with a positive economic foundation and access to a system that encourages and enables parents, other relatives, and the whole community to build strong economic futures for all, separate from the economic misfortunes and starting places of their parents. It is possible to see a future where all kids have the prospect of, in Abraham Lincoln's words, "an unfettered start and a fair chance in the race of life."[67] It is a politically feasible to create a universal, lifelong, progressive asset-building system of child accounts that are automatic and simple, coherent, adequate, and low-cost, and that also provide appropriate financial education/coaching.[68]

We should establish Generation Accounts by amending Section 529 of the Internal Revenue Code to provide nest eggs at birth to the 4 million kids born each year. Initial deposits and savings matches could be done on a sliding scale—initial deposits might range from $2,500 for newborns in the poorest fifth of families to $2,000, $1,000, $500, and $250 for the next four quintiles. The deposits should continue for five years, and be made available to kids under five years of age at the time of inception. This plan would result in endowments of $12,500 and $10,000 to the two poorest quintiles of children, and these endowments should double to $20,000–$25,000 or more by college—amounts equivalent to the average debt load of today's college graduates.

Though the savings capacity of low-income families is limited, encouraging all families to save in these accounts can help them grow more by connecting people to the financial system, augmenting their financial capability, and encouraging educational goals. Applying sliding-scale match rates makes it possible for savings to mount across the income spectrum. Matching rates of 4:1 for the poorest quintile, dropping to 2:1 for the second fifth, 1:1 for the middle fifth, and 1:2 and 1:4 for the wealthiest two quintiles, with maximum matchable savings of $500, could double the endowments over the course of the first five years.[69] If, for example, the family of a child in the poorest quintile was able to save $500 a year, when that amount was matched at 4:1 she would accumulate $12,500 in her 529 Generation Account by her fifth birthday. Five hundred dollars is four times what the average family saved in SEED, but contributions by the community, state and local matching policies, and a spreading culture of college savings could augment the savings of the poorest families, triggering the full federal match. Accounts would be managed using the essential infrastructure already established and proven in state 529 plans. Generation Accounts would simply attach a new, more robust, and equitable funding system to the accounts.

As suggested above, Generation Accounts are designed based on the experience with and lessons of Child Development Accounts across the country and the world over the last couple of decades. Though Generation Accounts deliberately include everyone, they are designed to level the playing field, with progressive benefits that recognize that kids are entering the race of life at very different starting points. And though the accounts are on their face race neutral, all the communities

GENERATION ACCOUNTS

who are disproportionately income poor—people of color, women, foster kids—are also more likely to be asset poor and disproportionately overrepresented in the quintiles receiving the greatest initial deposits and matches. Generation Accounts build on similar bold proposals for Baby Bonds and Opportunity Investment Accounts advanced by Darrick Hamilton and Sandy Darrity and by William Elliott and Melinda Kay Lewis.[70]

These accounts can fit into, utilize, and democratize the existing 529 federal-state, public-private system. They should be universal and created automatically, with public defaults. They should be used as prescribed by the existing 529 system—that is, primarily for tuition at accredited colleges, universities, and vocational training programs, and for related books, supplies, and room and board. But the accounts should continue throughout life and the permitted uses of the funds should be broadened to include business capitalization, homeownership, retirement savings, and inheritance after age twenty-five. These should be lifelong accounts that act as the foundation for intergenerational wealth. Account holders should be able to borrow their own savings from the accounts for up to a year at 0 percent interest or perhaps with a small penalty, which both prevents accidents, illnesses, or emergencies from requiring students to drop out and can dampen the increasing income and expense volatility afflicting families today.[71]

The amended 529 legislation should encourage states to include age-appropriate financial education in schools tied to the accounts. States and communities should take inspiration from Oakland Promise, Promise programs elsewhere, and other community strategies to build a college-going culture and high expectations and supports for the futures of all kids.

All of the above can be accomplished with just $40 billion of the more than $50 billion recouped by reinstating the estate tax. The remaining $10 billion could be used to provide transition benefits to older children, quality preschool to all kids, or other investments in the future of coming generation.

Generation Accounts are a big bet, especially as they are a bet across decades and generations. To the casual observer, in many ways universal child accounts can seem inert over twenty years. (If a tree falls in the forest and no one is there to hear it, does it make a sound?) In fact, the accounts are growing silently in amount, power, and direction—receiving quarterly personal statements will raise families' educational expectations, financial skills, economic security and resilience, and lifetime aspirations. Generation Accounts are an enduring foundation, quietly but insistently investing savings in the present to build for the future. Generation Accounts can lift the sights and aspiration of our most promising and vulnerable resource, underwrite their productive capacity, and establish a platform of intergenerational stability and mobility for generations to come.

Generation Accounts are an extraordinary gift from one generation to future generations. They are the essence of "gratitude for the next generation":

> If some messenger were to come to us with the offer that death should be overthrown, but with the one inseparable condition that birth should also cease; if the existing generation were given the chance to live forever, but on the clear understanding that never again would there be a child, or a youth, or first love, never again new persons with new hopes, new ideas, new achievements; ourselves for always and never any others—could the answer be in doubt?

> When we fear death's decree, let these bring us solace: the memory of loved ones who have gone before us; a vision of generations to come, through whom we reach far into the future—beyond our own lives.[72]

Let us reach far into the future—beyond our own lives. No legacy can be more significant or enduring.

4

Home

Building wealth begins at home. Homeownership has been at the core of the American dream, and its growth has been one of the great achievements of the past century. In 1930, fewer than half of all white households and less than a quarter of black families owned a home, compared to 64 overall percent today.[1] That's despite the fact that American families have lost 15 million homes since the Great Recession of 2008. The 64 percent, however, masks an ugly fact: while seven out of ten white families own their own homes, fewer than half of African American and Latino families do.[2] We are losing faith in homeownership. We no longer believe it is possible or even desirable. But every American family should be able to aspire to homeownership and have a reasonable chance of achieving that dream. Only then will we realize the full economic and social potential of the American people.

A home is different from enterprise or education or financial capital. It tends to be the largest investment a family will make, less liquid, more tangible, more enduring, and harder to achieve without existing wealth or support. But like other assets, it is fundamental to economic opportunity and social mobility. It is in many ways the crucible of future wealth and success.

Some commentators see the American dream of homeownership as a mirage. But the simple truth is that the opportunity to own a home is structured by regulation of the marketplace. Just as homeownership increased last century, so it can increase again, especially among communities of color if only we restructure the market.

The first definitions of the word *home* in the dictionary are what you would expect: "a place where one lives; a residence; the physical structure within which one lives." But go on and the definitions get more profound and suggest the centrality of home to development and democracy: "an environment offering security and happiness; a valued place regarded as a refuge or place of origin," and, my favorite, "the place where something is discovered, founded, developed, or promoted; a source." Home is where personal, social, and economic development begins.

Eighty-nine percent of Americans, nine out of ten, across racial, ethnic, class, and geographic lines, believe homeownership is a key part of achieving the American dream.[3] "The United States," observes Bruce Katz, "is essentially a nation of homeowners and people who aspire to be."[4] Home is at once the destination of the American dream and its nest. Matthew Desmond, author of *Evicted*, notes how home is essential to Americans' inalienable rights to life, liberty, and the pursuit of happiness, and he calls it "the center of life," "the wellspring of personhood," and a means of entering into civic life.[5] Homeownership is associated with reduced rates of crime and lower levels of teenage pregnancy. It is also connected to increased academic achievement and community engagement.[6] According to Desmond, "America is supposed to be a place where you can better yourself, your family, and your community. But this is only possible if you have a stable home."[7]

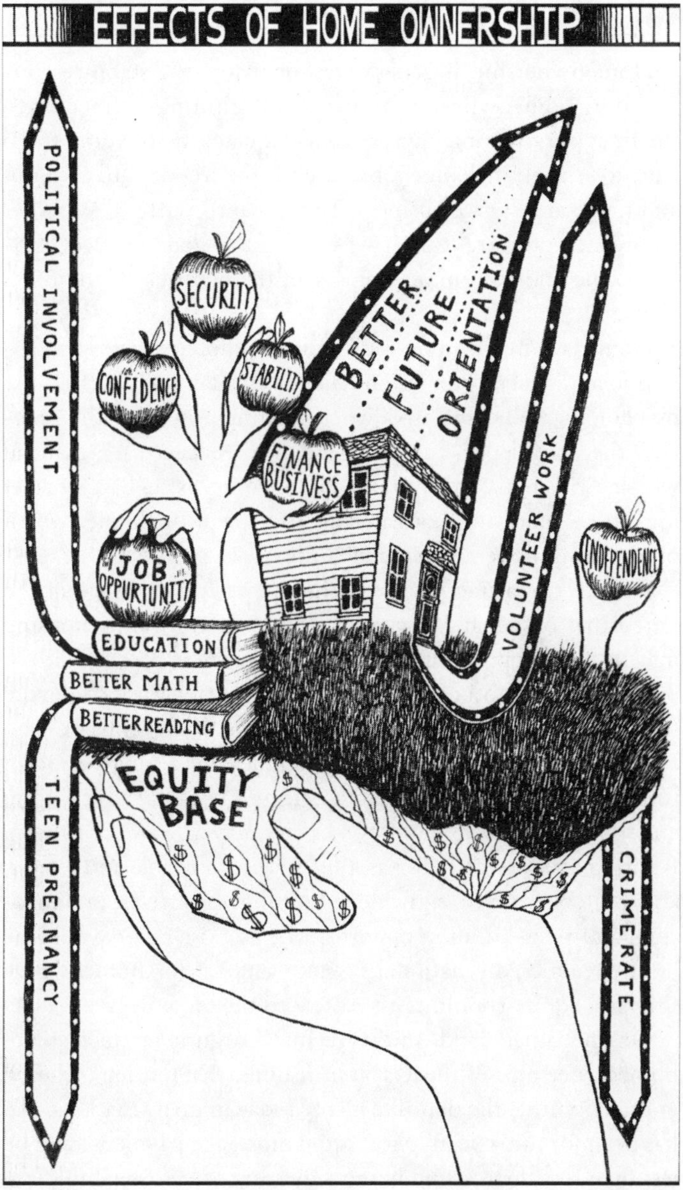
EFFECTS OF HOME OWNERSHIP
POLITICAL INVOLVEMENT
SECURITY
CONFIDENCE
STABILITY
BETTER FUTURE ORIENTATION
FINANCE BUSINESS
VOLUNTEER WORK
INDEPENDENCE
JOB OPPURTUNITY
EDUCATION
BETTER MATH
BETTERREADING
EQUITY BASE
TEEN PREGNANCY
CRIME RATE

Homeownership is generative: for many, the stability conferred by homeownership is only the beginning of freedom—the freedom to quit a job that is inadequate, the freedom to go back to school or change jobs, or even the freedom to cash out and move and start a business. Tom Shapiro writes, "Whether secured through renting, owning, or the generosity of others, home and community represent the bedrock of a family's future."[8]

Home is as much an outlook and a psychology as it is an economic and social foundation. Indeed, it may well be that the psychological and social value of owning a home—the security, the confidence, the independence—exceeds its financial worth. Still, make no mistake: home equity is the largest asset for most Americans, constituting 70 percent of the net worth of low- and moderate-income families.

Despite the attractiveness of homeownership, it should be noted that ownership is not for everyone, and rental housing may be more appropriate and desirable for some people who for one reason or another cannot afford or do not want to devote the time, energy, and money needed for ownership, or who cannot commit to a particular geography for a long period of time. Young people who are mobile and unlikely to stay long enough to see the value of homes rise may also prefer to rent. Renting can be stabilizing as long as it is affordable and secure, and renters deserve equivalent housing incentives, stabilization, and asset-building opportunities as existing or would-be homeowners. Any national or state support for homeownership and equity should assist renters to the same degree.

On the other hand, there are many arguments in favor of homeownership. While it is often assumed that renting is cheaper than owning, the opposite is true today in many markets, and has been for some years. Most often mortgage payments will be less than rental rates, and homeownership offers asset-building,

HOME OWNERSHIP BY RACE

capital appreciation, stability, control, and choices that renting does not. It offers attitudinal, psychological, behavioral, and community effects that renting does not. Homeowners are more likely than renters to be satisfied with their homes and neighborhoods, more likely to participate in voluntary and political activities, more likely to stay in the community.[9] Children of homeowners show significantly higher reading and math scores, decreased incidence of delinquency, and higher future earnings.[10] Two-thirds of renters believe that homeownership is essential to living the American dream, and cite assembling a down payment as the greatest barrier.[11]

For decades, spending 30 percent of income for housing —owned or rented—was thought reasonable. Today, however, a majority of renters spend more than half of their income on rent, and fully one-quarter spend more than 70 percent of their income on housing.[12] Moreover, the security of renting has been decreasing: millions of renters are evicted yearly, and an equal number are forced to leave their premises through informal pressure.[13] The impacts of eviction are often catastrophic. Matthew Desmond details the downward spiral eviction causes: "Eviction's fallout is severe. Losing a home sends families to shelters, abandoned houses, and the street. It invites depression and illness, compels families to move into degrading housing in dangerous neighborhoods, uproots communities, and harms children. Eviction reveals people's vulnerability and desperation, as well as their ingenuity and guts."[14] Indeed, the stress of the possibility of eviction exacts its own penalty.

Home equity is the largest source of net worth for a quarter of all American families. Home equity constitutes fully two-thirds of the wealth of the middle 60 percent of families.[15] For people of color, home equity is an even greater determinant of net worth.[16] Only in the wealthiest households do other investments exceed home equity. The poorest fifth of the population lacks this essential economic, social, and psychological bedrock.

The U.S. homeownership rate peaked at 69 percent in 2004 before the housing market collapsed in 2008; the rate has stabilized at 64 percent today. But this disguises the huge disparities in homeownership rates and home equity amounts among racial groups. Seventy-two percent of white families owned their own homes in 2017, while fewer than half of African Americans (42 percent) and Hispanic Americans (46.1 percent) did.[17] This is not for lack of desire, but because of differences in opportunity and financial means—and the lack of homeownership is an ongoing generator of inequality. Not only are people of color less likely to be owners, but the net worth of their homes is distinctly lower than the net worth of white people's homes, and their homes tend to appreciate more slowly.[18] Disparities in homeownership account for a large portion of the difference in net worth between white, black, and Hispanic families. In fact, if black and Hispanic families owned homes at the same rate as their white compatriots, the racial wealth divide would close by nearly a third, adding about $30,000 in net wealth. If rates of appreciation were equalized, the gap would close another 16 percent for black Americans ($17,000) and an astounding 41 percent ($24,000) for Hispanics.[19]

This highly unequal pattern is no recent phenomenon, but rather centuries in the making. The stunning disparity of homeownership rates and values between whites and people of color is the product of public policy and powerful private interests.[20]

Markets are made, not born. No clearer example exists than the U.S. housing market. One-quarter of the nation can trace its wealth to the Homestead Acts passed by the U.S. Congress more than 150 years ago, in 1862. From then until 1934, when the Federal Housing Administration created the long-term fixed-rate mortgage, people living in the United States could only buy a house if they had cash for the full purchase price. That condition changed with the creation of the long-term, fixed-rate mortgage. Backed by Fannie Mae, Freddie Mac, and other soon-giant government-sponsored enterprises willing to buy or insure millions of mortgages and extend hundreds of billions in credit, homeownership grew to encompass more than two-thirds of the country. From 1934 until 2008, homeownership expanded—and so did the wealth associated with owning one's own home.

Yet the Homestead Acts, fueled by land stolen from Native Americans and denying homeownership to most African Americans, enriched mostly white households. Redlining and housing segregation were the law of the land and standard industry practice during the heyday of rising homeownership in the middle of the twentieth century, and those problems extend to this day.[21] From 1934 to 1968, 98 percent of federally backed mortgages were made to white borrowers; all people of color shared less than 2 percent of federally backed mortgages.[22] As a result, even forty years later, fewer than half of households headed by men or women of color own their own homes—a full 33 percent less than whites.[23] Sales and lending practices that affected nonwhite citizens created and extended residential segregation and limited the appreciation of homes in those communities.

These disparities were exacerbated by the proliferation of variable-rate predatory mortgages and refinance loans that fueled the housing crash of 2008 and caused African American and Latino communities to lose half their net worth. African American and Latino families with good credit had been three times more likely to receive a subprime loan and, as a result, lost their homes with greater frequency: 76 percent more often for black families, 71 percent more often for Latinos.[24] Some 9.4 million homes were foreclosed from 2007 to 2015, disproportionately in black and brown communities.[25] When the U.S. government rescued the financial institutions that trafficked in worthless tranches of mortgage debt, it did not generally bail out most homeowners defrauded into entering subprime loans or address the systemic discriminations which depressed housing values in communities of color.[26] Though housing markets have recovered generally, home prices and ownership rates among communities of color have not.

The housing crash destroyed the burgeoning, if discriminatory, housing market that the thirty-year mortgage built. Many of these predatory companies are now extinct, but their shadows persist in our ever-larger financial institutions and in the breakdown of the larger government-sponsored enterprises such as Fannie Mae and Freddie Mac, which were so crucial to the expansion of housing in the early part of the century. Mortgage lenders have since tightened lending criteria, often more than necessary—thereby denying loans to some 7 million would-be home buyers who would have qualified with the perfectly adequate standards of 2001.[27]

Exacerbating the growing divide in homeownership wealth and opportunity in the United States today is the tax code, which overwhelmingly benefits the wealthiest Americans while generally ignoring the vast majority of low-, moderate-, and even middle-income families. It reinforces the racial wealth divide.

In 2017, housing subsidies in the federal tax code exceeded $250 billion. The wealthiest 5 percent of taxpayers get more than $200 billion in annual homeownership tax breaks—more than the bottom 80 percent combined. The lion's share of this goes to the wealthiest 1 percent, who command more than a third of the total. While the poorest quintile receives an average annual benefit of just $3 from these tax policies, the wealthiest 0.1 percent of taxpayers get on average $17,276—

more than 5,000 times as much. Ironically, too, we are taxing the third of all Americans who rent in order to subsidize the wealthiest homeowners.[28] This is Robin Hood in reverse, on a giant scale. It is obscene, especially when we understand this policy as the breeding ground of future inequality.

These upper-income housing tax subsidies are four times the entire annual budget of the federal Department of Housing and Urban Development (which focuses on the housing needs of lower-income Americans and tends to overlook homeownership).[29] These homeownership subsidies are as huge as they are regressive: they were expected to grow to more than $330 billion a year by 2019 before the passage of tax reform in late 2017.[30] The Tax Cuts and Jobs Act of 2017 reduced these tax expenditures on the margins.[31] Also, the deduction for state and local property taxes was limited to $10,000.

There are four major categories of homeownership tax subsidies in the code: the home mortgage interest deduction, the real estate tax deduction, the capital gains home sale tax exclusion, and the tax preference for homeowners over renters.

The best-known and most-loved, if not the largest, is the home mortgage interest deduction, worth $77 billion in 2016.[32] The home mortgage interest deduction is what the name implies: until this year it allowed taxpayers to deduct from adjusted gross income the interest on a mortgage on first and second homes up to $1 million. Interest on yachts and home equity lines of credit up to $100,000 were included in this deduction until the 2017 tax act. Thus, for example, the owner of a house with a $1 million mortgage with a 5 percent interest rate could deduct $50,000 from her gross annual income. The Tax Cuts and Jobs Act of 2017 capped the value of the home mortgage interest deduction to a $750,000 mortgage for new home purchases going forward, and eliminated the deduction for refinancing.

Mariana

As Mariana welcomes me into her two-bedroom 1926 home in Oakland, California, she casually discloses a larger truth: "I bought my house to provide stability to myself and my daughter, but that is only 20 percent of its value."

As Mariana proudly ushers me through the house, she points to the walls and the floor, each piece of furniture, her kitchen, her bedroom, even the doghouse in her backyard, describing the condition the house had been in when she bought it and how she had transformed it with her own hands. "Time," she explains, "is money. When you don't have money, you need to invest more time." Each piece of furniture—the bed her daughter uses that had been Mariana's at sixteen, the $2,000 couch bought for $300 on Craigslist, the side table rescued from the trash and painstakingly restored, the filing cabinet in which the documents of her life are carefully organized in alphabetized files—has a story, a history of meticulous effort.

Common knowledge suggests it is impossible for anyone who's not wealthy to buy a house in the San Francisco Bay Area, even if you're solidly middle-income. But Mariana did it, and she is not alone.

Mariana came from humble means. Her father is

an Argentinian immigrant who, she remembers, "was always making things," collecting other people's discards and transforming them into useful items. "From him I learned if I see something, I can re-create it." Her father always stressed to her that opportunity, not money, is what makes the person, and she credits him for teaching her the necessity of thrift. To this day, she does not buy anything at retail prices, and she has never had cable TV service.

Mariana did not have a stable home until she was eight—a rented apartment in Lake Merced. Until then she had bounced from her father to her grandmother to her mother, who suffered from mental illness and met Mariana for the first time when she was four. At thirteen Mariana gained U.S. citizenship. In 2003, Mariana gave birth to her daughter, Mia.

Mariana had never planned to attend college, which she regarded as a place "for privileged people." She knew it was a tool to advance, but as a single parent without a job, she couldn't afford it. She qualified for CalWorks but was discouraged by the program because "they push you into poverty and minimum-wage jobs." Still, through CalWorks, Mariana was able to get child care and work-study money. Combining Pell Grants, food stamps, cash aid, and cleaning jobs, Mariana went to City College and then San Francisco State, where she earned her bachelor's degree in social work in 2007. To get to this point, Mariana spent every available minute earning what money she could cleaning homes, typically patching together $200 to $500 a month, thereby staying within the income limits permitted by CalWorks.

Within a month of graduation, Mariana found a job at an independent-living program for foster children in San Francisco, where she started teaching soon-to-be-independent kids to budget and develop financial plans. She drew on her own skills: "If you operate with no margin for error, you become super-strategic."

It was while she was working there that she came across a flyer from EARN offering to match the savings of working families as long as they were used for business, purchasing a home, or education. At first she thought it was too good to be true, but she applied and was accepted. Using the program, Mariana saved money to pursue graduate education.

In late November 2007, program administrator Iliana Montalk notified Mariana that in order to remain eligible for the savings match, she had to complete at least two financial education sessions a year. Mariana had completed only one. The only qualifying class offered that December was an introductory course for first-time home buyers. Mariana had always thought "houses were for rich people," but in the class the instructor persuaded her that buying a house was possible for her with the help of an FHA mortgage.

As she described this to me, Mariana went to her file cabinet and pulled out her home-buying binder, stuffed full of documents. She explained to me how she had saved $100 a month to accumulate $2,000, which EARN matched with $4,000. She earned $2,000 more working for the Census that year, collected $5,000 in child support (a payment that was long overdue), and borrowed $3,000 from her mother. The total sum she accumulated, $16,000, would cover a 3 percent down payment and closing costs.

Every weekend for six months, Mariana looked at houses in the Bay Area in her price range. Ultimately, she found her current house. There were six other buyers making offers on the house, but Mariana wrote a compelling letter with her offer and established a relationship with the seller. Just a couple of years earlier, the sellers had offered the house for $450,000. The downturn in the housing market meant that Mariana could buy it for $180,000 in 2010. When Mariana and Mia moved in, they found the seller had left them the Virgin Mary, some apple cider, and a glass of champagne.

"I'd never lived in a house before. I didn't know what it meant. It took me six months to get used to the idea I could jump and scream and paint the walls whatever color I wanted." And that was just the beginning.

A couple of years after buying the house, Mariana lost her job when the program she worked for lost its contract. She spent a year without a job, surviving on unemployment compensation. "I financed it on my credit cards," she recalls. "I know, not an economical way to do it. I accumulated $30,000 in debt. But by that time my house had appreciated to $300,000. I refinanced with a $220,000 loan and paid off my credit card debt."

When I interviewed her, Mariana had just quit her most recent job—a choice made possible again by the house and the savings she had been able to put into her 401(k). "You don't know how much having to work a bad job takes out of you," she says. "I decided my well-being—and my time with my daughter—came first. This time I took out what I needed to pay the mortgage for four to five months, live, and finance a car. I'm using the car to drive for Uber. It frees me up to interview for jobs where I can really make an impact."

Several months later, the perfect job appeared, one that utilized all her experience and education as a financial social worker. "I now work at a very small office with a wonderful man who is a conservator and trustee for elderly and disabled people incapable of managing their assets and daily life. Even though this is primarily a financial job, he specifically wanted a social worker to handle the daily interaction with the clients because he saw value in having a good relationship with his clients in addition to managing their money.

"I've worked hard. Now I owe myself. I owe myself working on a safe street; people get shot in Oakland. I owe my family time. I just make it . . . but I have stability. I know how to live with, and without. If I'm too conservative, though, I won't move forward. But you need a tangible strategy and the capability to break through. This house is what lets us take chances. If your credit's good, you can do anything. In ten years, Mia will be through college. I'd like to rent out this house, which will more than pay the mortgage, move to the Caribbean, and start a business."

While the home mortgage interest deduction may seem even-handed on its surface, it is a windfall for upper-income whites who currently own a home. The more expensive the house, the higher the income and applicable tax rate, the more valuable the deduction. Meanwhile, this subsidy does not benefit renters or would-be home buyers at all. Ironically, while the lion's share of the deduction accrues to the very wealthiest homeowners, with the wealthiest 1 percent receiving an average of $10,000 a year in benefits, it still manages to bestow benefits of several thousand dollars a year to the top quintile, an average of $819 to the fourth quintile, and even an average of $260 to the middle quintile.[33] This helps account for its popularity. But the truth is that it is a regressive tax subsidy, showering more than two-thirds (70 percent) of its largesse on the wealthiest fifth of Americans. It is not even available to the majority of taxpayers who choose the standard deduction and don't itemize.

The home mortgage interest deduction was never intended as housing policy. It is a remnant of the deductibility of interest included in the original income tax legislation of 1913. Properly understood, it is a reward for *owing* on a house, not *owning* a house. It is certainly no help in buying a house, especially in its tendency to push housing prices higher.

The real estate tax deduction—$36.5 billion in 2017—allows homeowning taxpayers to deduct state and local real estate taxes.[34] Together these two deductions total over $113 billion a year. While providing a mere $18, on average, to working families, they deliver an average of $11,890 annually to the wealthiest 0.1 percent of taxpayers—more than a thousand times the benefit.[35] The Tax Cuts and Jobs Act of 2017 capped the state and local real estate tax deduction, which previously had been unlimited, at $10,000—effectively limiting the deduction only for the wealthiest 1 percent of taxpayers.

A third large homeowner tax incentive is the capital gains home sale tax exclusion, which cost the federal government $46.1 billion in 2017. This allows individual home sellers to exclude up to a quarter of a million dollars in capital gains on their homes from income (married sellers can deduct half a million), thereby paying no tax on that gain.[36]

The largest homeownership tax subsidy, making up more than a third of the total, is the tax preference for homeowners over renters.[37] Homeowners do not pay tax on the occupancy value of their homes, while renters must pay their rent in after-tax dollars. Let's put it this way: if a homeowner and a renter were each occupying a house worth $1,000 a month, the renter would pay tax on this $1,000 but the homeowner would not. This exclusion of "net imputed rental income" cost the government $72.4 billion in 2013.[38] In effect, renters are subsidizing homeowners to the tune of more than $70 billion a year.

Our current housing tax policy lines the pockets of the wealthy without inducing them to do anything they wouldn't have otherwise, except maybe to encourage them to buy a second or larger home while pushing up house prices. Meanwhile, it fails to help renters and would-be homeowners, pushing them further from their dreams. It does little to help middle-income homeowners. We are making the problem worse year by year at a rate of a quarter of a trillion dollars annually . We can no longer afford this counterproductive policy—if indeed we ever could. It is inimical to the country of opportunity we aspire to be.

If markets can be made and unmade, they can also be remade. Over the past thirty-five years, the emerging opportunity economy has shown how. Rising homeownership rates over the past century are testament to the ability of a well-formed market to enable not just the middle class but low-income people and families of color to own their own homes.

Four initiatives demonstrate how to build sustainable homeownership in a way that is advantageous to low-income and economically marginalized populations:

- The Center for Community Self-Help's Community Advantage Program
- Innovations in Manufactured Homes; Resident Owned Communities USA
- Individual Development Accounts
- Community Development Financial Institutions

These initiatives prove that homeownership is a realistic, profitable, and achievable goal for low-income families across the country. It shows that we can unlock the promise of widespread homeownership by assisting with down payments, offering counseling on homeownership, and providing long-term fixed-rate mortgage credit through established financial

David and Heather Greer

David Greer is an African American man in his mid-forties.[39] He hit bottom at the turn of the millennium: unable to control the hard-drinking lifestyle he learned in the army while stationed overseas, he became homeless, sleeping under the moorings of the San Francisco–Oakland Bay Bridge and in the parking lots and alleys around the Transbay Terminal.

David never met his father. His mother died when he was eight years old, overcome by illness, alcohol, and prescription drugs. He was raised by his aunt in Southern California with his two brothers and seven other kids, some her own. She expected him to graduate from high school and stay out of trouble. He looked up to the eldest of his cousins still in the house. When one of his cousins went to college at the University of California, David took notice.

School came easily to David. In high school, David qualified for independent studies, earning top grades while playing football, baseball, and basketball. High school offered him an introduction to college via college tours, and it encouraged and prepared him to take the SATs. He wanted to go to the University of Southern California, but it was prohibitively expensive. Instead, he attended the University of California, Berkeley, with a "nice" package of grants and loans, which, when combined with summer and part-time jobs, enabled him to attend. David majored in business, but he struggled in college. During his first year, his grades dropped from his high school grades. In his sophomore year, David dropped out. He tried community college, but that didn't work out either, so he joined the army. Stationed first at Fort Bragg and then overseas, he began drinking, and he even received a couple of DUIs. After two years, he and the army came to a mutual decision to part ways.

David went back to Southern California, and then drifted to the Bay Area. His drinking got worse; again he got in trouble with the law and ended up with the choice of rehabilitation or jail. He chose rehab at the Veterans Administration in Menlo Park. David reflects, "When you're down here to try to catch up, and fall down, it's a much bigger trip back up." The recovery program paired David with another veteran, who introduced David to an older woman from the Philippines. That woman showed David a picture of her daughter, Heather, who was still in the Philippines, and David began to talk with Heather on the telephone. Six months later, at Christmas in 1997, David flew to the Philippines to meet Heather in person. David proposed to Heather before returning home.

Back in San Francisco, however, David started to drink again. That was when he hit bottom. By New Year's Day 2002, David "had had it," he says. He returned to the VA for help, this time to live in a group home in Ingleside, where he spent eight months, and then on to a facility on Treasure Island.

Rehab included job training. He was given thirty days upon release to find a job, and he found one in the mailroom of a local hospital. He then worked as an assistant manager until a deposit turned up missing and he was blamed. After that he got another job, one that has anchored and powered him for the last fifteen years, working in and subsequently running a department in a business in San Francisco's financial district. During his tenure, David's responsibilities have grown from just being a clerk to managing the whole operation. Finally, when he was able to bring Heather and her son to the United States, he became a stepfather. Then his wife got pregnant.

That started David thinking of buying a house. He wanted his stepson and new daughter to have the stability he had never had. He scoured the internet for information and attended homeownership fairs. He found EARN and learned about its Individual Development Account program, which offered to match up to $2,000 in savings at a 2:1 rate. Both David and Heather signed up, taking courses on budgeting, credit repair, credit management, and saving. Each began saving $150 to $200 a month. By 2007, they had saved the limit together, and they had a $12,000 nest egg. In April 2007 they purchased a condominium in Daly City, taking advantage of a thirty-year fixed-rate mortgage from Bank of America. Within five years David had gone from homeless to homeowner in the San Francisco Bay Area.

The Daly City condo was not the last house David and Heather would buy. After the 2008 crash, they fell behind on their mortgage payments and the bank was about to foreclose on their home, but they were saved by refinancing provided by Ocwen, a leading mortgage servicing company. Through this program, part of the mortgage was forgiven, enabling David and Heather to resume their payments and keep their home. As a result of this second chance, in 2015 David and Heather were able to purchase a larger house in Hercules, a small city about ten miles north of Berkeley, which offered enough space for their daughter, Denise, her half-brother, Chris, and David's mother-in-law to have their own rooms. They rented out their old condo in Daly City for enough to cover the payment on their new house, and learned they could deduct its expenses and taxes on their tax returns. When the long commute got onerous they sold their Hercules home, moved into the condominium briefly, and then, in January 2016, bought and moved into a new house in Daly City. David and Heather still own that original condominium and continue to rent it out.

David says, "Now we can focus on getting Denise ready for college and teach her what she needs to know to take control of her life: career choices [Denise wants to be a social worker], car, student loans, budgeting." Asked to describe the value of their houses, David explains how it keeps him "thinking about the future and possibilities out there beyond where I am today. It enables me to spend time helping Denise with her school assignments. The IDA has helped me in my job too—it taught me to think ahead, manage a budget, manage people, billing, supplies, and create a profit for the business."

David says the future looks bright. "I'm hopeful. As long as I'm blessed to have a job and can keep the houses, everything's possible. You gotta live somewhere, but it's better feeling like house expenses are an investment and a tax break." And he reflects, "I think it would be great for everyone to have access to an IDA. I'd like to see others have the opportunity I had. We spend a lot on the effects of not investing in people, like building more prisons."

David and Heather both know that, as David says, "you don't live in the past, and you can't shut the door on it." But when challenges arise, a little money in the bank and a safe place to call home can make an enormous difference. David summarizes this philosophy: "Fall down. Get up."

institutions and the emerging network of community development financial institutions.

In the Community Advantage Program (CAP), the Center for Community Self-Help used a $50 million grant from the Ford Foundation as a reserve to protect against potential losses that could arise from loan defaults to back 52,000 mortgages to low- and moderate-income home buyers, leveraging some $4.74 billion.[40] The loans were thirty-year fixed-rate loans advanced to home buyers with a median annual income of $30,792. Fifty-three percent of the home buyers had credit scores below 680, deemed by the mainstream market as too risky to be expected to repay. Thirty private lenders applied their own screening standards, accepting down payments that were lower than usual—generally less than 5 percent and as low as 3 percent of home value. These were down payments that were achievable by lower-income families. The result was that two-thirds of these low- and moderate-income borrowers never missed a payment, and the 4.8 percent foreclosure rate was comparable to the loss rate on conventional mortgages. Delinquency rates were similar to those seen with conventional prime mortgages. In fact, subprime loans advanced by the larger market were three to five times more likely to default than the CAP mortgages.[41] The inescapable conclusion: low- and moderate-income families, including a disproportionate percentage of families of color, can and will buy and keep homes if they have access to low down payments, thirty-year fixed-rate mortgages, home buyer training and counseling, and rational underwriting standards.

The Community Advantage Program began in 1998 and bridged the Great Recession and housing collapse of 2008. By 2012, the average home buyer had gained $22,000 in equity. The comparison group of low- and moderate-income renters who continued to rent throughout the fourteen-year period

Lillian Bowie Singh

Like many African American and Latino homeowners, Lillian Singh lost a home in the wake of the housing crash of 2008, and blamed it on herself.

She bought her first house in 2007, at the age of twenty-five: a two-bedroom, one-and-a-half-bath condominium in Prince Georges County, Maryland. She was making a good salary at a research firm and had saved several thousand dollars, which she combined with a $5,000 inheritance from her brother to purchase the condo for $260,000. She thought she had purchased with a thirty-year fixed-rate mortgage with affordable $1,200 monthly payments. She felt very accomplished; she had achieved something her parents only dreamed.

Six years later, when she got married to David Singh, a digital analytics and marketing professional, they began looking for a larger home for their growing family. Lillian discovered then that her loan had been a seven-year, 6.5 percent interest-only variable-rate mortgage, and that she was upside-down in her mortgage: she owed a quarter of a million dollars on a house now worth only $100,000. In addition, she had to pay property taxes and the homeowners' association fees, which totaled an additional $600 per month. Her income was too high to qualify for a mortgage modification, so after months of agony and the help of the Financial Freedom Center, operated by the NAACP, she arranged a short sale. She took the hit; her credit score plummeted from a creditworthy 732 to a subprime 610.

The financial impact of the short sale was great, but the psychological impact was greater. She was deeply ashamed and embarrassed: she was a Stanford University dual-degree graduate, yet she had allowed herself to sign such a predatory mortgage loan document. As national data verify, her experience and reaction were not singular. More telling are the personal testimonies of several leaders of color like Lillian, who also achieved homeownership early in their careers, then lost those homes, and blamed themselves. In fact, these losses, perhaps abetted by bad decisions on the part of the dispossessed owners, were mostly a result of structural factors—bad timing, the collapse of the housing market nationally, predatory lending by mortgage brokers, discrimination in the provision of long-term fixed-rate loans, residential segregation, lower home values, and the low appreciation rates in the communities to which purchasers of color were steered.

Lillian was born in rural Mississippi, and when she was six her parents divorced and her mother relocated with her children to California, joining her siblings, who had migrated to the West Coast. The trade-off was that the cost of living was far higher in Los Angeles than in Mississippi. However, when she was twelve years old, it became clear that her mom's move to Los Angeles to provide more opportunity would pay off.

In the sixth grade, she applied and was accepted to USC's Neighborhood Academic Initiative. A rigorous seven-year pre-college enrichment program designed to prepare low-income neighborhood students for college, "The Academy," as it was called, worked to remove barriers to educational opportunities through enhanced classes at USC on weekday mornings, Saturday classes, after-school tutoring, and workshops on time management and study skills. This program proved to be very successful. Many of her peers in this program went on to attend Yale, UC Berkeley, Columbia, Brown, or USC. They are now employed as successful attorneys, advertising executives, school principals, doctors, and health care administrators. Thanks in part to this private-public partnership, she became the second college graduate in her family and the first to receive a graduate degree, both from Stanford University.

Lillian transformed her shame about the loss of her first home and her ignorance of the financial markets into knowledge and action. Determined to help other families avoid predatory financial advisers and mortgage lenders, she professionalized her own financial expertise by first acquiring her life insurance broker license in 2015, because she had experienced firsthand the importance and relevance of having a life insurance policy in place at the death of a loved one. Then she pursued her securities and investment broker license and became a licensed registered representative in 2017.

Professionally, Lillian stays committed to helping families avoid wealth-stripping mechanisms and encouraging them to focus on economic mobility solutions. She co-led the NAACP National Economic Department's Financial Freedom Center, focused on strengthening the economic security of communities of color, from 2010 through 2015. Then in partnership with Dedrick Asante Muhammad, she joined Prosperity Now to launch the Racial Wealth Divide Initiative in the fall of 2015.

Personally, Lillian successfully short-sold the condominium with the support of a HUD-certified counselor and with her husband purchased another home in Prince Georges County—something that she acknowledges might not have been possible had it not been for his separate income and credit score. Her credit score now exceeds 750 and she continues to partner with families to help them get the protection they need at a price they can afford, to invest for the future and get out of debt.

"Families need to be empowered with information; they need someone to trust, because financial markets are complicated and discriminatory. I will continue to work at the intersection of practice and personal finance for families to be a part of the solution," Lillian vows.

had only $2,850 in median net worth in 2012, while owners who started the period as renters had eleven times as much ($32,097), and owners throughout ended the period with nearly twenty-five times as much wealth ($70,985). Indeed, homeownership can be a wealth-building opportunity for low- and moderate-income home buyers the same way it has been for their wealthier compatriots. The median annualized return on equity was 27 percent per year—meaning that wealth doubles every three or so years, as compared to the Dow Jones rate of 2.4 percent and ten-year Treasury rate of 5.4 percent through the same period. Housing is one of the most profitable investments a family can make, exceeding gains in bonds and stocks—even for low-income households—if the market is structured right. An evaluation of CAP by the North Carolina Center for Community Capital concluded: "When done right, i.e., with long-term, fixed-rate, amortizing loans that are carefully underwritten, homeownership can help lower-income families build wealth."[42] Recall that housing wealth and security are not the end of expanding opportunity for homeowners, but the foundation of future opportunity too—the foundation of childhood aspirations and accomplishment, the nest egg for new business ventures, the impetus for community involvement and improvement.

After the 2008 collapse of the housing market, many people

were left with the impression that homeownership is unwise for low- and moderate-income families, a risky proposition that will set them, their financiers, their communities, and indeed the larger economy on its heels in the next inevitable downturn in the market. The success of 52,000 low- and moderate-income homeowners during one of the greatest housing downturns in our history—homeowners who made use of the thirty-year fixed-rate mortgage and rational underwriting—ought to refute arguments against homeownership as a route to economic stability and opportunity for the middle class.

For further proof of homeownership as a vehicle for greater stability and opportunity, consider a very different segment of the U.S. housing market: manufactured homes. Manufactured housing, commonly known as mobile homes, is the largest source of unsubsidized affordable homeownership in the United States, providing homes to more than 17 million people, 7.9 million of whom are members of families earning an average of $29,000 a year. It is the source of 43 percent of homes selling for under $150,000 a year and 75 percent of those selling for under $100,000.[43] About two-thirds of these homes are located on single plots of land owned by their residents. A third are located in communities frequently referred to pejoratively as mobile home or trailer parks.

The manufactured housing industry was spawned by automobile manufacturers as a way to sell more cars—in this case, trailers on a chassis. They are sold by dealers, are generally located in communities where the land is owned by investors instead of the homeowner, and are financed by higher-rate "chattel" loans, which are more like car loans than mortgages and generally have less favorable terms than real estate mortgages.[44] Despite being referred to as mobile homes, they are really not transportable; moving costs often exceed the value of the homes. Since the federal government adopted its building code in 1976, the quality of manufactured homes has improved markedly, and now they are energy efficient and architecturally distinctive and attractive. They can be built in one-fifth the time of site-built homes and at one-half the cost.

The economic interests of investor-owners, community managers, and homeowners are not aligned. Without controlling the land under them, homeowners are unable to build and realize long-term gains. High-interest chattel loans further mitigate sustained appreciation, and no tax advantages accrue.

This is a market that can be modernized and transformed, and with it the financial futures of millions of low-income homeowners. The most fundamental reform is to provide manufactured-homeowners the opportunity to own the land under them and build equity, and then to extend mortgage loans at lower long-term rates that encourage and reward responsible homeownership and improvement.

Since 1984, the New Hampshire Community Loan Fund (NHCLF), stepping in where no private lender was willing to venture, advanced more than a hundred loans to cooperatives of residents organized to purchase their communities when they came up for sale. One hundred communities, one hundred loans, zero defaults.

In 2008, the Loan Fund, Prosperity Now, Capital Impact Partners, and NeighborWorks America joined to form Resident Owned Communities USA (ROC USA) to provide loans and technical assistance to residents of mobile home communities across the country to buy and manage their communities. To date, ROC USA and NHCLF have lent $86 million to residents of two hundred communities in fourteen states covering more than 14,000 homes. New Hampshire and four other states have adopted laws to give the right of first refusal to residents wanting to buy their complexes in the event an owner wants to sell.[45] A model state code to rationalize the financing and management of manufactured home communities has been ratified, which could spread best practices across the nation. Innovations in Manufactured Homes (I'M HOME) is a network of activists across forty states acting and advocating for transformation of the industry to realize its potential as a source of affordable, appreciating homes for millions of families. I'M HOME partners not only advocate for policy but also develop new and replacement homes, conserve and preserve communities, and promote single-family and community financing.

A third key social enterprise working to transform the manufactured housing industry is Next Step Network, Inc., whose mission is to put "sustainable homeownership within reach of everyone, while transforming the manufactured housing industry one home at a time." Next Step provides home buyer education, Energy Star–certified homes on permanent foundations, transparent life-cycle financing, fair mortgages that enable families to build wealth, and advocacy to ensure that manufactured-housing homeowners have the same rights as owners of site-built homes. Next Step has partnered with the leading factory-built home manufacturers, including Clayton Homes, Champion Homes, Cavco Industries, and KIT HomeBuilders West, to supply state-of-the-art homes. The replacement of older manufactured homes with Energy Star–certified homes saves homeowners an average of $360 a year, and owners of pre-HUD-code mobile homes can save as much as $1,800 a year.

Social entrepreneurs Andrea Levere, George McCarthy, Paul Bradley, Stacey Epperson, and Doug Ryan along with hundreds of partners across the country are leading a growing and multifaceted effort to transform the manufactured housing marketplace from a disappearing, stigmatized, and equity-destroying industry to a vibrant source of badly needed unsubsidized, appreciating, affordable homeownership for millions.[46] With the supply of affordable housing plummeting across the country—the number of affordable rental units dropped 60 percent in six years from 2010 to 2016 alone—this kind of transformation is crucial.[47]

Levere suggests that five elements are crucial to the transformation strategy: social enterprise and innovation; policy development and advocacy, especially for the right of first refusal and the uniform code; technological advances, such as Energy Star–certified homes; market evidence and communication to raise the appreciation of the value of manufactured housing; and data analysis and collection to document the rise and returns of manufactured housing done right. This transformation can be seen in states such as Oregon and New Hampshire. Another key will be to shift the ownership of manufactured housing communities and the land under manufactured homes from investors to homeowners. This requires increasing the capacity of manufactured housing residents to build savings and equity so that they can afford down payments and equity investment in their communities.

Down payments are the chief barrier to home purchase for low- and moderate-income buyers. Individual Development Accounts are a prime way to amass a modest nest egg to cover the down payment. They also bring with them tailored home buyer education. Homeownership was always the most popular choice of Individual Development Account holders, even if it was the hardest and most expensive option. Homeownership was the initial goal of half of all participants in the American Dream Demonstration and for participants in the federally funded IDA demonstration, the Assets for Independence Act. As savers realized the savings requirements, sacrifices, and

Lowry Grove and Park Plaza

Lowry Grove, a mobile home community in the St. Anthony neighborhood of Minneapolis, closed on June 30, 2016, after seventy years.[48] Many of the ninety-plus residents had called it home for more than a decade, but they received notice of the sale of the community only a few months prior, in a letter stuffed in their mailboxes.

Frank Adelman, who is in his eighties, had lived in Lowry Grove for over thirteen years. It was the only place he had ever owned himself. When his daughter asked him what he was going to do, he replied, "This is my home. I'm not going to leave Lowry Grove." On June 20, ten days before the community closed, he took his life.

Another resident in her eighties, Jean Christianson, had also lived at the park for more than a decade. Her chief concern was moving her piano, even though she could not afford to have it tuned.

Just days before the closing, Bill McConnell, a resident for thirty-one years, had no idea where he would go. Tongue-in-cheek, he described himself as "coming soon to a Walmart parking lot near you."[49]

What was evident in the closing of Lowry Grove was how much of a community it had become. Residents helped each other pack, ensured that everyone had a place to go, helped each other find refuge.

Since 1991, no new mobile home communities have opened in Hennepin County, where Lowry Grove is located, and half of the existing ones have closed. The economic, social, and human loss that occurs when a community closes cannot be underestimated. Unsubsidized affordable housing units are disproportionately the home of people of color, whose kids could attend some of the better schools in the state. In Hennepin County, 25 percent of mobile home community residents are Latino, more than four times their presence in the population.

In Minnesota, as in half a dozen other states, mobile home community residents are required to be given the right of first refusal to buy the land their homes are located on for the same price offered by another buyer. The residents of Lowry Grove organized and found a nonprofit, Aeon, Inc., to forward an offer to buy the community's land for $6 million. However, the park was sold the next day to The Village LLC, a developer with plans to build seven hundred units of mixed-income housing on the spot.[50] The move was subsequently blocked by the St. Anthony City Council, but it was too late to save Lowry Grove, even though the development that was to supplant it has yet to win approval.

Across town from Lowry Grove is another mobile home community, Park Plaza, a nine-acre development divided by a car dealership. Owned by the same man, Phil Johnson, as Lowry Grove, Park Plaza had a very different outcome.

In 2010, the eighty-four homeowners in Park Plaza received a letter in their mailboxes informing them that Johnson was selling the complex, but that the residents had the right to buy it. The price: $3.85 million. More than 80 percent of the residents had incomes less than half the median family income; half had lived there more than five years, and nearly a third had been there for more than ten years.

"I remember getting that notice and thinking, where are we ever going to get that kind of money?" said Natividad Seefeld. At that point she had already lived in Park Plaza twelve years and loved it. Now she had been joined by her disabled daughter and three grandchildren. "Where else could you live in

Minneapolis for $285 a month, near to all the necessary city services and some of the highest-quality schools in the state? I was not moving."

Born in East Los Angeles, Natividad has managed to pack a dozen occupations and lifetimes into her fifty-seven years. Currently a Logistics Coordinator for General Mills, she has also been a mother at sixteen, a truck and limo driver, a pet store owner and employee, a shipping and receiving clerk, and a burn unit volunteer. She was married for twenty years to "a wonderful man—we never argued," and for a while was, at least on paper, a millionaire, co-owning a 3,200-square-foot home with him. She fell in love with someone else and left her marriage amicably, with only a couch and a dresser. Natividad was diagnosed with an incurable brain tumor in 2007 and underwent several surgeries. Her health is still good, but with an annual income then of $20,000 to $21,000, she figured she could not afford to move anywhere else.

Upon receiving Johnson's letter, Natividad went to City Hall, purchased the property plan for $16, and checked out the city records on Park Plaza. She found that the water and sewer bills ran $12,000 a quarter and were regularly paid late at a 10 percent penalty. This was no surprise: there were regular leaks at the complex, water outages, disruptive repairs, and potholes in the street.

Armed with this information, Natividad attended

a community meeting where Kevin Walker from the nonprofit North Country Foundation (NCF), one of nine regional technical assistance affiliates of ROC USA, briefed the residents on how they might form a cooperative to buy the housing complex, but a majority of the residents had to agree, and they had to establish a cooperative that night and elect its officers. When Walker asked who would be president of the owners' association, everyone pointed to Natividad.

The organizing that followed made Park Plaza even more of a community. Residents had to come up with $200 each in membership fees. The mayor of the area taunted, "You will fail." Natividad answered, "We will not fail."

With help from Kevin at NCF, the residents secured a $4.235 million thirty-year 6 percent mortgage loan through ROC USA and proceeded to buy the community. Though the loan provided for $200,000 in maintenance and improvements on top of the purchase price and fees, the reserve was insufficient to keep up with $40,000 in annual repairs to the neglected infrastructure of the complex. Unable to raise grants or loans for the necessary upgrade, the community elected to refinance the development in 2015. In those five years, the value of Park Plaza had increased almost $1 million, and the community secured a $5.1 million new mortgage at 3 percent. With that, they replaced the ailing water and sewer system, repaved the streets, and generally upgraded the community infrastructure. In 2017, the residents unveiled a new playground for children of the community, a longtime dream, and dedicated it as "Natividad's Dream."

Today, Park Plaza residents and owners pay $487 a month, well below the market rate. As residents die or move on, the cooperative makes the units available to new entrants for as little as $2,000. Two of those new families came from Lowry Grove. Last Christmas, every member of the community received a $25 Walmart gift card from the association. The community also gets backpacks and school materials donated to kids at the beginning of school each year, maintains a community garden, and is building a community storm shelter. Residents from the two sides of the park know each other now. "We're like a giant family with crabby uncles and aunts, but now we take care of each other and face the future with hope and confidence," says Natividad.

So, will the remaining 50,000 manufactured housing communities across the country go the way of Lowry Grove, or will they succeed the way Park Plaza has? ROC USA is expanding as a sustainable and profitable social enterprise, hoping to convert fifteen or more communities to resident ownership each year. If Fannie Mae and Freddie Mac are allowed to rejoin the fight for home opportunity, the field could take a quantum leap forward, converting hundreds per year.

Private financial institutions, banks, insurance companies, and states, once strangers to this emerging marketplace, are increasing their investments now that the risks have been substantially reduced. More states are passing the uniform code and enacting right-to-purchase laws. Perhaps someday there might be developments designed to engender prosperous communities of owners from the outset.

learning involved in securing housing, the numbers of home seekers declined by a fifth or more. Still, within two years of the start of the American Dream Demonstration, some 46 percent of account holders—half of whom had incomes under the poverty line, and a fifth of whom were living on less than $9,000 for a family of four—purchased assets; 28 percent of the account holders chose homeownership and 18 percent chose home repair. More than half of the 111,000 Assets for Independence Act account holders bought assets, and half of those—26,000 low-income families—chose homeownership. Similarly, 21,512 participants in the Office of Refugee Resettlement IDA Program purchased homes.

Given the history and depth of racial disparities in homeownership, it should be noted that African Americans, Latinos, Asian Americans, Native Americans, and women are disproportionately represented in IDA programs—with success rates equal to or better than their white counterparts.

How did new, low-income IDA homeowners fare after 2008? In partnership with the Urban Institute, CFED studied a sample of 831 IDA home buyers in seventeen states supported by six different state, local, and community programs who

Robin Craig

Robin Craig was born in southeast Washington, DC, in 1958. Her father worked for the U.S. Government Printing Office and her mother for Sears. "We were not rich, but we had a house and we ate every day. I went to private school—the Immaculate Conception Academy in Georgetown."

Robin never thought she'd own her own home. "My parents did, but they were old people, and who wants to mow the grass anyway?" she jokes. She was also a single parent with limited income and "not the best credit." She didn't think she could afford it. "I knew that buying was cheaper than renting if you had the down payment, but where was I going to get the down payment?" But she soon set her mind on buying her own home. The reason: her son, Brandon, wanted a home so he could get a dog.

Robin bought her first home in 1997. She had just started working for the Marshall Heights Community Development Corporation as an assistant property manager. By then she had graduated from Langston College in Oklahoma and worked for several private property management firms, including Dreyfus Management and Gates, Hudson & Associates.

Robin's timing was perfect. The Capital Area Asset Building Collaborative (CAAB) had just launched its first Individual Development Account program, and Marshall Heights CDC was one of their first partners. As a $30,000-a-year facilities manager and single mom, Robin qualified. Under the terms of the IDA program, Robin's savings were matched dollar for dollar. She proceeded to save $500 a month for nine months, earning an additional $4,500 for a $9,000 home reserve. She also completed home buyer classes—"I had no idea about home purchase, brokers, inspections," she says. She went looking for houses during her lunch breaks, and eventually found a fixer-upper in the neighborhood. It was valued at twice the $100,000 she bought it for. She put $6,000 down, reserving the remaining $3,000 for repairs, and secured a thirty-year fixed-rate mortgage. She found she was eligible for a five-year tax abatement and secured it. Three months after buying the house, Robin and Brandon got Pepper, a black Lab.

Today, twenty years later, Robin still lives in that home. "The best thing about owning a home is being part of the community. When you own, you're invested in this community. You want the best for the community. You don't let anybody disrespect it because you own. You don't allow people to come in and sell drugs. You contact the police. You get involved in solving problems. I got involved and raised money for the school Brandon attended [H.D. Woodson]. I got involved in the Advisory Neighborhood Committee for the area. Brandon got to grow up in this neighborhood. I think it gave him a sense of stability. He still is friends with the group of kids he grew up with. I'm still very active in the community. Now I'm acting president and CEO of Marshall Heights CDC. We're helping neighborhood residents keep their homes, advocating for inclusionary zoning, developing transitional housing. I'm talking to CAAB about partnering on a first-time home buyer IDA program.

"Everyone should have the opportunity to have what they so desire. Everybody should be educated in opportunity."

bought their homes between 1999 and 2007.[51] Only 3 percent of account holders lost their homes. At least 93 percent of IDA home buyers showed no evidence of payment problems. The reasons for this were the cost of down payments, the quality and cost of the loan product, and home buyer counseling and assistance. By inviting account holders to contribute substantial amounts of savings and multiplying those savings at an average match of 2:1, IDAs were instrumental in providing down payments—the largest barrier to homeownership for low-income families.[52] Account holders overwhelmingly held high-quality thirty-year fixed-rate mortgages, and a mere 1.5 percent of IDA home buyers got saddled with subprime, high-interest loans. This was probably the combined result of educating and counseling account holders, as well as program oversight and negotiations with banks originating the loans.[53] Home buyer education has been shown to reduce delinquencies by 23 percent.[54]

Besides down payments and home buyer education, another key to opening up homeownership to low-income home buyers is access to reasonable mortgage loans with reasonable underwriting criteria. Here the emergence of community development financial institutions—financial institutions that provide credit and financial services to underserved markets and populations—over the last twenty-five years is particularly instructive and propitious. In 1992, Bill Clinton ran for the presidency in part on the promise of creating "a thousand microloan programs and 100 community banks" in the country. The result was the establishment of the Community Development Financial Institutions Fund in 1994, to underwrite the expansion of microenterprise loan funds, community development credit unions, community banks, community development loan funds, and other hybrid community-based financial institutions dedicated to providing loans and technical assistance to low-income and minority entrepreneurs, home buyers, students, and nonprofits. In 1996, there were 196 CDFIs in the country. Twenty years later, there were 1,049 such institutions across the country with $108 billion in capital.[55] To date, the CDFI industry has invested in the development or rehabilitation of 1.5 million housing units.[56]

We must—and we can—restore the dream of homeownership for all Americans. In doing so, we can establish for all households a foundation for future prosperity, matching their work, talents, and aspirations with their fair share of housing incentives. The idea that homeownership is within the reach of every American has faded in the face of reality. But we cannot accept that reality. We must change it, and we can, but only if we boldly assert that every person in America should have the opportunity to buy and enjoy a home in her or his lifetime.

If we build on proven practice, policy, and tools, millions more middle- and low-income families can own their own homes. Even if the United States doesn't spend a dollar more than it does now, reforms to tax codes to promote popular homeownership and asset-building will enrich the country as a whole, and particularly people of color and renters who have been left out. As an added benefit, these policies will lay a foundation for increased entrepreneurship, education, retirement security, and wealth creation. Central to unlocking this promise is the establishment of Home Accounts.

The key to expanding homeownership, with its multiplicity of benefits, is to open up access to and effective demand for it. The steps are simple:

A down payment for every household. Down payments are the key to homeownership—an elegant, effective gatekeeper ensuring that the owner will take full responsibility for stewarding and building the value of the asset and will repay the loan. Most Americans, especially low-, moderate-, and even middle-income families, have no reasonable way to assemble them. Our experience with IDAs over the last twenty-five years argues for establishing Home Accounts with matching incentives—the Home Credit—for every would-be homeowner in the country.

Home Accounts would be established in private and non-profit financial institutions, with a federal default—a MyHome Account, along the lines of the MyRA account introduced by the Obama administration. These accounts should have low fees, low minimum deposits, and uses limited to home buying, home repair, or home improvement, with provisions for rollover to other uses in event of hardship, and they should earn interest and provide prudent investment options.

A refundable Home Credit should be established, which would provide a savings match for savings in Home Accounts.[57] All taxpayers would be entitled to the Home Credit, which would match up to $1,000 a year in savings or rent on a sliding scale. A progressive sliding scale might, for example, begin with a 3:1 match for the poorest income quintile (making below $19,000 in 2017), decreasing to 2:1 for the second-poorest quintile ($20,000–$40,000), 1:1 in the middle quintile ($40,000–$60,000), 1:2 in the second-highest quintile, and finally 1:3 in the highest. With this scale, the poorest households who could save the maximum $1,000 (contributions from family, friends, the community, and state and local government could be included) could accumulate $4,000 per year, enough for a 5 percent down payment for a median-priced house (about $300,000 nationally) in three to four years. Since people of color are so much more likely to be poor and renters, it would disproportionately benefit them, helping to close the racial wealth divide significantly.[58]

The Home Credit would be funded by phasing out all or some of the home mortgage interest deduction, the deductions for state and local real estate taxes, and, perhaps, the exclusion for capital gains in home sales, replacing them with the Home Credit and a 15 percent refundable credit on homes up to $500,000 in value. The universal, refundable home credit proposed here would be fairer and more productive and could reach all Americans, rather than just the wealthiest homeowners. It would also reduce the effective tax on renters.

Open fair access to homeownership. Strengthen and enforce fair housing and nondiscrimination laws and ban or change practices and policies that lock out people of color from entry. Institute reasonable and proven underwriting and credit standards, building from the perfectly adequate standards of 2001 as informed by discoveries of community groups at the

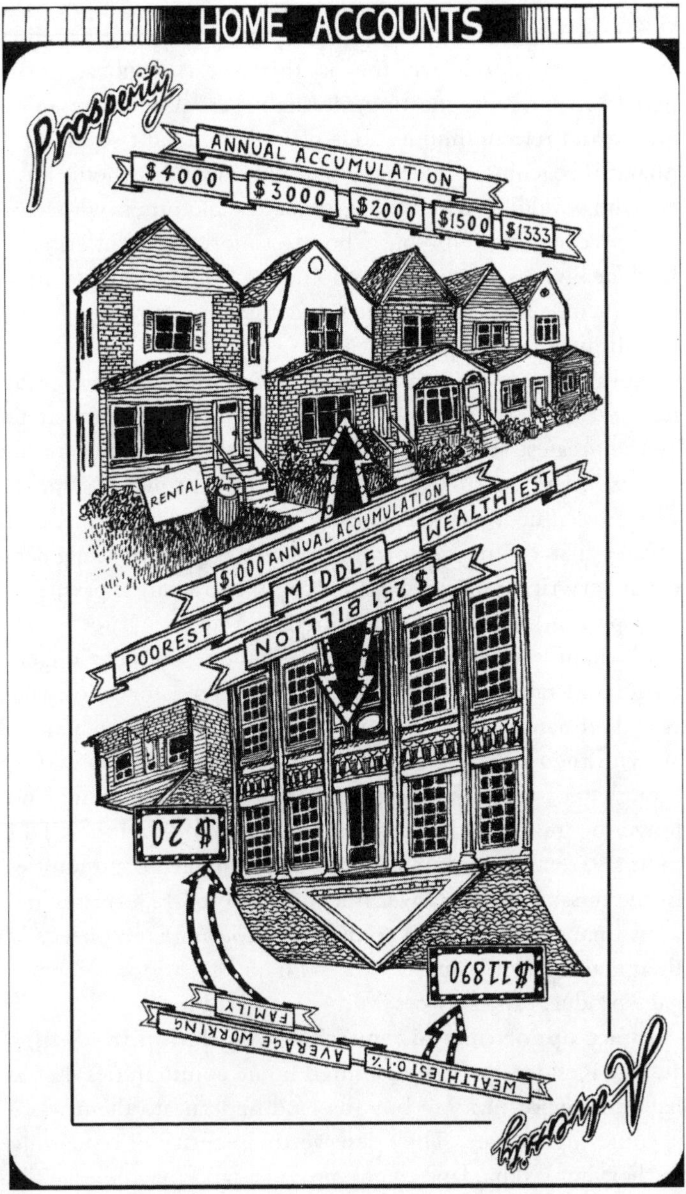
HOME ACCOUNTS
Prosperity
ANNUAL ACCUMULATION
$4000
$3000
$2000
$1500
$1333
RENTAL
$1000 ANNUAL ACCUMULATION
POOREST
MIDDLE
WEALTHIEST
$251 BILLION
$20
$11890
AVERAGE WORKING FAMILY
WEALTHIEST 0.1%
Adversity

local and state levels over the last thirty years: innovations in underwriting, rent reporting, alternative credit measures (e.g., utility and telecommunications payments), credit repair, and financial coaching.[59] Let in the 7 million would-be home buyers who would have met those standards, and others who have credit scores below 700 but who meet more stringent criteria. Exclude savings designated for homeownership from asset limits in income support programs, and raise or remove applicable asset limits more generally.[60]

Reinvigorate the thirty-year fixed-rate mortgage at fair rates. The thirty-year fixed-rate mortgage proved to be the greatest tool for asset-building and homeownership in the twentieth century. This brilliant, elegant piece of inclusive government market-making can be the centerpiece of twenty-first-century opportunity as well, especially using better underwriting standards and accepting low down payments (3–5 percent). Fannie Mae and Freddie Mac, or whatever succeeds them, should finance and guarantee responsible longer-term fixed-rate loans. Variable-rate loans, predatory mortgages and refinancing, and discriminatory underwriting practices, all with their risks assumed by Fannie Mae and Freddie Mac, brought down the housing market in 2008, and should no longer be guaranteed. We should continue to build the CDFI industry, renew the duty to serve disadvantaged communities in the mission of the Government-Sponsored Enterprises and press financial institutions to meet the housing credit needs of their marginalized communities with quality, affordable mortgage products and services.

Enact opportunity-to-purchase legislation in all fifty states. Residents of manufactured home communities should have the opportunity to buy the land underneath them when it comes up for sale. They deserve the security of remaining in their homes that land tenure provides, and they deserve the incentive to improve their homes and communities and build wealth.

Will the reforms above ensure that every American who chooses can buy and own a house? No, but they can give everyone a reasonable chance for a clear path to homeownership—and a reason to hope and work and save to this end. That hope, moreover, is grounded in cash. Through these reforms we should be able to generate millions more homeowners and entrants to the middle class each year, without spending any more than we do now in the name of homeownership.

Is this achievable in the next decade? Yes—if, and only if, common Americans demand their share of the federal tax largesse. Only if common Americans insist on making their homeownership dreams real. Only if we decide to opt for hope and opportunity for all over greed and narrow self-interest.

Then we can come home.

5
Business

> Our country has been and will be built on the enterprise of our people—on their ideas, their energies, their willingness to take risks, their willingness to pursue their dreams. And with the right opportunity, those kinds of dreams can become real for countless numbers of people to support their families and strengthen their communities and build our country into the kind of nation we want in a new century.
>
> —*President William J. Clinton*[1]

Entrepreneurs, people who start and grow businesses, combine resources in new ways to add value to communities. They are at the center of economic dynamism, growth, and job creation in the United States. Entrepreneurial small businesses and their founders should be at the center of any employment or economic development strategy. Expanding entrepreneurship is a key to creating an opportunity economy, where everyone plays and everyone benefits.

Almost all net new jobs created in the United States over

the past three decades have come from new businesses. The National Bureau for Economic Research found that nearly all job creation in the United States over the last thirty years has been in new and young businesses under five years of age.[2] New businesses, not existing businesses. New businesses not only create jobs but also introduce innovation: new industries, new technologies, and new (and global) horizons. And at the beginning of entrepreneurship is capital.

Entrepreneurs do not generally come from the comfort of soft living; they come from the margins of the economy. Entrepreneurs come in all sizes, races, genders, ages. They are very often immigrants and new entrants to the economy. Sometimes the easiest way to find a job is to create it for yourself.

In most policy circles, self-employment is not understood as having macroeconomic effects. Yet it does, and entrepreneurship has demonstrated an almost unlimited power to grow the size, productivity, and vitality of the economy.

"New businesses fail" is invariably the first objection to a policy that promotes entrepreneurship. Yet 100 percent of all people die! The value of a business, or a marriage or a life, cannot be measured by its length; rather, it must be assessed by what it does during its existence and by the legacy it leaves. Even business "failures" leave a legacy: an entrepreneur or an economy that learns and, as a result, does better the next time. Though 40 percent of new businesses cease operations before their fifth birthday, the surviving 60 percent grow enough to replace jobs lost, so the gain in year five is the same as in year one.[3] The Freelancers Union projects that by 2020, freelancers—independent entrepreneurs—will command $1.4 trillion in revenue, up 30 percent over today, and include half of millennials. Only one-tenth of this workforce of 57.3 million people will be temporary and part-time gig economy workers.[4]

Given the central role entrepreneurial small businesses play in the growth and dynamism of the economy, it is startling that the rate of new business formation in the United States has been falling for more than thirty years.[5] During the early 1980s, the new business formation rate hovered around 13 percent.[6] In those years, new businesses created nearly 3 million jobs each year.[7] For the past five years, the new business formation rate has fallen to 8 percent a year, generating only 2 million new jobs a year—a 40 percent decline.[8] This decline costs the country 1 million new firms and 1.5 million jobs a year. It is essential, and possible, to reverse this decline.[9]

The greatest sources of underdeveloped entrepreneurial capacity are people sidelined by the mainstream economy today: women, people of color, the young, people with disabilities, immigrants. The number of women-owned firms has tripled from 1 million in 1997 to 3 million in 2015.[10] Recent immigrants make up 13 percent of the population, but they start more than a quarter of all new businesses.[11]

Perhaps even more dramatic, and reflecting the growth in immigrants' and women's entrepreneurship, is the rapid rise in Latino entrepreneurship. In the last two decades, Hispanics became entrepreneurs almost ten times faster than the overall population.[12] Under current market conditions, however, Latino businesses fail to scale in size and revenues relative to white-owned businesses, primarily because of lack of start-up and growth capital. The Aspen Institute Forum on Latino Business growth estimated the macroeconomic loss of this growth gap to be $1.38 trillion![13] The cascading effects of this shortfall can be measured in employment, income, taxes, and growth opportunities lost.[14]

Even this evidence of entrepreneurial vitality among excluded groups likely understates their potential contributions. The Family Independence Initiative, which encourages low-income

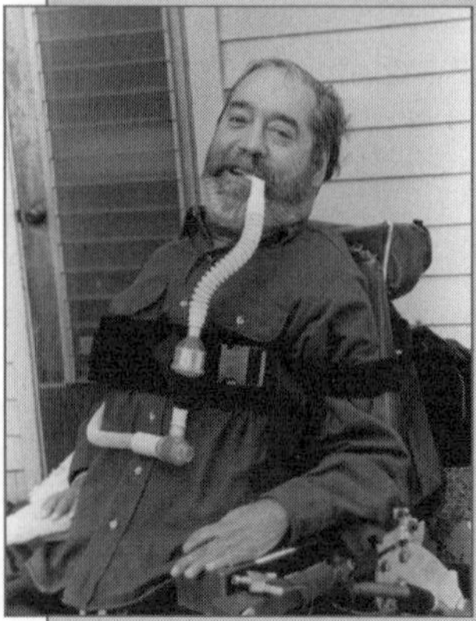

Ed Roberts

In 1953, a doctor counseled a young mother named Zona Roberts, "You should hope he dies, because if he lives, he'll be no more than a vegetable for the rest of his life." The doctor was assessing the potential future life of Roberts's fourteen-year-old son, Edward Verne Roberts. Ed was a lanky athlete and freshman football player. He contracted polio in 1953, two years before the Salk vaccine virtually obliterated the disease from the planet. As a result of Ed's bout with polio, he was paralyzed from the neck down except for two fingers on one hand and several toes. Ed slept inside an iron lung, a large respirator that forced air into his lungs because he could not breathe on his own while asleep. During the day, Ed used a respirator to assist his breathing.

Overhearing this prognosis from the doctor, Ed thought, "If I'm going to be a vegetable, I'm going to be an artichoke—prickly on the outside, with a good heart."

Ed spent nine months in the hospital, then another nine months at a polio center. His mother insisted that he go back to school and that Burlingame High

School readmit him. Ed feared returning to high school and being subjected to the stares of students and teachers alike. He steeled himself by seeing himself not as a "helpless cripple," to use the language of the 1950s, but as a star. Ed excelled in high school, academically and socially, but the school administration refused to let him graduate because he had failed to complete the phys ed and driver's education requirements. Zona and Ed prevailed by going to the school board.

After high school, Ed enrolled at the College of San Mateo. He deepened his interest in political science, earned his associate's degree, and set his eyes on attending the University of California, Berkeley. Ed spoke to a dean at Berkeley about his desire to matriculate; the dean told him, "We've tried cripples before and it didn't work." Ed was admitted in 1962, but for the first year he had to live in Cowell Hospital, the only place on campus with an 800-pound iron lung. During that year, he converted his hospital room into a dorm and created the Cowell Residence Program, which became the point of entry to UCB for a stream of students with disabilities. These students soon began calling themselves the Rolling Quads. They advocated for the first curb cuts and established the Physically Disabled Students Program, the first student-led disability program in the country, which, among other things, provided attendant referral and wheelchair repair. To solicit and secure federal support for the Physically Disabled Students Program, Ed flew cross-country without respiratory support (he used a technique called "frog breathing" that involves gulping air into the lungs). Ed earned his bachelor's degree in 1964 and his master's in 1966 in political science from Berkeley.

With others in the program, Ed helped establish the Center for Independent Living (CIL), the first center run by and for people with disabilities. Ed ran the center for three years, from 1972 to 1975, during which time the center spawned a movement. Soon there were hundreds of CILs around the world. Ed spearheaded advocacy for the Rehabilitation Act of 1973, which proclaimed that "no handicapped individual shall, solely by reason of his handicap, be excluded from the participation in, be denied the benefits of, or be subjected to discrimination under any program or activity receiving federal financial assistance." The act was the first national legislation to protect the rights of people with disabilities to obtain rehabilitative services and accommodations from federally supported educational institutions, medical providers, and other federal subcontractors.

In 1976, Governor Jerry Brown appointed Ed director of the California Department of Vocational Rehabilitation. Eighteen years earlier, in 1958, this same agency had told him that he was too severely disabled to ever get a job. Ed served eight years as director of the department. In 1983, he founded the World Institute on Disability, which he led for the rest of his life. Ed is often called the father of the independent-living movement. His work provided a foundation for the successful passage of the Americans with Disabilities Act in 1990.

In 1983, Ed traveled to the Soviet Union, Australia, Japan, and France to see how other countries treated people with disabilities. I met Ed shortly after he returned from that trip. Much to my chagrin, my office on Folsom Street in San Francisco was not in an accessible building, but Ed was determined to take the meeting in my office. We eventually found a way in, enabled by the portable ramp he carried with him. I have no doubt that if the only way in had been for him to break a hole in the concrete wall, he would have.

Knowing of CFED's work to promote self-employment and entrepreneurship, Ed told me that he had discovered on his trip to the Soviet Union that 20,000 disabled Russians were running businesses. This fact confirmed that entrepreneurs come from the most unlikely of circumstances; one should never underestimate the capacities, talents, abilities, dreams, and potential of all manner of economically marginalized and denigrated people. Ed made me promise to work with him to ensure that every person with a disability had a reasonable opportunity to bring her skills and drive to the marketplace and realize their potential. I agreed, figuring Ed was such a force of nature that I wouldn't have to do much. Together we, but mostly he, brought the self-employment and disability rights fields together, making sure that the growing self-employment field saw and served people with disabilities, and that people with disabilities saw that they could create jobs for themselves.

On March 14, 1995, I sat stunned in my car at the news that he had died of cardiac arrest at the age of fifty-six. Today Ed's wheelchair sits in the National Museum of American History, complete with its Porsche seat, portable ramp, mobile respirator, and headlights for night driving. The museum did not acquire it in the formal ways of museums; rather, his longtime personal assistant and five hundred members of the National Council on Independent Living simply dragged it in. "You can't leave that here," docents objected, but history prevailed. Ed married and divorced, fathered a son, Lee, swam with dolphins, and rafted down the Stanislaus River. He won a MacArthur Fellowship; in 2011, he was inducted into the California Hall of Fame.

It has been twenty-two years since Ed's untimely death. Ed believed in social change and the potential of all people, and he would be glad to see the growth of the disability rights movement, of self-employment and microenterprise, of the asset-building field, of the marriage of the disability rights movement and the economic development field. But Ed would not be satisfied until every American—every person—has a chance to bring his or her dreams, abilities, and work to the mainstream economy as entrepreneurs, students, skilled workers, homeowners, and creators of wealth. Ed is the symbol of the potential of every human being who is routinely underestimated and excluded.

families to move forward relying on their own resources, finds that almost one-third of families engage in some form of part- or full-time business activity to move ahead—four times the average rate of business formation in the country today.[15]

Yet from an economic policy perspective, the United States does not capitalize on this dynamism. Black-, Latino-, and women-owned businesses are undercapitalized; they are smaller and less able to access financing than white, male-led businesses.

Most entrepreneurs start their businesses with personal savings or savings from friends, family, and associates, and often with less than $5,000.[16] Three-quarters of businesses that were started in 2004 began with substantial owner's equity, though women- and black-owned businesses were 5 percent and 16 percent, respectively, less able to assemble this equity.[17] Family Independence Initiative families start theirs with an average of $2,000. They do not access the formal market for loans or venture capital until they are much larger. Without liquid savings, a financially capable social network, access to markets, expansion loans, and relevant business skills and planning, starting and growing a business become impossible. The entry point for small businesses is household liquid savings and social networks.[18]

Capital is both input and output. In addition to all the other benefits of business, small business ownership provides long-term and significant differences to the net worth of households. Overall, business owners have a median net worth two and a half times that of non–business owners. For a black woman, owning a small business increases her net worth by ten times. For a Latino man, the increase is five times.[19]

Growth, innovation, job creation, business formation, and certainly the diversity and inclusiveness of all of those depend on would-be entrepreneurs having liquid savings to invest. Most Americans do not have those funds. Their dreams, their visions, their talents, and their energies are denied because they lack a few thousand dollars. A few thousand dollars can secure licenses, buy supplies and equipment, and justify business dreaming and planning. Without a few thousand dollars, American capitalism is capitalism without capitalists.

Tax breaks for existing corporations (including those passed in the 2017 Tax Cuts and Jobs Act for pass-through Schedule C, partnerships, and unincorporated business income) may help the bottom line of those businesses, but they are not likely to generate new businesses or new jobs for our economy. Promoting new business creation will require bolstering individual and family savings across the population.

Existing tax breaks, including those introduced by the 2017 act, do not increase paychecks in most companies or for most people. According to former Young & Rubicam CEO Peter Georgescu, while corporate profit margins are at an all-time high of 11.5 percent and productivity has more than doubled since the 1970s, household income has increased less than 1 percent in the last twenty-eight years.[20] That is because corporations devote 91 percent of earnings to stockholders and a meager 9 percent for all other things, including R&D, wages, and benefits.[21] Georgescu attributes this to Milton Friedman's "shareholder primacy manifesto" and the focus on steadily increasing quarterly profits to the detriment of the traditional broader array of stakeholder groups—employees, customers, and the larger community as well as shareholders.

Derek "Pete" Hansen, California's deputy director of banking, distinguished between capitalism and entrepreneurialism. Increased returns to capital do not ensure or necessarily even encourage investment in entrepreneurs and early-stage ventures, where the returns are longer-term and uncertain, and the bet is more on a person than on a business plan. Entrepreneurial business policy addresses the barriers that stand in the way of small business creation, including decisions concerning whether or not to start a business, grow a business, rescue a business, or end a business. While there is great need for more loans for expanding business, an effort in which both Community Development Financial Institutions and mainstream financial institutions can play crucial roles, the core economic issue for small business formation is individual entrepreneurs' nest eggs. The path to enterprise, and particularly that essential individual equity (as distinguished from institutional debt), begins with an individual's cash.

This focus does not mean that U.S. economic policy should not address wages and benefits of employment; full-time jobs should yield reasonable security and stability. Raising the minimum wage, encouraging CEOs to manage for the long term for all stakeholder groups, providing benefits to independent contractors and entrepreneurs, organizing labor, expanding wage and hour protections to restaurant and home workers, and enforcing employer responsibility are vital economic goals in the United States.

Some question whether tiny independent entrepreneurs and businesses can compete in a global economy. The question has become more acute with the globalization of the economy along with the expansion of the internet. Companies can export anywhere in the world, and they must compete everywhere in the world. In many regions, notably northern Italy, Denmark, and parts of the United States, firms join to do together what they cannot do alone, setting up flexible manufacturing networks with network hubs to achieve global best standards of market intelligence, technology, production, and design, with each firm specializing in a critical niche.[22] These new structures will only become more essential as the economy changes.

For more than forty years, economic policies have been evolving to support small business ownership and entrepreneurship. In particular, a new understanding of the kind of economic or business climate that breeds vital business start-up and growth and the evolution of the self-employment and microbusiness fields show us the way to cultivate economic vitality from the bottom up.

Each June for more than ten years, from 1979 to 1989, the accounting firm Grant Thornton issued its *Annual Study of the General Manufacturing Climates of the Forty-eight Contiguous States of America*, effectively defining what constituted a good business climate. Governors and state policy makers anticipated the results with exhilaration as well as fear and trembling. States that ranked high proudly proclaimed their standing in national advertising campaigns aimed at luring footloose businesses, while states that ranked poorly tried to defend themselves, their policies, and their economies.

Grant Thornton measured the cost of doing business in a

state; lower wages, lower taxes, lower welfare benefits, fewer regulations, and fewer unions were considered better. The results were absurd: North Dakota, Utah, and Nebraska, not exactly manufacturing hubs in any sense, and poor states such as Mississippi routinely ranked at the top, while economic powerhouse states, including Maryland, Massachusetts, Michigan, New York, and Pennsylvania, routinely ranked at the bottom.

In 1986, with the support of business, labor, and private foundations, CFED took on Grant Thornton. The CFED study, "Taken for Granted: How Grant Thornton's Business Climate Index Leads States Astray," was front-page news in the business section of almost every newspaper across the country, priming a new debate about the real determinants of a good business climate.[23]

Critiquing a bad theory and misguided policy, however, was not enough. After two years combing through the economic literature and best studies of what made for healthy and resilient economies, CFED issued "Making the Grade: The Development Report Card for the States." This report emphasized strengthening the chief sources of new jobs and wealth: the state's own existing businesses and potential entrepreneurs. It emphasized investment—in education, training, infrastructure, technology, amenities, and other sources of development capacity—to build international competitiveness. Finally, it recognized government as a partner responsible for building the basic foundations of an economy.[24]

Grant Thornton ceased issuing its study three years later, although the misguided policies it embraced seem never to die. Kansas recently repeated the tax-cutting, service- and investment-gutting practices recommended by Grant Thornton, resulting in deep and continuing deficits and eventually a reversal of those detrimental policies, including tax increases.

Going forward, it will be crucial that we learn the lessons of this history, understanding the role of new and young entrepreneurial businesses and entrepreneurs in creating jobs and wealth, and the kinds of policies that enhance that development.

Bottom-up economic development is a vital understanding from the past forty years. Welfare policies in the United States are the second place from which economic development policies must draw important lessons in order to define a future path.

In 1984, virtually every welfare code in the country had a provision dealing with self-employment. This almost universal recognition was a good indicator of the existence and breadth of entrepreneurship among poor Americans. But the policies offered no endorsement of the upwardly mobile strivings of men and women on welfare, nor did they offer any assistance to poor people in their search for gainful employment. On the contrary, these provisions ensured that all income was accounted for, and that welfare support was reduced or eliminated in the face of self-employment income. The value of any equipment or supplies—think the cleaning supplies of a housecleaner, the flour of a baker, or the food of a chef—counted against asset limits so low that even a few hundred dollars in value could make a family ineligible for support.

The most promising and commonplace job creation strategy, self-employment, was the least appreciated. The idea that unemployed people might create jobs for themselves, and the reality that for many low-income people the only way forward was to combine multiple forms of income and employment, including starting a business, was unimaginable.[25]

In the early 1980s, most people I talked to thought the idea of welfare mothers starting their own businesses was patently crazy. Most people; not all. Kathy Keeley founded Women's Economic Development Corporation (WEDCO) in St. Paul,

Minnesota, in 1982. Over the next few years, WEDCO nurtured hundreds of women-owned businesses a year and dozens of similar efforts in cities across the country.

The Self-Employment Investment Demonstration (SEID) involved nascent self-employment programs for welfare recipients in five states (Minnesota, Mississippi, Michigan, Maryland, and Iowa) that petitioned the federal Department of Health, Education, and Welfare for waivers from welfare rules prohibiting recipients from owning even a minimal amount of assets.

SEID businesses yielded income and jobs for welfare recipients, and participants displayed all of the nine effects of asset ownership.[26] The results of SEID demonstrated these dramatic outcomes:

- Nearly one-third of the welfare mothers eligible for SEID ended up starting businesses.
- Four out of five businesses were still operating two and a half years after starting.
- Business income as the primary form of income increased sixfold.
- Welfare dependency fell by two-thirds.
- Business owners nearly doubled their assets in less than three years.
- Each business created on average one and a half jobs.
- Sixty-nine percent of SEID entrepreneurs said they could not have started their businesses had welfare rules remained the same.
- People of color participated in proportion to their presence in the welfare population, and way above their current representation in the marketplace.

A key finding of SEID was the multiplicity of positive effects of self-employment and business investment. A major change in one aspect of a person's life is unlikely to occur without other related changes. Marked change in tangible economic indicators—employment, income, assets—is likely to be accompanied or preceded by other, less tangible, but no less important psychological, behavioral, and social changes. These changes are so intertwined that it seems easier to understand them as a linked web or a circle of changes—clearly connected but with no single sequence of impact.[27]

The stories of the participants provide richer details of the positive outcomes. Jean Peters, who had relied on welfare (Aid to Families with Dependent Children, or AFDC) for five years, started a video rental store in her small rural community, discovering the booming demand for video games before most were aware of it. Within a year she was off welfare. Conscious that her son would soon be of college age, and doubtful of her ability to save but confident now of her ability to grow a business, she opened two additional stores after careful planning and additional loans; she sold both stores two years later for contracts that paid for her son's college.[28] A former Detroit bank clerk went on AFDC when she was laid off by General Motors; with the help of the Detroit Self-Employment Project and Cathy McClelland, she applied building skills gained from her parents and went on to found perhaps the only construction business in Detroit owned and run by an African American female. A Latina teen mom in Minneapolis, with the help of WEDCO, started a successful Mexican catering business and then went on to take a restaurant manager job at a much higher salary for an established Chinese restaurant chain.[29] Other welfare moms in SEID started a video production business, a flower shop, a telecommunications business, housecleaning ventures, a day care center, a fix-it enterprise, a restaurant, a retail bakery, a vinyl repair service, two commercial janitorial services, a nanny employment service, a bookkeeping service,

Marguerite Sisson

Marguerite Sisson stared at the jar of Skippy peanut butter and burst into tears: She had the peanut butter but not the bread to spread it on.[30] She felt like she had missed the last two years of her son's life, working nights from 10:00 p.m. to 6:00 a.m. as a van driver for the railroad at $5.35 an hour. Even though she worked a full forty hours a week, she made too little to support herself and her son, so little that she still qualified for welfare—so little, in fact, that her welfare caseworkers demanded she get a better job or lose benefits. She found a factory job that paid $7 an hour, but she still had to work nights and largely miss her son. She vowed to take the first day job she could find near her home in Clinton, Iowa. It was cleaning a medical clinic.

She was so good at it that the doctors praised her thoroughness and asked why she didn't start her own business. "Yeah, give me a break, how could I ever do that?' she countered, but a few days later half-jokingly told a co-worker, "I think I'm gonna start a cleaning company." Her co-worker told her boss, who confronted her for even considering becoming a competitor, and promptly fired her. How was she to support her son now?

Marguerite used her last paycheck to buy insurance coverage. The night yardmaster at the railroad helped her buy some cleaning supplies. She put an ad in the paper, and in a few days got a call from a woman who needed her house cleaned, and then a call from Foley Construction Company. Over the next few months, she acquired more cleaning contracts. After six months in business, she filed for a tax identification number; she bought stationery and a briefcase. Marguerite recalls, "That's when I said, 'I'm a businesslady.'"

Marguerite had been on her own since age thirteen. When she was five, her father left for the bank and never returned. Marguerite and her mom survived on a nurse's aide's salary and welfare. Marguerite never was in school much; she moved with her mother's different husbands, none of whom really acted as a father toward her. Her father came back into her life for six months before he died of cirrhosis of the liver when she was fifteen. When she received a $9,000 death payment from Social Security, she gave half to her mother to put a down payment on the house she had always wanted, and decided to go back to school. She entered ninth grade when she was eighteen. She lasted two years, dropping out when she became pregnant with her son, Will, at twenty. Marguerite went on welfare when Will's father disappeared. She taught herself how to drive, and bought a car; she learned how to change spark plugs, how to use computers, and how to do her own taxes. She earned her GED.

Marguerite's welfare caseworker referred her to the Institute for Social and Economic Development (ISED), which had just started to provide entrepreneurial training and counseling to Iowa Family Assistance recipients who were starting businesses as part of the national Self-Employment Investment Demonstration. The state gave Marguerite a waiver that allowed her to continue receiving public benefits while trying to grow her business, and provided a $500 Promise Jobs grant that allowed her to purchase a cleaning cart and repair her car. ISED helped Marguerite get her financial records in order and pushed her to market more, helping her design flyers to distribute and even write a press release. Within three months Rapid City Cleaning had several clients, including the local police department, and had hired its first employees. A year later she had nine employees, all earning $8 to $9 per hour. Rapid City Cleaning had contracts with a medical complex, the Visiting Nurse Association, and the Union Pacific Railroad, as well as the police department and Foley Construction. Marguerite bought herself a dependable 1995 Chrysler Sebring and was on course to clear $65,000 a year.

Then everything went wrong. She lost her biggest account and two employees. Her housing benefits ended in July 1999 and her rent tripled from $120 to $315 a month. Her welfare grant ended; two months later, her medical coverage was withdrawn. Taxes and insurance premiums came due. She lost more customers. Only when she finally talked to customers did she find out that they were quitting because her employees weren't doing a good job. Like many start-up businesses, Marguerite knew how to do her business—in her case, clean—but she did not know how to run or build a business, and particularly how to recruit, interview, train, manage, and oversee employees and do quality control.

She rebuilt the business by doing most of the cleaning herself along with just two colleagues: a longtime employee and her fiancé. She took out a loan to diversify into lawn care and snow removal. She built back client by client. In two and a half years she was off welfare. She got married in 2001 and bought a home. Four years after starting her business, "Marguerite is beginning to experience what self-employment has brought millions of other Americans: stability, security, a buffer when things go wrong, a nest egg for the future. After years of struggle, Marguerite is finally doing well. And if things should turn out badly, she is in a much stronger position to weather the change that she has been at any point before. Both the house and business are in her name. She has assets against which she can borrow, a support network on which to rely, and a newfound sense of personal confidence."[31]

In 1999, Marguerite made her first flight out of Iowa through Chicago to Washington, DC, where she testified, after Senator Ted Kennedy, to Congress about the difference starting a business had made in her life. She said: "I learned more than to run a business. I learned that I am important. I learned that I am a strong and intelligent person. My son is very proud of me, and tells his teachers that I own a small business. And being a role model to my son is one of the most important achievements, setting aside everything else. I am showing him that anything is possible, and that when he grows up. He will understand that hard work can take you anyplace you want to go."[32]

Marguerite noted, "I can go to the grocery store and buy bread and peanut butter and milk. I can eat steak and roast and chicken and whatever for supper, not hot dogs or macaroni. You know what I'm saying? I'm living a lot better."[33]

a publishing company, a housing rehab company, and a dry cleaner.[34]

Part of the strength, creativity, and wholeness of the entrepreneurial small business field in the United States was because it was an outgrowth and economic expression of the women's movement, and the movement of women—by necessity and choice—into a growing but challenging economy.[35] The self-employment movement that swept the country during the

1980s flourished into a hundred self-employment programs in almost every state, changed state and federal policies, and generated tens of thousands of new entrepreneurs: mothers and fathers on welfare, unemployed industrial workers, poor kids. They were overwhelmingly women, whether African American, Latino, Native, Asian, or white, drawn from the margins of the economy.[36]

U.S. self-employment efforts met international microenterprise programs in the mid-1980s, though Nobel laureate Muhammad Yunus's Grameen Bank, BRAC, and other international efforts were at least a decade older.[37] Today, microenterprise and low-income entrepreneurship programs continue throughout the United States and the world. Two million businesses are created each year in the United States, yet programs reach barely one out of a hundred. How many additional businesses (and jobs) could we produce if we could address critical bottlenecks in the formation and maturation process of small businesses?

Gene Severens always had his eye on scale. Coming from the Center for Rural Affairs, he surveyed best practices in the field in order to come up with the remarkably effective Rural Enterprise Assistance Program (REAP) in Nebraska. Not content to operate at the local level, he went on to lead the Nebraska Microenterprise Partnership, a statewide public-private partnership and framework—a first of its kind, which created a capacity and process for spreading microenterprise support services to every county in the state.[38] In an attempt to extend the model to other states, Gene came to CFED to lead the National Fund for Enterprise Development and spread the Nebraska model, which proved to be more difficult than expected, mostly because states at the time were not looking for new ways to invest state funds, however promising. Undeterred, Gene struck upon another platform for scaling and universalizing microenterprise support.

At the beginning of the twenty-first century, the U.S. microenterprise field was reaching 250,000 microentrepreneurs a year with business technical assistance and 25,000, about one out of ten, with microloans. In any given year in the United States in this period, 15 percent of U.S. taxpayers—some 20 million returns—filed Schedule C reporting self-employment income. A full 10 percent of those filers were filing for the first time, adding 2 to 3 million jobs a year.[39] This was not only a large field to play on, as it turned out, but one uniquely challenged and widely served (and underserved) by a national service and delivery platform.

Start-up businesses, constrained by lack of capital and in need of seed equity, had to pay both the employer and employee shares of payroll taxes—a significant, unpredictable, and often unexpected cost and barrier. But the upside was similarly high: "While they represent a relatively small share of economic activity, non-employer firms are important as a gateway to becoming employer firms, providing flexible work opportunities and a path to economic prosperity."[40] Perhaps, reasoned Gene, we could tackle both barriers simultaneously with a tax credit for the self-employment or new entrepreneurs, which would create a three-year tax holiday, perhaps on a sliding scale, for the newly self-employed, and a business savings match. Gene's Self-Employment Tax Credit has unfulfilled promise, especially in a world where three-fifths of businesses are started with less than $5,000.

More than anything else, there is potential here: millions of would-be entrepreneurs, ready and able to take their ideas and energy to the marketplace, and millions more of established businesses ready to take root and grow, if only they

Dion King

"When you live and have a story to tell, you don't hold back," says Dion King. Dion is a native DC resident whose integrity is the product of thirty-eight years of learning and mistakes.

Dion grew up without a father and was taken away from his abusive mother at age nine. For the next six years he lived in three group homes and four foster homes. When his last foster mother was jailed for neglecting her charges while collecting state support, Dion entered DC's Independent Living Program. It was a relief to be on his own.

At age sixteen he was hired to assist at Expressly Portraits and fell in love with photography. "I love people's smiles and what you get out of pictures. It goes way beyond words. A portrait is art; it's about feelings." He has been photographing ever since. Soon after starting to assist at the studio, Dion began to work at the radio station WKYS. He has photographed many a star, including Janet Jackson and Beyoncé, and photographed President Obama seven times. He contracts with several historically black colleges and a school for mentally challenged kids. He continues to try to build his business while holding down low-wage jobs at parking lots and discount stores. About ten years ago, his electricity got cut off because of an unpaid bill. In order to cover it, he went to shoot a house fire. Confronted by a police officer who grabbed him around his throat to push him back, he resisted. He was charged with assault and was convicted. He served time, and then tried to straighten out his life, but with a record, he found it hard to get hired. He went without a job for two years before entering Project Empowerment for citizens returning after incarceration, where he learned of the Capitol Area Asset-Building Collaborative's IDA program.

"It's hard to save, working at minimum wage. Especially with five kids. But it's crucial. You never know what will come. It's important to save." Still, saving is easier said than done. "Every time I saved $500, something would come up, some emergency, some repair, and I would spend it. My IDA, with its 8:1 match, was my chance, and I took it." Dion saved $500 over a year, and used the $4,500 he amassed to buy the photo equipment he needed to grow his business. Today, he says, the future looks wonderful. Business is steady. He's about to qualify for a second IDA, which will allow him to upgrade his videography software. He has begun to employ his thirteen-year-old son, Damari, adding his son's DJ services to King D Photography's offerings and purchasing used DJ equipment for Damari.

He now saves by having his current employer,

Costco, directly deposit $50 a month into a hard-to-access savings account and an additional $3 monthly to an emergency account. As another savings trick, he will "forget" checks he receives for photography jobs. He hopes to qualify for another IDA program so he can start a 501(c)(3) nonprofit, the Reach 4 It Foundation, to help foster kids establish and pursue their goals.

had the savings to underwrite start-up and growth. These entrepreneurs are disproportionately people of color and low- and middle-income people most in need of an economic path forward. There is a nation of development institutions and individuals who understand this potential and are ready to advocate for and support it. The data, methods, policy designs, and even the beginnings of market foundations exist to bring the innovations of the past decades to scale. Perhaps most promising of all for this policy is that this is a potential that need hurt no one and can benefit everyone, including the economy as a whole, while addressing the lack of real economic opportunity in this country. Key to this policy is ensuring that every American with an idea and desire to bring a new good or service to the economy has the seed capital she needs to start a business. The path ahead builds on the lessons, experience, evidence, and innovation of the last thirty-five years.

First, we must understand the role and dynamics of entrepreneurship in the economy. Broad-based grassroots entrepreneurship is the source of innovation, value-added growth, and job creation. Unless there is a general recognition of these dynamics, future policy will tend to focus on existing firms, large and small, which are unlikely to add jobs on net. For example, the tax cuts of 2017, focused on reduced corporate tax rates and reduced rates on pass-through income of unincorporated business, largely missed the new and young business leverage point. Entrepreneurs come in all colors, genders, ethnicities, ages, and citizenship statuses, all across the income spectrum. The entrepreneurship rates among the economically marginalized may be even higher, through necessity if not choice, than among their better-off counterparts. By understanding the potential for entrepreneurial expansion and the barriers holding it back, policies can begin to address it on the scale necessary.

Second, it is crucial to remove the penalties to entrepreneurship buried in federal, state, and local policies that affect income maintenance programs, social services, employment and training, and housing. When addressing means-tested programs, policy makers should raise or eliminate asset limits for business assets. Never again should a welfare recipient be denied benefits because she is building assets and net worth in a new business.

Third, policy makers must ensure that every entrepreneur, especially new and young entrepreneurs, can assemble the few thousand dollars it takes to launch a business.

Today in the United States there are incentivized savings accounts for retirement, homes, and education, but none for business. A business use should be added to existing retirement accounts: 401(k)s, 403(b)s, and the like. Standalone business accounts might also be established in community and mainstream financial institutions, or a default set of accounts established, as in the MyRA program. Schedule C of the income tax return could be used to allocate and enforce tax credits for savings earned by the accounts.

Paty Cruz

Paty Cruz hasn't slept much in the last ten years, since she fled her abusive ex-husband in order to provide for her three children. She came from her native Oaxaca, Mexico, to Washington, DC. After a few weeks of a futile job search, she decided to rely on the secret mole recipe her grandmother had whispered in her ear, and her culinary and entrepreneurial skills. She began El Sabor del Taco, making tacos, tamales, agua fresca, and mole at home and selling them on the street; a year later, she began selling them at two downtown farmers' markets. She hired two other Mexican women to distribute and sell her food.

The Latino Economic Development Corporation provided her with business counseling and training. In 2007, the Mexican ambassador discovered her and invited her to cook for the embassy for a month and a half. By 2014, she was residing at the embassy and serving as resident chef. After sixteen hours of work at the embassy, she would take an Uber to a restaurant that allowed her to use its kitchen in the wee hours of the night. There she spent three to six hours preparing the day's supply for El Sabor del Taco.

Now El Sabor del Taco generates $1,600 a day, and Paty nets $600 after expenses, taxes, and licenses, on top of her employment income. Most of her business earnings have gone to support her three children. Her oldest son is now a lawyer, her middle daughter an accountant. Now most of her financial and emotional support goes to her youngest son, a talented dancer.

Paty's grandmother's Heritage Mole requires twenty-three ingredients and a complex process that involves roasting, grinding, and mixing the ingredients. For her first seven years, Paty burned out a home blender every week, at a cost of $100 to $120. In 2013 she heard of the Capitol Area Asset Building Collaborative's Individual Development Account program. She saved $80 to $85 a month for eight months to earn an 8:1 $4,000 match, which she used to buy a commercial blender, a turbo mixer, a VitaMix for dry ingredients, and warming drawers. She continues to rely on the $1,500 commercial blender to this day, though she confesses its days are numbered. "An opportunity like this is a life-changer," she concludes.

Paty dreams of someday opening her own restaurant. She may qualify for another IDA, which she intends to use to begin a matched savings program for foster kids. "I want to pay my good fortune forward."

Reallocating our existing investment tax incentives—the preferential 20 percent tax rate on capital gains, dividends, and carried interest—would provide a sliding-scale match for Matched Business Accounts (MBAs) for all aspiring and start-up entrepreneurs.

Matching money in these accounts would help potential entrepreneurs grow their nest egg more quickly and provide an important tool for addressing growing income and asset inequality. By matching (through refundable tax credits) the first $1,000 saved in MBAs, at a 2:1 rate for the poorest third of Americans and 1:1 for the middle third of Americans, people could build enterprise savings of $2,000 to 3,000 per year. These MBAs could be added to existing retirement accounts, or simply added through reporting on Schedule C on individual returns.

In addition, instead of requiring the newly self-employed to pay both the employer *and* employee shares of FICA, let's have a tax holiday for these entrepreneurs and provide a three-year on-ramp—a New Entrepreneur Tax Credit—with no employment taxes owed the first two years, and just the employer share during the third year. This policy should be largely self-funding, since it would close the largest of business tax gaps, encouraging informal businesses to register. Establish a tax-advantaged matched savings account for business, or add an explicit business use in larger systems of retirement savings accounts. Provide every American with a savings match or refundable tax incentive to save for business start-up and expansion, funded as part of our incentives for investment and capital gains.

Fourth, in order to ensure that the entrepreneurs who fuel this growth of businesses and jobs have employment benefits and that businesses are competitive, it is vital to separate systems of benefits (health insurance, disability insurance, unemployment insurance) from employment. Increasing business start-up and growth is not a strategy to further privatize risk and deny fringe benefits to new gig economy workers. Entrepreneurs accounted for a full 20 percent of new enrollees in the Affordable Care Act.[41] Lack of family health coverage has stopped many a potential entrepreneur from assuming the risk of starting a new business. The Freelancers Union in New York City has pioneered the way for self-employed entrepreneurs to band together to advocate for and purchase critical benefits, such health insurance, for themselves. The Freelancers Union is expanding to twenty-three cities to allow networks of freelancers and small businesses to learn from one another, collaborate for comparative advantage, and supply portable benefits.[42] Untying the provision of employee benefits, including health care, sick leave, retirement savings, and savings in general, from employers (without weakening existing employer-based systems) is a powerful vision for U.S. social policy. The Freelancers Union and Upwork project that within ten years more than half the workforce will be freelancers, described by labels such as "independent contractor," "moonlighter," "diversified worker," and "temporary worker."[43] If they are to have decent health care, savings, and sick leave, U.S. policy will have to create portable, employer-independent systems of support, like the progressive matched account systems advanced here.

Fifth, ensure that new and growing businesses can access growth capital. Continue to expand Community Development Financial Institutions that lend to businesses in and of poor communities, such as HOPE Enterprise Corporation in the Mississippi Delta and Craft 3 in the Pacific Northwest, and spread these practices. Encourage the development of inclusive

MATCHED BUSINESS ACCOUNTS
Prosperity
IDEAS
MBA's
PLANS
BUSINESS
12 MILLION NEW BUSINESSES
27 MILLION NEW JOBS
$ 1000
WEALTHIEST
MIDDLE
$ 3000
POOREST
$18 BILLION
$200 BILLION
$10
WORKING FAMILIES EARNING LESS THAN $ 50000
BANKS
FINANCIAL INSTITUTIONS
STOCK MARKET
BIG BUSININESS
$138 280
WEALTHIEST 1%
Adversity

financial products and services. Regulate financial institutions to encourage business lending.

Sixth, ensure that, along with capital, entrepreneurs have access to high-quality and relevant entrepreneurial training, business planning, and technical assistance resources as well as the advice of their peers. Spread online and school-based business and financial capability skills training and business networking. Excellent resources exist and are increasingly available online.[44] Time and again, all over the globe, entrepreneurs demonstrate their power to help their peers, from the "if he can do it, then certainly I can" phenomenon evident in the Family Independence Initiative to the small-firm networks of Italy, Denmark, and Germany, where small firms do for themselves and achieve unprecedented levels of quality, innovation, competitiveness, and resilience.[45]

These conditions—putting capital in the hands of would-be entrepreneurs—could result in an additional 1 million new entrepreneurs and businesses in the U.S. economy, and with them an additional 1.5 million jobs. The United States achieved this rate for five years per decade in the 1980s and 1990s, but in only two years since 2000. It is a rate we could achieve again if the disappearance of family savings following the 2008 recession is reversed.

If we provide MBAs as incentives to all new and young entrepreneurs of firms under five years of age, about 18 million entrepreneurs would be eligible for an average refundable credit of $1,000 by the matching formula proposed above. The cost would be about $18 billion a year, less than one-tenth of current investment tax incentives, yet this would be the most likely to generate jobs.

There is abundant reason to think that if we simply allow millions of low- and moderate-income would-be entrepreneurs straining on the margins of the economy without the liquid savings to be able to take an entrepreneurial leap the entrepreneurial economy of the United States would leap forward. Open the doors to enterprise in this way, harness the full entrepreneurial might of the American people, and, if history is any guide, we can expect millions more businesses and jobs to be created each year—businesses and jobs that will be a continuing source of vitality in the economy for years to come.

6

Prosperity

Prosperity is simply economic well-being or, in more traditional terms, the pursuit of happiness. It need not connote vast wealth. Prosperity is the legitimate and realistic hope for a modicum of financial stability and freedom, which includes the ability to:

- Pay this month's bills
- Retire past debt
- Withstand inevitable financial accidents, repairs, unexpected bills, and illnesses
- Have the financial resources to imagine, achieve, and invest in lifetime financial goals
- Leave something to succeeding generations[1]

Prosperity—that is, economic well-being—is both an individual and collective goal; it is the promise of America, the fulfillment of our legitimate common quest for life, liberty, and the pursuit of happiness for all. In these times, prosperity requires that every American possess at least a few thousand dollars of disposable wealth—to stabilize, to inspire, and to power choice and action.

How can we make prosperity a reality for all Americans? Simply by redeploying in smarter ways the tax incentives already devoted to building family wealth. Restructuring existing tax incentives will unleash the full entrepreneurial energy of the American people—to start businesses, buy homes, raise families, seek higher education, become skilled and productive citizens—for the benefit of all.

We in the United States cannot give up on widespread prosperity. Complacency suggests that only the lucky few will be wealthy beyond the wildest imagination, while the bulk of Americans will struggle just to make ends meet each month and those at the bottom of the pyramid will fall into an endless whirlpool of debt that consumes all hope. A zero-sum view of the world compounds these ideas: if the pie is fixed in size, some must lose in order for others to gain. Yet the experiences relayed in the previous chapters of this book demonstrate that we do not live in a zero-sum world. If we unleash and harness the productive capacity and dreams of all people, the United States will find innovation and growth (and even consumption) that we could never have imagined.

Prosperity for all is not an impossible dream. History reveals patterns of disenfranchisement that dismay us, but it also demonstrates that widespread prosperity is possible through democratic investments in the common genius. Major investments in literally millions of people in each of the preceding three centuries suggest a path for renewed investment in the American people to invest in the American dream and endow everyone with the opportunity to earn a down payment on that dream.

Thomas Piketty's encyclopedic study of the global dynamics of wealth and income since the eighteenth century reaches a stark conclusion: "The past devours the future."[2] Returns to capital exceed the rates of growth of income and growth; in other words, "Once constituted, capital reproduces itself faster than output increases."[3] Piketty proposes a progressive global annual tax of 0.1 to 10 percent on capital to address inequality.[4]

I have no quarrel with the wisdom of this approach, but its political prospects in the United States are not good. Instead of a progressive global annual tax, a rational reallocation of the United States' current wealth-building tax incentives could put basic capital in the hands of all Americans. Adopting a Prosperity Bill—something like a GI Bill for the twenty-first century—would enable all Americans to reap capital returns and grow with them.

Debt, in the form of loans, has been the primary workhorse of economic development in the United States for quite some time. Loans, sometimes low-interest and subsidized, support microenterprise, housing and homeownership, business, education, community facilities, infrastructure. But debt pays off only if the return exceeds the interest rate incurred. This is almost never the case when debt is used to support consumption; $1 spent on consumables today costs $1.10 or even $2 tomorrow, plunging the borrower further into debt with few prospects of paying it off. Debt can be a result of both necessity and desperation; for this reason, almost all religions have condemned usury. On the other hand, if debt is used to finance high-return investments, such as in education or business, it can pay off if the return on the investment exceeds the cost of the loan. Long-term, fixed-rate, sensibly underwritten mortgage loans have worked out well for millions of Americans and have often led to increased saving as the principal is paid down. So have small microenterprise loans.

While debt has a role in economic in development, equally important is deploying U.S. wealth-building tax incentives to match the savings of low- and middle-income Americans. Capital in the hands of everyday people can harness and unleash vast new sources of entrepreneurial energy and productive investment. Hundreds of thousands of low-income and even very poor Americans, disproportionately people of color, women, immigrants, foster youth, and citizens returning after incarceration, as well as white men, have transformed a few thousand dollars of equity into savings, businesses, jobs, homes, educations. With a few thousand dollars, people build better lives for themselves, their families, their communities, and the nation.

The promise of America—that everyone will have a chance—recognizes the promise of Americans: that through their work and genius they will not only help themselves but also expand the richness of the country, its culture, economy, society, and politics. The political promise of America—that the country will do best if everyone has a voice and a vote—has an economic corollary: America will do best if everyone has a chance to participate. From our earliest days, the connection between political liberty and economic opportunity was recognized. The "life, liberty, and pursuit of happiness" described in the Declaration of Independence in fact derived from earlier versions that read "life, liberty, and property." It is impossible to be totally free if one is economically shackled.

In every century of our history, the United States has enacted large-scale policies to empower millions of our forebears. Investments in economic opportunities for common American families gave rise to some of the most significant, widely shared, and enduring increases in economic well-being and growth in our history. Universal public education, the Homestead Acts of the nineteenth century, the creation of the thirty-year mortgage, and the GI Bill powered economic growth throughout the centuries of our existence. While these policies opened opportunity for some people, mostly white men, they often failed to expand opportunity for people of color, women, and others. It is time for a Prosperity Bill that underwrites

Bill Bynum

The Mississippi Delta as a region is both rich and poor: rich in soil and culture, poor in economic conditions, reflecting a history of oppression. Eleven of the poorest twenty-five counties in the United States are in the Mississippi Delta. After the Civil War, black families, not allowed to own property elsewhere, sought the rich unfarmed soil of the Delta. Oppression in the form of Jim Crow laws was not far behind.

"This is our industrial park," our guide said. At first I thought I was looking in the wrong place. Then I realized the flat green field was the industrial park—without industry. That field is a testament to one hundred years of state economic development policy led by Mississippi's legendary Balance Agriculture with Industry program of state tax incentives designed to lure footloose northern manufacturing plants to such fields. And it is testimony to the failure of that policy in improving the lives of the people that lived there.

In spite of past failures and the seemingly intransigent poverty in the Delta region, today Hope is growing. A trio of organizations—Hope Community Credit Union, Hope Enterprise Corporation, and the Hope Policy Institute—are leading the way forward. More than $2 billion has been channeled to more than a million residents of the Mississippi Delta and other poor communities in Mississippi, Louisiana, Arkansas, Tennessee, and Alabama because of those three entities. Between their founding in 1994 and 2014, the Hope organizations have financed 143,000 businesses, 934,000 jobs, 1.5 million housing units, and 9,800 community facilities. Three-quarters of Hope's members and beneficiaries are low-income, half are people of color, and half are women. Seventy percent of Hope's branches are in areas where more than 30 percent of the population has been desperately poor for thirty years. Thirty-six thousand people, most of them formerly unbanked and unserved by financial institutions, are members of the Hope Credit Union (growing by 6,000 members a year), underwriting $60 million in investments to the community.

Spearheading the Hope organizations is William Bynum. He still bears the last name of the master who owned the town where his forebearers were enslaved. Bill was the second employee of Self-Help Community Credit Union in North Carolina, one of the godparents of community development in the United States. Founded by Martin Eakes in 1980, today Self-Help boasts credit unions and associated community institutions in North Carolina and California as well as the city of Chicago and has lent $6.8 billion to more than 100,000 entrepreneurs, homeowners, and low-income customers. Self-Help also birthed the Center for Responsible Lending, which has led the national fight against predatory mortgage and consumer lending, and conducted the Community Advantage Demonstration, discussed in chapter 4, which definitively proved that low-income homeownership was viable. After six years of leading Self-Help's business development and credit union organizing efforts, Bill moved to North Carolina's Rural Development Center, where he orchestrated a pioneering statewide program for microenterprise development, experimenting with both nonprofit loan funds and peer-group lending. In 1994, he answered a call from Mississippi to assume the helm of a nascent development effort envisioned by a Pew-funded commission chaired by Bill Moyers and championed by private-sector leaders including the Walton family (of Walmart), Entergy, and visionary ex-governor William Winter. Bill built that organization into Hope, with $360 million in assets and 200 employees leveraging $3.8 billion in development.[5]

Bill has no illusions about what it takes to sow lasting bottom-up development in the region. "We have to make up for the gaps in collateral, credit, and trust that plague Delta residents, especially black entrepreneurs. We need to develop and use nontraditional tools and flexible underwriting standards. This is necessarily more labor-intensive and higher-cost. When the wind blows hard, we'll take a bigger hit. But we build that into our models. All in all, we write off less than 1 percent of all loans we make. As we grow, the closer we get to our communities. The closer we are to the community, the more we know what's working, what's not, how to get a good outcome, and the more trust we develop. There is always a gap between what people can do and what they think they can do. We try to close that gap through technical assistance, training, interacting. At our best, we are dot connectors—connecting isolated residents and entrepreneurs to resources, networks, foreign places and people. People pay more for everything to live in the Delta. Eighty percent of all transactions are in cash in convenience stores, unlike elsewhere, where 80 percent of transactions are plastic." As a result, over the last several years, Hope has been acquiring bank branches abandoned by mainstream banks and reopening them as credit union branches that enable residents to manage their money safely, reducing crime, loss, and fees for money orders and cashier's checks. Forty percent of their credit union members have never had a bank account before. Consider the range of products available to the new member when she walks into the Itta Bena branch: a whole range of affordable checking, savings, loan, credit card, home, and insurance products.[6] What's more, customers are owners, and tellers know customers by name and are ready to counsel them.

It will be easier to see the cumulative impact of

Hope and the co-investment and partnerships it has fostered as the streams of development, trust, and enterprise enlarge over coming decades. But already the impact is palpable. Before Hurricane Katrina, the Central City neighborhood of New Orleans was an economic wasteland where homelessness, poverty, drugs, and crime were rife. No financial institution had served Central City for generations. Hope established a credit union there in 2004. Today, thirteen years later, Central City is full of supermarkets, restaurants, tourists, businesses, and owner-occupied homes, and in fact is in danger of gentrification.

One indicator of future success is a narrow failure: in 2006–7, led by Hope, Mississippi nearly became the first state to establish and fund $500 child college savings accounts for every child in the state. Shortly thereafter, however, the recession derailed the economy, the state budget, and those hopes. Still, the chair of the State Ways and Means Committee offered to fund the program with a state bond; knowing that that was not the way to fund a permanent program, Hope demurred.

Still, Hope grows. "None of us get there by ourselves," Bill notes. "This is necessarily a multigenerational effort. As the demographics of the nation shift, it will become only clearer and clearer that a successful future will require investment in communities like this. People matter. These people matter. We need to help everybody understand that."

savings, educations, homes, businesses, and the aspirations of all people. This new prosperity plan must be based on savings, not debt.

In 1785, President John Adams declared, "The whole people must take upon themselves the education of the whole people and be willing to bear the expenses of it." Universal public education did not come from a presidential edict or an act of Congress, however; it happened in a much more organic, decentralized, bottom-up, American way. Starting first in New England and beginning with religious denominations, localities, and ultimately states, universal public education spread, powered by the understanding that our democracy and our economy could not rise without it. By 1870, all states had tax-subsidized elementary schools, and the United States had achieved one of the highest literacy rates in the world. Educators argued that mere literacy was insufficient; additional education beyond the age of fourteen was needed to improve citizenship and develop higher level skills. During the next seventy years, a system of public high schools and then colleges developed; by 1940, half of America's youth were earning high school diplomas. Spurred by the Morrill Land-Grant College Act in 1862, public universities were established.

In typical American fashion, first in line for schooling were white male children, but the "Republican Motherhood" movement, led by Lydia Maria Child, Catharine Maria Sedgwick, Lydia Sigourney, and others, brought girls into public education. In 1851, the Cherokee Nation opened the first college for women west of the Mississippi River. Until the Civil War, education was illegal for slaves. After the Civil War, the Freedmen's Bureau created a thousand schools across the South; by 1865, 90,000 freed slaves were enrolled. Republicans led the creation of the first system of taxpayer-funded (though segregated) schools across the South in 1867. With the end of Reconstruction, Democratic state legislators cut funding for black schools in the 1870s. Historically black colleges and universities emerged toward the end of the nineteenth century. But in 1896, with its infamous *Plessy v. Ferguson* decision, the Supreme Court ruled that separate-but-equal schools were constitutional; of course, there was no equality of funding or educational quality. Between 1914 and 1930, philanthropists including Julius Rosenwald and an active African American community established 5,000 schools across the South for African American children. And in 1954 the *Brown v. Board of Education* decision struck down the separate-but-equal doctrine. Even then equality did not prevail.

Education and economic development are intertwined. In 1957, Nobel laureate Robert Solow found that increasing levels of education were even more important to national growth than the increase in capital stock.[7] Edward Denison estimated that between 1929 and 1982 in the nonresidential business sector, increasing levels of education were responsible for 16 percent of growth in output and 30 percent of employees' productivity growth.[8] More recently, Dale Jorgenson and Kevin Stiroh attribute to education 8.7 percent of total growth and 13 percent of growth in output per worker from 1959 to 1998.[9] One can wonder what the contribution would have been had we educated all our people, rather than just some.

The important and lasting lessons of universal public education are three: education pays off in lasting ways, there is widespread support for public education, and the United States has found it continually challenging to provide that education equitably across class and racial lines.

Like public education, homeownership emerges over

time and with strong government and private economic interventions. The Homestead Acts of the late nineteenth and early twentieth centuries were great acts of democratic wealth-building; they were also limited because they built wealth primarily for white Americans. The Homestead Act of 1862, as signed by Abraham Lincoln, provided free 160-acre tracts to U.S. citizens and veterans over age twenty-one or to heads of household who had never taken up arms against the country, provided they were willing to live on and work the homestead for at least five years. Over a seventy-seven-year period, from 1863 to 1939, the Homestead Acts distributed 246 million acres to 1.5 million households.[10] Trina Shanks estimates that 46 million Americans today can trace their wealth to these acts.[11]

In the middle of the nineteenth century, 1.5 billion acres of public-domain land, tens of thousands of hungry immigrants and settlers and speculators, unregulated banks, rising land values, easy credit, and a raging appetite for federal land sales (and their revenues) all drove a frenzied marketplace. Land speculators, fueled by cash and East Coast banks, purchased large tracts of western land, which they then sold or rented to squatters moving west. They set the value of land, sold it, and repossessed it if and when the new farmers, facing mortgage interest rates of 20 to 40 percent, couldn't pay their debts. Large numbers of questionable roads, canals, railroads, and other infrastructure projects ensued.[12]

There were explicit efforts to ensure that freed slaves and black people benefited from the Homestead Acts. During the Civil War Lincoln ordered 20,000 acres confiscated in South Carolina to be sold to freedmen in twenty-acre plots. In 1865, General Sherman issued Special Field Order No. 15 providing land along the Georgia and South Carolina coasts for black settlement in forty-acre tracts. (He also lent settlers army mules, leading to the phrase "forty acres and a mule.") Within six months of the order, 40,000 former slaves lived on 400,000 acres of southern land. These land grants were supposed to continue, but President Andrew Johnson remanded the order and decreed that the land should be returned to the original owners, dispossessing thousands of black landowners. The Southern Homestead Act of 1866 explicitly included black people, but its provisions expired with the end of Reconstruction and the rise of Jim Crow.[13] The rise and fall of the Freedmen's Bank, into which freed slaves were urged to deposit what money they had saved, is no happier a story. Always managed by whites, its funds were allowed to be invested recklessly, and only when the bank was on its last legs was Frederick Douglass, one of its depositors, put in charge to go down with the ship.[14]

African Americans were not the only people of color passed over by the Homestead Acts. The Chinese Exclusion Act of 1882 prevented Chinese immigrants from participating, as did agreements with the Japanese government limiting Japanese immigration and economic participation.[15] Other immigrant groups—Mexicans, Filipinos, Bahamians—worked the land but were generally unable to get title. Of course, the people who lost the most in westward expansion were Native Americans; they had claim to much of the land given away. In 1823, the U.S. Supreme Court in a unanimous opinion authored by Chief Justice Marshall in *Johnson v. M'Intosh* effectively adopted as U.S. law the "doctrine of discovery," initially promulgated by the Vatican in the fifteenth century, which removed any Native right and title to land.[16] The Dawes Act or General Allotment Act of 1887 extinguished tribal title to land in return for privatizing allotments of a portion of it. When the act was passed, Native American lands totaled more than 138 million acres; fifty years later, only 48 million acres remained in Native hands. Wilma Mankiller, former principal chief of the Cherokee Nation, called it "one of the most massive thefts in American history."[17] It was neither the first or the last of these takings. When gold was discovered on Cherokee lands in Georgia, those lands were seized, and the Cherokee and other nations were forced to march 1,200 miles across the country in the Trail of Tears to what would become Oklahoma in 1838–39; more than 4,000 died along the path.[18]

Most troubling to Chief Mankiller was not the magnitude of the theft but the undermining of tribally owned and managed community property. Henry Dawes visited the Cherokee Nation in Oklahoma in the early 1880s, concluding, "The head chief told us there was not a family in that whole nation that had not a home of its own. There was not a pauper in that nation, and the nation did not owe a dollar. It built its own capitol . . . and it built its schools and its hospitals."[19] Despite the shock of removal, the Cherokee Nation reconstituted its government, established a free and compulsory school system, established a college for women, and installed the first telephone west of the Mississippi. Cherokees were more literate than surrounding whites and graduated more students from college between the end of the Civil War and statehood in 1907 than did Arkansas and Texas combined.[20] Those achievements did not dissuade Dawes and his congressional allies. Dawes said of the Cherokees: "The defect of their system was apparent. They have got as far as they can go, because they own their land in common . . . and under that there is no enterprise to make your home any better than your neighbors. There is no selfishness, which is at the bottom of civilization. Till this people will consent to give up their lands, and divide them among their citizens so that each can own the land he cultivates, they will not make much more progress."[21]

At first the Cherokees were exempted from the provisions of the Dawes Act, though other tribes in the Indian Territories were covered. But subsequently they were included; many tribal members got individual allotments, but more than two million acres of "Unassigned lands" became the locus of the Oklahoma land rush—for non-Natives.[22]

The Homestead Acts suggest that making a bet on the productive capacity of people and providing a free stake, in this case land for a homestead, to people on condition they work to improve it can make an enormous difference to the country over generations.[23] Requiring families to add their sweat and drive, in this case by working the land for at least five years, but bearing the up-front cost of investment as only the government is able to, can generate large long-term returns. Individual stakes can build communities and community institutions.[24] The very success of the Homestead Acts and the enduring costs of their exclusions argue that future investments of this kind should not exclude but instead must be aggressively inclusive.

The Homestead Acts corresponded with a remaking, over time, of the mortgage markets in the United States. Fearing a replay of the Wild West banking that preceded the Homestead Act of 1862, the National Banking Act of 1864 prohibited national banks from financing long-term loans and mortgages.[25] As a result, mortgage loans remained short-term and high-interest with loan-to-value ratios under 50 percent, requiring buyers to come up with down payments of half or more the value of the homes.[26] High down payments and low loan-to-value ratios protected banks, which could recoup their investments by foreclosing and reselling properties, but kept homeownership beyond the grasp of most Americans. In 1895, average loan-to-value ratios were 30 to 48 percent; interest

Wilma Pearl Mankiller

Wilma Pearl Mankiller, born on November 18, 1945, grew up on Mankiller Flats, the 160 acres allotted to her grandfather, John Mankiller, in the late 1800s. The family name derives from a Cherokee military title, usually entrusted to a person who was in charge of "safeguarding a Cherokee village."[27] Her father, Charley, was a full-blood Cherokee and labor organizer; Irene, her mom, was white and willful. Wilma remembers exploring the woods and streams of her native land.

At age eleven, unable to support the family in Oklahoma, Charley took the offer of the Bureau of Indian Affairs to relocate the family to San Francisco. This was part of the federal government's termination policy—an effort to get rid of the "Indian problem" by getting rid of reservations so that Native Americans could work in urban areas "like white people."[28] The policy was the brainchild of Dillon Myer, who had come to the Bureau of Indian Affairs fresh from overseeing the relocation of the Japanese in internment camps during World War II and who would later move on to directing insurgent efforts in Central America. Charley, Irene, and their eleven children were dumped in the Bayview/Hunter's Point District of San Francisco, as dreary then as now. It was their first introduction to city life; they stared as the first elevators they had ever seen seemed to eat people, who entered but disappeared by the time the doors opened again. There Wilma would grow up, marry her first husband, Hector Hugo Olaya de Bardi, and have two daughters, Gina and Felicia; during this time she often passed as Latina. Her political coming-of-age coincided with the Indian occupation of Alcatraz. She shunned her role as housewife, assumed her Native identity, divorced Hugo, and began volunteer work with the Pitt Indian Tribe to regain their homelands.

Wilma valued community and communal ownership, especially of land, perhaps because she had been deprived of it before rediscovering it in California. Wilma regarded the Dawes Act, which dispersed tribal land into individual private allotments, as the single greatest blow to the Cherokee nation and way of life. Of course, there were many others.

Whenever Wilma spoke to Native audiences, she would remind them of the Trail of Tears, "the trail where we cried," ordered by President Andrew Jackson upon the discovery of gold in Cherokee country of Georgia, quickly adding, "I tell you this not so that you will hate, but so that you don't hate yourselves."[29] She would go on to emphasize the positives the Cherokee made out of that cruelty:

> We are a revitalized tribe. After every major upheaval, we have been able to gather together as a people and rebuild a community and a government. Individually and collectively, Cherokee people possess an extraordinary ability to face down adversity and continue moving forward. We are able to do that because our culture, though certainly diminished, has sustained us since time immemorial.[30]

To Wilma, community came first. Of the movie that grew out of her autobiography, she would say, "Remember, this is not about me."[31] She revered the heritage of which she was a part:

> There are over 550 very distinct tribal governments in the United States, each with their own unique history, culture and language. Tribal governments have a very long history of governance. Governments such as the Hopi here in Arizona, and the Umatilla in Oregon, have lived on the same land for more than 10,000 years. Other tribal governments, such as the Cherokee and Choctaw, have been forcibly removed from their homelands and have almost had to reinvent their communities and nations in unfamiliar territory. Yet, despite a history of extreme adversity, our tribal governments remain strong and continue to maintain a govern-

ment to government relationship with the United States government.[32]

And she revered the land:

> When the United States was in its infancy it recognized tribal sovereignty in formal treaties with tribal nations. These treaty agreements often involved the United States government taking tribal land. According to the First Nations Development Institute, by the early twentieth century, the U.S. took more than 2 billion acres by treaty or official government confiscation. Though land was and is critical to the cultural survival of tribal people and their governments, tribal governments now hold only a tiny fraction of their original land holdings. The land base and population of tribal governments range from those with millions of acres to some with less than 25 acres of land.[33]

Taken from Oklahoma at an early age, she never learned Cherokee, but she lived the Cherokee value of *gadugi*—working together for the common good. Upon returning to Oklahoma with Gina and Felicia, she worked with her eventual husband, Charlie Soap, to start community self-help projects to build water lines, community centers, ball fields, and communities.

Mankiller valued asset-building for its capacity to recognize and liberate the dreams and abilities of common people. She explained:

> The relationships developed and the learning processes undertaken during the course of most assets programs enable participants to acquire an asset—a savings account, a business, a home, a college education or even a working automobile—and simultaneously encourage people to trust their own thinking, to believe in themselves and their ability to change the circumstances in which they find themselves. Asset projects create situations and circumstances that encourage individual improvement and success.
>
> Acquiring a sense of self-efficacy is no small feat for low-income people of color, many of whom have endured the most outrageous oppression and exploitation for generations. Without assets, any short-term crisis or social disruption creates havoc in the lives of low-income people. We saw the most horrific example of that very situation on a large scale in New Orleans and the Gulf Coast over the course of the past year.
>
> Self-efficacy is an asset that is just as important as a savings account or a house. A great deal of research indicates that people who believe in themselves and their capabilities tend to perform

better in every aspect of their lives. And early research on individual development account participants supports the notion that people who acquire assets view themselves and their communities very differently than they did before they acquired assets. Once they have assets and a sense of self-efficacy, they are much more willing to view obstacles and barriers as challenges to be mastered instead of reasons to give up.[34]

Mankiller faced poverty, dislocation, single motherhood, muscular dystrophy, leukemia, renal failure, two kidney transplants, cancer, and slander, among many other affronts that might have stopped a lesser human being, or made her less caring or appreciative or optimistic. Not Wilma. For her, resilience was the more salient quality. She would entitle her second book on the wisdom of Native women *Every Day Is a Good Day*. Her favorite ceremony as chief was her time with the "Original Enrollees," the first generation of Cherokee whose names were inscribed in the tribal records when the Cherokee Nation was reestablished in Oklahoma, and who are now in their eighties and nineties.[35] She would say that "things have a way of working out the way they're supposed to."

I was with Wilma during the last few weeks of her life. Wilma faced death with characteristic courage, honesty, and grace, accepting only a fraction of the prescribed painkillers. She believed that while we can't control what happens to us, we can control how we view it and what we do about it. This is the Cherokee value of "being of good mind," and Wilma mastered that. She invited me saying we would cook a meal together as we had before, once spending a day making a wondrous chili stew that proved too spicy for anyone to eat. Wilma imagined, in the Iroquois tradition, that she would make her way across the Milky Way, picking strawberries as she walked. On the day that she died, spring broke. It seemed as though her life spread to the budding trees, the birds, the wind, and the blue sky.

rates varied between 6 and 10 percent; the average duration of a loan was less than four years except in New England, where it averaged just under six years.[36] Between 1910 and 1920, the nation shifted from being majority rural to being majority urban. As a result, a new type of ownership policy was required.

This market was able, eventually, to achieve overall homeownership rates of about 40 percent. But then the Great Depression hit, and property values declined by half, triggering widespread foreclosures. A quarter of a million homeowners defaulted each year from 1931 to 1935, a default rate exceeding 10 percent, causing homeownership rates to decline for both whites and blacks to below 50 percent and 20 percent, respectively.[37]

To save the housing market from the rippling foreclosures

of the Great Depression, the federal government remade the U.S. housing market. Three new government agencies were created: the Home Owner's Loan Corporation in 1933, to refinance mortgages; the Federal Housing Administration in 1936, to insure mortgages; and Fannie Mae in 1938, a secondary market tapping private finance. Together these agencies supported a new type of mortgage, the long-term, fixed-rate, self-amortizing mortgage, and brought homeownership within the purview of the American middle class.[38] This basic structure of homeownership—long-term loans with federal guarantees—was expanded over the ensuing decades. In 1948 the FHA increased the mortgage time limit to thirty years from a standard of twenty; in 1956 it raised the maximum loan-to-value ratio to 95 percent, lowering the minimum down payment; and other entities and regulations harnessed the power of the private sector to offer expanded financing.[39] These structural reforms, together with GI Bill mortgage support for World War II veterans, resulted in the transformation of the country from a nation of urban renters to urban and suburban homeowners, with the homeownership rate climbing from 43.6 percent in 1940 to 64 percent by 1980.[40]

Unfortunately, this great expansion of wealth-creating opportunity once again favored white Americans and excluded African Americans and other racial-ethnic groups. The FHA limited its financing to white neighborhoods and instigated "redlining," essentially denying to African Americans and other communities of color the primary wealth-building opportunity of the twentieth century.[41] Private market actors, including financial institutions, real estate brokers, and state and local public authorities (particularly zoning and redevelopment agencies), exacerbated this discrimination. The Home Mortgage Disclosure Act of 1975, the Community Reinvestment Act of 1977, and the Financial Institutions

Recovery, Reform and Enforcement Act of 1989 redressed some of this discrimination.[42] Yet structural exclusions and inequality still plagued the U.S. mortgage markets. In 2000, black mortgage holders were two to three times more likely than whites to hold high-cost subprime mortgages, Hispanic borrowers were 50 percent more likely, and other people of color were more than twice as likely—even when they should have qualified for conventional loans.[43] Not only has this resulted in homeownership rates for blacks, Hispanics, and other communities of color that are 30 percentage points less than comparable rates for whites, but it has limited the appreciation and wealth-building contributions of homeownership to communities of color.

The verdict of this history is that the government can make a housing market capable of expanding homeownership and wealth-building opportunities for wide swaths of the American people; it can also restrict those opportunities and allow private market actors and institutions to do so.

Of all the democratic wealth-building moments in our history, the greatest, perhaps, was the Servicemen's Readjustment Act of 1944—commonly known as the GI Bill. Historian Edward Humes summarizes the fundamental changes the GI Bill effected: "A nation of renters would become a nation of homeowners. College would be transformed from an elite bastion to a middle-class entitlement. Suburbia would be born amid the clatter of bulldozers and the smell of new asphalt linking it all together. Inner cities would collapse."[44]

The direct and indirect impacts of the GI Bill—both for good and for ill—can hardly be overstated.[45] Two hundred thousand businesses. Eight million students who received training and college degrees. Five million homeowners. The bill tripled the middle class and changed the shape of income distribution from a pyramid to a diamond within a decade.[46]

The GI Bill was a huge investment, with its costs accounting for more than 15 percent of the federal budget by 1948, but, according to the Joint Economic Committee of the Congress, each $1 of that investment yielded $7 in economic returns.[47] Though the GI Bill was neutral on its face, its benefits were effectively denied to most women and people of color, reifying the fissures of economic and social discrimination in the country at a time when they could have been transformed.

The prospect of millions of returning veterans—one-eighth of the nation—was certainly top-of-mind for Harry Colmery, commander of the American Legion, as he drafted the outlines of what would become the GI Bill on a Mayflower Hotel napkin. As it emerged, the bill provided unemployment benefits and home, education, and business loans and support to 16 million eligible returning World War II veterans. Most of the debate that took place in Congress focused on the provision of unemployment benefits, which ended up as $20 a week for up to fifty-two weeks (leading to it being known as the 52/20 Plan).[48] At the time there was great fear not only of recessionary unemployment that might (and did) follow when all those veterans lost their defense jobs but also of a return of Depression-era unemployment, a problem that had been solved only with the movement to wartime footing. So not only was the cost of the 52/20 Plan of concern, but there was also the fear that it would further weaken incentives to work. In fact, the unemployment benefit was the least used; veterans claimed it only for an average of eighteen weeks.

Demand for education benefits, however, was more than fifteen times what had been expected.[49] Education supports were for living stipends as well as tuition expenses and books—a full ride—enabling 8 million GIs to access vocational education and college. Among the 2.5 million college graduates were 91,000 scientists, 238,000 teachers, 67,000 doctors, 450,000 engineers, 240,000 accountants, 17,000 journalists, 22,000 dentists, and 1 million artists, lawyers, entrepreneurs, and writers—enough to help spur growth in the American economy for the next fifty years.[50] By effectively transferring the power to make college admissions decisions from college administrators to the broad middle class, the GI Bill transformed higher education from the province of a privileged elite to the rightful aspiration for all. Enrollment tripled; by 1947 half of college students were attending classes thanks to the GI Bill.[51]

The GI Bill's transformation of the housing sector was equally profound. Five million veterans bought homes with low-interest, long-term, no-down-payment mortgages through the GI Bill. For a solid decade after the war, half of new homeowners each year used home loans financed or guaranteed by the GI Bill. The GI Bill grew the American suburbs while simultaneously redlining these communities for white people and creating levels of racial segregation in housing that had never before been seen in the United States.

Although the GI Bill was race- and gender-neutral on its face and didn't explicitly hurt women and communities of color, the design of the bill combined with existing institutions of American life denied its transformational benefits to millions of women and people of color who could have benefited from it. While it moved white Americans to college and the suburbs in their own homes, it built upon the discriminatory tectonic plates of the racial and gender wealth divide at a time when it might have altered the geography of wealth in America and narrowed the divide.

Only 2 percent of the military personnel who served during World War II were women—350,000 women compared to 16 million men.[52] It is perhaps no wonder, then, that the overwhelming share of GI Bill benefits went to men. But even the women who did serve in uniform were often not apprised of the benefits they qualified for, and banks and colleges were reluctant to accept them as customers and students. In general, the culture of the time deemphasized the education of women, instead pushing family formation and the birth of the baby boom generation. One-third of eligible women servicemembers claimed education benefits, as opposed to three-quarters of eligible men.[53] And while the GI Bill made no distinction between combat and non-combat positions in the military, considering both equally necessary to the war effort, the 19 million women who swarmed into the workplace to assume positions in the "Arsenal of Democracy" after men had left those jobs for the military were not considered eligible for benefits, even though their roles were just as crucial as those of the non-combat military. Furthermore, many of these women workers—a third to a half—wanted to keep their jobs and their "newfound economic clout" after the war, but they were not given that option.[54]

Why weren't domestic defense industry workers, disproportionately women, included in the GI Bill? There are undoubtedly many reasons, including cost, a return to traditional gender and family roles, and a bow to urgent necessity over longer-term possibility. But what is certain is that the economic and social costs of not including the 19 million women who contributed to the war effort were considerable. The exclusions of the GI Bill "left women as second-class citizens after the wartime economy had lifted them up, if briefly, to near equality."[55]

Discrimination against African Americans and other people of color was largely outsourced in the GI Bill by leaving implementation to local and state administration in a country where segregation was still the law. But this was by deliberate design. John Elliott Rankin, chair of the House Committee on Veterans Legislation, was the primary force behind the version of the bill that eventually passed. He was also a racist, anti-Semitic, Red-baiting, New Deal–bashing, pro-lynching, anti-union future Dixiecrat who had supported the internment of Japanese Americans during World War II. A descendant of successful planters ruined by the Civil War and son of a poor white family in northwest Mississippi, Rankin never owned a house. He believed in economic development for the benefit of his poor white fellow Mississippians, and he was a crucial force behind creating economic opportunity for his white fellow countrymen in the form of the Tennessee Valley Authority. But he did not believe that black people deserved any of these opportunities. Claiming to support "the natural order of things," Rankin even blocked black GIs from voting in 1944. Furthermore, he was among the conservative coalition who voted to exclude farm and domestic workers—the largest categories of black workers—from Social Security.

Rankin's most important act of discrimination in designing the GI Bill was to block federal oversight and leave implementation to local and state authorities, which, especially in the South, were firmly in the hands of segregationists. It was these local authorities that were given the power to deny home loans, business loans, and education loans to black applicants. The Veterans Administration (VA) was not allowed to make loans directly and could only serve as a guarantor or co-signer; thus the decision to make loans was left to banks, under pressure to mind redlining guidelines and not inclined to make loans to black borrowers, however qualified. The results: out of 3,000 VA home loans made to veterans in Mississippi in 1947, two went to black families.[56] Up north, in New York and New Jersey, the results weren't much better: out of 67,000 mortgages insured by the GI Bill, fewer than 100 went to black families.[57] Thus, overall, while the GI Bill allowed homeownership to soar among white families from less than half in the 1940s to two-thirds by 1960 and three out of four later, it kept homeownership by blacks, Latinos, and other communities of color stuck at much lower levels.[58]

The result, based on a comprehensive econometric analysis, was that while the GI Bill had substantial positive benefits for black as well as white veterans outside the South, "those from the South made no significant gains in educational attainment." An act that "fostered a 'true social revolution' within the white population served as perhaps the greatest instrument for widening an already huge racial gap within postwar America."[59] A greater proportion of the 1.3 million black veterans actually participated in the GI Bill's education benefits than their white counterparts—49 percent versus 43 percent.[60] However, "it is almost impossible to separate the pure effects of the G.I. Bill from the fact that its benefits were dispensed and used inside a society expressly designed to cheat, belittle, and oppress black Americans. The rose itself might have been hearty and bountiful, but its roots were planted in poisoned soil."[61]

Racial disparities showed clearly in other areas as well. Though college and vocational training increased significantly for black GIs after the war, the gains paled compared to those of white veterans, who saw double the increase. Predominantly white colleges admitted fewer than 5,000 blacks in the late 1940s, with underfunded historically black colleges and universities responsible for 95 percent of black college-goers.[62] Sharecroppers were denied business loans because sharing profits with their landlords was construed to disqualify them from self-employment status.[63]

The GI Bill reached one-eighth of Americans directly; add in other family members who benefited, and it reached one-fifth of

Americans. Add in the number of non-veterans who benefited from the "G.I. Bill's domino effect—lowered barriers to college, the rapid growth of vocational and on-the-job training programs, the boom in affordable suburban housing, the booming economy"—and it reached at least 40 percent of the country.[64]

Today, the impact of the GI Bill has shrunk: it reaches less than 1 percent of Americans, and with a much less robust package of benefits. Still, the effects of the GI Bill after World War II leave us with a concrete demonstration of the potential to transform an economy from the bottom up, a host of important lessons and precedents, and living proof that even now, the United States could—this time intentionally and with remedies for previous exclusions—remake opportunity and prosperity in America.

Six key lessons and precedents emerge from the GI Bill:

1. **A hand up, not a handout.** GI Bill benefits were earned by service, and they were translated into economic gains through the self-directed efforts of individual beneficiaries: "the individual G.I., not the government, picked the college, the neighborhood, the job, the vocational school, the paint color of the garage."[65]
2. **Education, homeownership, business.** The GI Bill invested in education, entrepreneurship, and homeownership—engines of economic growth. The GI Bill's "true power came in directing the largesse into the beneficial realms of education, homeownership, and the creation of responsible, productive citizens with firm stakes in their communities and country."[66]
3. **Capital.** The GI Bill enabled millions of GIs to build lasting economic foundations for their families in the form of growing home and business equity and human capital.

4. **Transformation.** The GI Bill did transform the economy and society of the country, ushering in the postwar era of "effortless superiority" based on the empowered productive capacity of the American people, even while it reified racial and gender inequality.
5. **Inclusion.** The GI Bill teaches that democratic investments in the common genius need to include all. Surface neutrality is insufficient when confronting entrenched institutional and cultural discrimination and exclusion.
6. **Return on investment.** The GI Bill, expensive as it was, represented a value-added investment that returned many times the initial investment. Just the education investment of some $51 billion then yielded $260 billion in increased economic output from those educated GIs, and an additional $93 billion in taxes, as well as unquantified innovation, inspiration, and inheritance.

The initial Declaration of Independence presaged the 150-year quest for universal public education to provide all citizens the base of knowledge and learning inherent to exercising freedom. The Homestead Acts of the mid- to late 1800s distributed 270 million acres—10 percent of the land area of the United States—to 1.6 million households. With 10 percent of American homes in foreclosure during the Great Depression, we created the Federal Housing Administration, the Federal National Mortgage Association, and more, which established the thirty-year fixed rate mortgage as the standard—bringing homeownership within the purview of average families, and financing those dreams. Then the GI Bill, unleashing the entrepreneurial and intellectual energy of one-fifth of a nation, opened up twenty-five years of prosperity for many late in the last century. In each century, the United States expanded the range of Americans who could participate and profit.

These are very different historical acts with very different impetuses and effects. In them, justice and injustice combined. Each gave additional millions of Americans a toehold, a stake, an economic place from which they could enter the American economy. Each resulted in significant macroeconomic growth in the economy as a whole. Each underscored and underwrote the productive capacity of common people. Each contained a case against its own discriminations. Now that most American families are being left behind, the question is squarely this: What will the United States do in the twenty-first century to realize the American promise of prosperity for all?

Two great lessons emerge from our four past waves of investing in the common genius. First, we can unleash the productive and entrepreneurial capacity of common people. This time, we should embrace the full proven potential of these kinds of investments and do it for everyone. Everyone deserves a down payment on the future. Everyone, regardless of age, race, gender, ethnicity, ability, or geography, deserves an investment in the American dream. A new prosperity policy should help the unemployed steelworker or coal miner just as much as any person of color or woman at the same income or asset level.

Second, prosperity policies must be deliberately inclusive or risk exacerbating current inequities. The GI Bill did not discriminate on its face, but the institutions and officials charged with implementing it effectively, if not always intentionally, translated its lofty goals to disparate effect. Women, people of color, and others were often left out of our previous waves of large-scale family asset-building; this fact impels us to make sure this new wave is affirmatively inclusive. This inclusive imperative need not be based on our assuming responsibility for the shortsightedness or sexism or racism of our past; it need only rest on our determination to harness the full productive

Adnan Bokhari

Adnan Bokhari remembers the moment he arrived in the United States: "The most terrifying experience of my life was when I walked out of the terminal at JFK in 1994." He had just flown for the first time from his native Pakistan. He was fifteen years old. His few belongings were in a battered suitcase; in his pocket were a visitor's visa and a few hundred dollars, barely enough to get him to Alexandria, Virginia, where his older brother lived.

At first Adnan shared the floor of a tiny room with his older brother. He slept on a futon that a salesman had told his brother he "wouldn't buy for a dog." He worked delivering pizzas, distributing flyers, waiting tables at a diner, as a hotel clerk, and as an administrative assistant. With the help of his family, he bought a ten-year-old car so he could do more deliveries. It was years before he could afford to put a full tank of gas in that car. He regularly worked twelve- to fourteen-hour days, and then he would study for another four hours. Like his fellow new Americans, he was often overworked and underpaid. Unfortunately, there are people who hire immigrants and, as he puts it, "don't mind the law"—they are willing to pay people less money than what is legally required for work—

and often cheat workers out of wages due to them. Adnan notes wryly, "The last paycheck is a myth."

Uncertain if he had enough money to pay all his bills, and to avoid overdraft fees, he did not open a bank account for four years, despite working multiple jobs all that time. He lived in the cash economy, using check-cashing services that charged usurious fees—part of Adnan's early accounting education.

Adnan entered the country on a visitor's visa, which he then changed for a student visa when he began studying accounting at Strayer University. He was caught in a no-win vise: he was supposed to study full-time, but he could not afford the three courses required for a full-time load. His family helped. He earned his bachelor's degree in 2003, and his CPA a year later. Why did he study accounting? "Because that's where the jobs were. They had just changed the accounting rules, and I found officials were projecting 50,000 to 60,000 job vacancies in the next few years." A shortage in the job market meant an opportunity for entry-level candidates such as Adnan.

Goodwill and luck played roles in his success as well. A network of Pakistani immigrants in the metropolitan Washington, DC, area helped connect him to jobs. Colleagues who saw potential in him recommended him for jobs for which he lacked the education and experience required but which he was capable of performing.

While Adnan was working two jobs and simultaneously studying to complete his degree and certification, his typical day began at 5:00 a.m. For two to three hours he would listen to cassette tapes he had recorded with class notes as he drove to work and after he arrived. At 8:30 he would start working until lunchtime at 1:00 p.m. He would take the first ten minutes of his lunch hour to eat, then spend the remaining fifty minutes studying. He was back to his desk from 2:00 p.m. until 4:30 p.m. Then he studied for another two hours until 6:30 p.m., when he would drive either home or, most evenings, to school. He would work a second job on the weekends. During these years, he took off only during federal holidays and tried to squeeze in a four-day vacation over the Thanksgiving holiday. Though he was working a full-time job and a part-time job, he was barely keeping his head above water.

His financial condition didn't improve until he obtained his certification and moved into public accounting. That was the start of a new chapter in Adnan's life that, due to his work ethic and desire for continuous improvement, would prove fruitful.

His father had always impressed upon Adnan the value of education. Descended from a long line of Sufi clerics, his father was a respected lawyer and judge in Pakistan. He put Adnan in the best schools in Pakistan, and then urged him to continue his education abroad: "As an immigrant, you'll need to work harder, earn more credentials. You can't take anything for granted." Adnan worked long hours that helped him climb the corporate ladder. He recalls an email exchange with one of the firm's partners: the partner commented on the late hours Adnan worked, to which Adnan responded, "I have read that most successful people work twelve hours a day. I figured if I averaged thirteen hours I would get there faster."

Some colleagues told Adnan he did not need to seek further education once he had earned his CPA. But Adnan continued his education and earned a master's degree while serving as chief financial officer for Prosperity Now. With many depending on him, he could not take the chance that his skills and credentials would grow stale.

Adnan's story is the quintessential immigrant-made-good one, complete with incredibly hard work, sacrifice, hardship, luck, and, ultimately, reward. Of course, it is also an unfinished story: the immigrant story in the United States continues with new waves of immigrants and refugees coming to the United States to make a better life for themselves and for all Americans. For other Adnans, and indeed for the good of the country, we make sure this sort of rise continues to be possible and, more than that, likely.

Adnan says, "I remember now everyone who helped me out, who opened a door for me. It is for me to pass on that opportunity. That's why I work at Prosperity Now and serve on the boards of the National Immigration Law Center and the Golden Key International Honour Society—to open paths for others, especially new waves of immigrants, including those who have lived here for generations, but have never really been admitted to the mainstream economy."

capacity of all our people, not just some. It rests on us assuming the responsibility of recognizing that our current tax policy does not only accept huge, growing, and toxic racial wealth inequality but actually invests massively in widening the divide. To the extent we can, we should ensure that new policies try to close the racial and gender wealth divides at the same time as they open up economic opportunity to everyone regardless of race, gender, disability, history, or demographic circumstance.

History and disparity argue for racial reparations, but it is politically difficult and might not meet constitutional muster; the Supreme Court decision in *Regents of the University of California v. Bakke*, banning affirmative action based on race, still stands.[67] In spite of this, a universal basis for saving and asset-building in the country—automatic account opening, savings matches and other incentives, access and investment choices, and so on—is the essential foundation for renewal of the American dream for all.

By giving everyone the opportunity to build a nest egg, we put in place the architecture for differential investments that take account of the fact that people do not start from the same place. Some people need and deserve greater incentives. Income proves to be an imperfect proxy for asset-holding and history, and net worth is even more reflective. More than half of black and Latino families are in the poorest income quintiles. More than 60 percent of both African Americans and Hispanics

FIVE WAVES OF INVEST
UNIVERSAL PUBLIC EDUCATION
HOMESTEAD ACT
A FEW MILLION
1.5MILLION
GROWING TO
46MILLION
10-20
MILLION

IN THE COMMON GENIUS
G.I. BILL
PROSPERITY ACCOUNTS
BUSINESS
15 MILLION GROWING TO 30 MILLION
326 MILLION

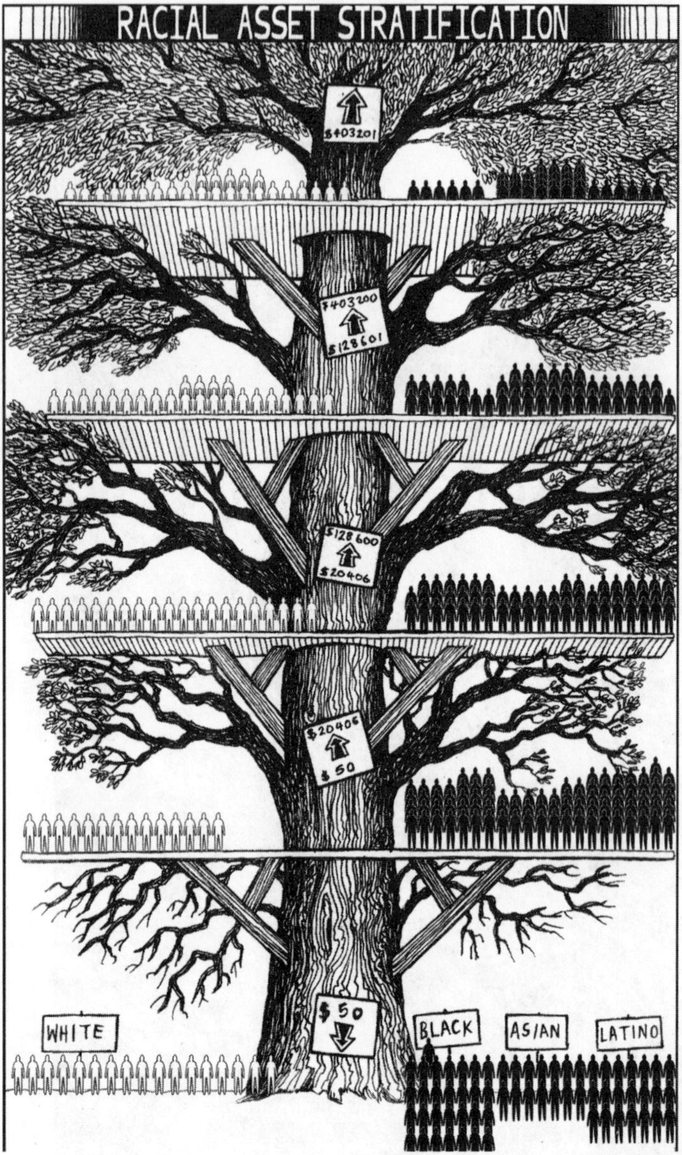

RACIAL ASSET STRATIFICATION
$403201
$403200
$128601
$128600
$20406
$20406
$50
$50
WHITE
BLACK
ASIAN
LATINO

cluster in the two lowest asset and net worth quintiles (that's 50 percent more than an egalitarian distribution would suggest) and only 6 percent were present in the highest net worth quintile (less than one-third what equality would suggest).[68] Differential savings matches are not the only way to make wealth-building incentives sensitive to need, but they are probably the most effective and acceptable way of closing the racial wealth gap (as well as gaps due to gender, disability, and/or age) while extending real wealth-building opportunity to all.

What would a comprehensive, inclusive Prosperity Bill look like? First and foremost, savings matches would be earned; no savings, no match. Widespread experiments summarized in the preceding chapters demonstrate that low-income and even very poor people can and will save for both short- and long-term needs. That said, poorer people can save less. Depending on the demonstration, the immediacy of the use (emergency savings, business, retirement, for self or for kids), income level, the effectiveness of outreach and financial education, and the use of opt-in or opt-out provisions, somewhere between a tenth and a majority of low-income families can be expected to save \$10 to \$40 a month (between \$120 and \$480 a year). Sliding-scale matches, such as 3:1 or 2:1, become an efficient and progressive way of delivering incentives and leveling the playing field. Moreover, when the federal government prods savings through effective policies, nonprofit community groups, private philanthropy, corporations, state and local governments, and business and housing organizations could offer matches targeted to low-income, low-wealth groups—whether racial or ethnic communities, people with disabilities, citizens returning from incarceration, or foster youth—to augment the few hundred dollars they are able to save up, to the match limit.

Donna Brazile

It is not the widely renowned veteran Democratic political strategist Donna Brazile I profile here, but the economic one, who has built assets for herself, her family, and a larger community all her life.

Donna Brazile has participated in more than fifty political campaigns to date at every level, including becoming the first African American woman to run a major presidential campaign. Her political career began more than four decades ago, at the age of nine, when she campaigned for and won a local playground.

It has been a remarkable career, not finished yet, in which she has tasted great victories, great defeats, and always gets back up. What unites her political and economic work is that her feet and heart are still firmly planted in her native New Orleans, among family and community, and that she is dedicated to the American promise of life, liberty, and the pursuit of happiness for all.

She has always recognized that there is an economic dimension to liberty and opportunity. She listens to, relates to, and works for all people, across lines of age, race, and political persuasion. Mary Matalin is one of her best friends, as are Condoleezza

Rice, George Will, and Karl Rove. This profile of Donna does not focus on the widely renowned veteran Democratic political strategist but on the economic success she has demonstrated in her life, building assets for herself, her family, and a larger community.

In 1972, at age twelve, Donna was running four businesses she had started: a prescription and grocery delivery service and check-cashing business, a recycling business, a bait-and-tackle business, and a landscaping business—each built on recognizing the needs of others, each marketed with charisma. Realizing that older folks had trouble getting their prescriptions and groceries and cashing their checks, Donna became their legs and courier: she would run their prescriptions to Mr. Burton of Burton's Pharmacy, then collect and deliver their medicine. She clipped coupons from the *Times-Picayune*, which enabled her to take advantage of the Tuesday chicken specials and generally secure food for less. Similarly, she would take paychecks to Lloyd's Furniture Store, cash them, make monthly payments on balances for appliances, and bring the proceeds home, for which she would be paid $2 or so a trip—"real money in those days."

She recycled cups, cans, bottles, paper, cajoling neighborhood boys to build her a wagon and assist in the collection. She purchased dented cans of soda from the local Shasta bottler for 5¢ apiece and resold them for 10¢. She even recycled chicken guts as bait for crawfish and crab seasons and delivered them to the local bait-and-tackle shop twice a week. Her return was not only financial but also in catfish, croakers, trout, or shrimp, depending on the season.

When Mr. Jimmy, whom she would help care for in a fifth business, died and left her his lawnmower and tools, having taught her to fix and maintain lawnmowers, she started a landscaping business, employing her brothers, cousins, and friends; six to eight yards a weekend yielded a profit of $80 or more, but her mother thought she didn't pay the boys enough.

Her nickname back then was "Dollar Brazile." Also "Paper Chaser," as she transformed care for Mr. Jimmy and Ms. Olive into doing taxes, reading legal papers and notices, and providing general financial assistance for many in the community. She specialized in meeting the economic and financial needs of seniors, as well as teaching her contemporaries how to save their money.

During all this time, Donna's bank was a handkerchief, her constant companion, in which she saved her pennies, nickels, quarters, dollars. She would leave the money with her mother, who borrowed from it to pay for surgeries for her sisters; Donna never asked for that money back. In 1973, at age thirteen, Donna opened her first bank account at the Merchant Trust Bank with over $1,500.

Asked where she acquired her entrepreneurial and financial values and affinity, Donna mentions her grandmother Frances. "There were plenty of lessons my grandmother Frances taught my eight siblings. The biggest was the power of owning land. She told us that we all needed to have a place to lay our heads." Born in Mississippi two scant decades after the formal end of slavery and the Civil War, Grandmother Frances was an accomplished seamstress who could produce whatever she saw, a homemaker and cook who "continued to face racial hostility and mistreatment in her early days, bitterness deeply swallowed so that it never overshadowed the prospects of hope and renewal. Grandma also taught us how to live, thrive, and even become prosperous. It started with not wasting anything, especially our food and clothing. Everything could be recycled; everything had a price. Today it's chicken; tomorrow it's broth, a soup, jambalaya. One chicken could produce multiple meals."

Donna's mom, Jean, and dad, Lionel, met at a basketball game in 1956. Her mom was a second-year student at Southern University who intended to become a social worker or teacher; her dad was a student at Grambling University. They married a year later and had six girls and three boys over the next ten years, of whom Donna was the third. Jean and Lionel had to drop out of college, as the needs of the kids proved dominant, but they always taught their kids that college was the path to success. Lionel, who had been recruited to Grambling to play sports, was drafted and sent to Korea, where he earned four stars and a UN medal for valor. He went to work for Boh Brothers Construction, where he was injured; for Dobb's House, where he was reinjured; and then to serve as a custodian engineer ("a fancy name for a janitor," says Donna) at Riverdale Senior High School. He did odd jobs ("he was very talented") until he retired in 1989 after more than thirty years. Jean worked for the Hilbert family six days a week for more than thirty years, for $100 a week without benefits or health coverage. They worked around the clock, earning a total of about $15,000 a year. When Grandma Frances died in 1975, though her house was fully paid for and intended for Lionel and Jean and their family, an inheritance dispute forced the family to move out and rent a house back in New Orleans. "They say you can't work too hard. But I think both my parents died of overwork."

Donna reminisces that she was a "Head Start baby," having gotten her head start with the inauguration of the program in 1965. She excelled in school, especially reading and math, and in sports—track and field, basketball, volleyball, and softball. The sports gave her a path to college: "I got into LSU on my body, and graduated by my brains."

Before graduating from LSU in 1981, Donna continued to own and operate the four businesses as well as working for the Jefferson Parish Recreation Center, Pizza Hut, and the U.S. Food and Drug Administration as a paid summer intern for two consecutive years. While a student, she did work-study programs to earn enough to live on campus and was a part of the Student Government Association; for a while she served on the Baton Rouge Fair Housing Commission.

Once Donna got to Washington, DC, she had less than $1,500 in college debts but was low on cash. In order to make the trip to Washington, where she had been promised a job, she borrowed $150 in cash from her sister Lisa and promised to pay it back within weeks.

Once settled in Washington, Brazile served as a Capitol Hill intern for House Democratic Caucus chairman Gillis Long. She worked on the campaign to designate the third Monday in January in honor of the Rev Martin Luther King Jr. and began helping Democratic candidates across the country. In 1983, she landed a job as an organizer for Jesse Jackson's historic presidential campaign. While it took some time to find steady work as an organizer, Donna continued to find consulting work in between campaigns to pay off her student debts and begin to save up for a house.

It took her ten years to save up enough money for a down payment and closing costs for her first home, which she bought in 1992 for $165,000. She sold it twenty years later for $800,000 and bought another home, which is now worth $600,000 more than when she purchased it in 2012.

Following Al Gore's presidential campaign in 2000, Donna decided against taking a job as a lobbyist and went back to her entrepreneurial roots. In 2002, she opened Brazile and Associates, using her savings, and it quickly became a boutique strategic consulting and training firm that focused on grassroots organizing. The business started with two interns and a research assistant to help with proposal writing and more. Within two years, she had clients ranging from the Urban Library Council to the U.S. Telecom Association, for which she would hire consultants in more than twenty states to expand broadband.

In 2005, when Hurricane Katrina forced her extended family to flee their homes (they wound up spread over eight states and fourteen cities), she remembers paying $10,000 a month in rent to house her father, siblings, nephews and nieces, aunts, uncles, and numerous cousins. In 2008 and 2010 she bought two houses in Louisiana to help resettle her family; the total cost was $258,000, and the houses have appreciated by $100,000 since then.

She has financed the college and sometimes high

school educations of some of her siblings and most of her nieces and nephews, sometimes with outright gifts, sometimes by matching their college savings. All have graduated or will soon. She routinely endows scholarships at universities, especially historically black colleges and universities (where she often speaks), and has backed a generation of Donna Brazile Scholars at the Louisiana Leadership Institute. She has also helped in emergencies, with Thanksgiving, Christmas, and birthday checks, and to pay for extraordinary health care.

Donna matches sources and uses of her money. She divides her revenues from 2002 through 2016 into six pots: Brazile Associates revenues, speaker or lecture fees, commentator fees from CNN and ABC News, additional writing fees, fees from acting (she has appeared on *The Good Wife* three times and *House of Cards* twice) and fees for her political activities—"the empty pot," she calls it, as, except for two years on the Gore campaign, she never charges for her political work (including serving as an officer of the Democratic National Committee and twice being its chair) so that there will be no conflicts of interest.

She keeps her basic living expenses under $1,600 a month, an amount covered by her fees from ABC and from teaching part-time at Georgetown. Her CNN fees used to pay for tuition, family emergencies, and what she refers to as her personal charities, including homeless shelters and local food banks. Her speaking fees, mostly from unions, corporations, nonprofits, and trade associations, are devoted entirely to an education fund to grant scholarships; today its balance stands at $250,000, but hundreds of thousands of dollars have already traveled through it. She has done asset-building on the community and national levels too, serving on the Louisiana Recovery Authority board after Hurricane Katrina, and was appointed by former president Barack Obama to serve on the J.W. Fulbright Foreign Scholarship Board.

Today, Brazile's assets continue to grow through the ownership of two homes (she maintains what she calls a "safe house" outside New Orleans in case the city is evacuated because of another natural disaster), and her passion for helping young people go to school continues with her philanthropy work. With one exception, all her family are proud homeowners. Her niece Janika, whom she helped raise, is now the proud owner of a house as well as a condo that she rents out.

For Donna and her siblings, this journey to financial independence started with her grandparents, who believed in homeownership, and her own parents, who preached the gospel of getting an education.

How would a comprehensive, inclusive Prosperity Bill be funded? The United States has a current wealth-building policy and budget that is huge, regressive, and ineffective: its systems of tax breaks and incentives. In 2017 the United States spent more than $709 billion on tax advantages—enough to average $2,200 per year for every man, woman, and child in the country. At present, however, the wealthiest Americans get the lion's share of these tax benefits. But those benefits could be redeployed to give everyone a chance without the country needing to spend a dollar more than we do now.

In 2017, this $709 billion in tax incentives broke down into four categories:

Savings and investment incentives	$251 billion
Housing incentives	$251 billion
Retirement Savings incentives	$178 billion
Education incentives	$28 billion

Source: Based on research by *Prosperity Now* using data from Office of Management and Budget, "Analytical Perspectives: Budget of the U.S. Government Fiscal Year 2018."

The Tax Cuts and Jobs Act of 2017 included some significant changes to the nation's tax code. While the changes to corporate taxation are fundamental and enduring, the changes to individual asset-building tax incentives are significant but marginal. The most significant were to limit the mortgage interest tax deduction to $750,000 for new purchases, eliminate the deduction for up to $100,000 in refinance loans, limit the state and local property tax deduction to $10,000, and double the estate tax exclusion to an inflation-adjusted $11.2 million for individuals and $22.4 million for couples in 2018.

Over the last decade, the United States government has spent more than $5 trillion subsidizing the assets of American families. These subsidies generally support families who have the ability to create their own futures. The wealthiest 1 percent of taxpayers receive more benefit from these tax expenditures than the bottom 80 percent combined. The wealthiest 1 percent command more than a third of the total expenditure; the wealthiest 5 percent command more than half; the least wealthy 60 percent share less than 10 percent of these economic benefits.

Overall, the wealthiest 0.1 percent of Americans, those making over $1 million a year, collected $160,190 on average from these wealth-creating tax breaks, 744 times the $226 seen by the average working family.[69] This huge annual investment in the wealth-building activities of wealthy families is actually an outsized investment in wealth inequality.

Moreover, there is not much evidence that this spending achieves its aims. The savings and investment incentives generally miss the new businesses and middle-income entrepreneurs who start companies, spawning innovation and creating jobs. Homeownership incentives reward homeowning, or more accurately home *owing*, as the chief incentive is the deduction for mortgage interest—so the bigger and more valuable the first and second homes (up to $750,000), the greater the deduction.[70] In the $251 billion in 2017 housing incentives, there is nothing that helps renters to buy houses. Similarly, the retirement incentives don't really reach the majority of households that have the least in savings and earnings out of which to save. The Urban Institute suggests that each dollar in retirement savings incentives induces an additional penny in retirement savings—a 99¢ loss.[71]

The tax structure that invests in the economic futures of families in the United States should be seen for what it is at present: a system that that feeds our gaping racial wealth divide. It rewards the rich, misses the middle, and penalizes the poor to the tune of more than $5 trillion a decade. If homeownership, business and job formation, postsecondary education, retirement savings, and family nest eggs are legitimate areas for public encouragement and investment, then all families should be given the opportunity to participate.

While the 2017 tax act didn't attack most of the incentives that support the existing wealth inequality, it did show that these tax incentives are neither permanent nor immutable: it limited both the home mortgage interest deduction and the state and local tax deductions, once thought sacrosanct. The door is open for a redeployment. In fact, the Tax Cuts and Jobs Act of 2017 was so large, addressed so many fundamental elements, was passed so fast along partisan lines, and is so deficit-prone that it virtually ensures the need in the not-so-distant future for corrections and further reform.

There is a twenty-five-year history of bipartisan support for universal progressive savings and wealth-building accounts and incentives, built on across-the-aisle support for more traditional retirement savings proposals. Jack Kemp was the first high-level public official to laud Individual Development Accounts. Orrin Hatch (R-UT) and Bill Bradley (D-NJ) co-authored early IDA legislation. The today unthinkable team of Rick Santorum (R-PA), Jon Corzine (D-NJ), Chuck Schumer (D-NY), and Jim DeMint (R-SC) all supported variants of matched savings accounts for children and adults for a variety of purposes.[72] Jeff Sessions, then a senator, proposed PLUS Accounts—universal retirement accounts for all kids, seeded with $1,000—in 2006.[73] Perhaps the era of bipartisan accomplishment is gone, or perhaps when the country looks around again for practical solutions, the benefits from investments in the common genius will unite policy makers across the spectrum. There is reason to suspect that social, economic, and political congruence might make rare consensus possible. In other words, the time to redeploy our family wealth–building tax incentives is upon us.

To unleash the full productive capacity of the American people in the way the GI Bill and other investments in common genius have done over the past centuries, the United States needs to invest in the education, business, home, savings, and investment dreams and down payments of all Americans. Lessons from forty years of experimentation with seed capital and savings matches demonstrate that when they are given a reasonable opportunity—a few thousand dollars—common people will expand the economy with their ideas and their labor. And that is why the United States needs a Prosperity Bill: a legislative and economic intervention to reduce and eliminate economic inequality and enable everyone to participate fairly in the economy, built on savings and on Prosperity Accounts, and funded by existing revenue.

Previous chapters reviewed ways specific existing tax expenditures aimed at promoting business, savings, education, and homeownership could be redeployed as effective capital incentives for all Americans, particularly those desperately searching for an economic places to stand. Universal Savings Accounts (USAs) match saving for a range of purposes on a sliding scale for all adults (paid for by redeploying existing tax incentives for investment and savings). Matched Business Accounts match savings for starting new ventures and stabilizing and expanding young ones. Reinstating inheritance and estate taxes converts a windfall for the wealthy to an endowment for the education of all children and their progeny in Generation Accounts. To reinstate the American dream of universal homeownership, Home Accounts enable every family to save for a down payment on the dream. Those policy recommendations unite with a more inclusive and overarching frame: Prosperity Accounts.

There are ample reasons to completely revamp our wealth-

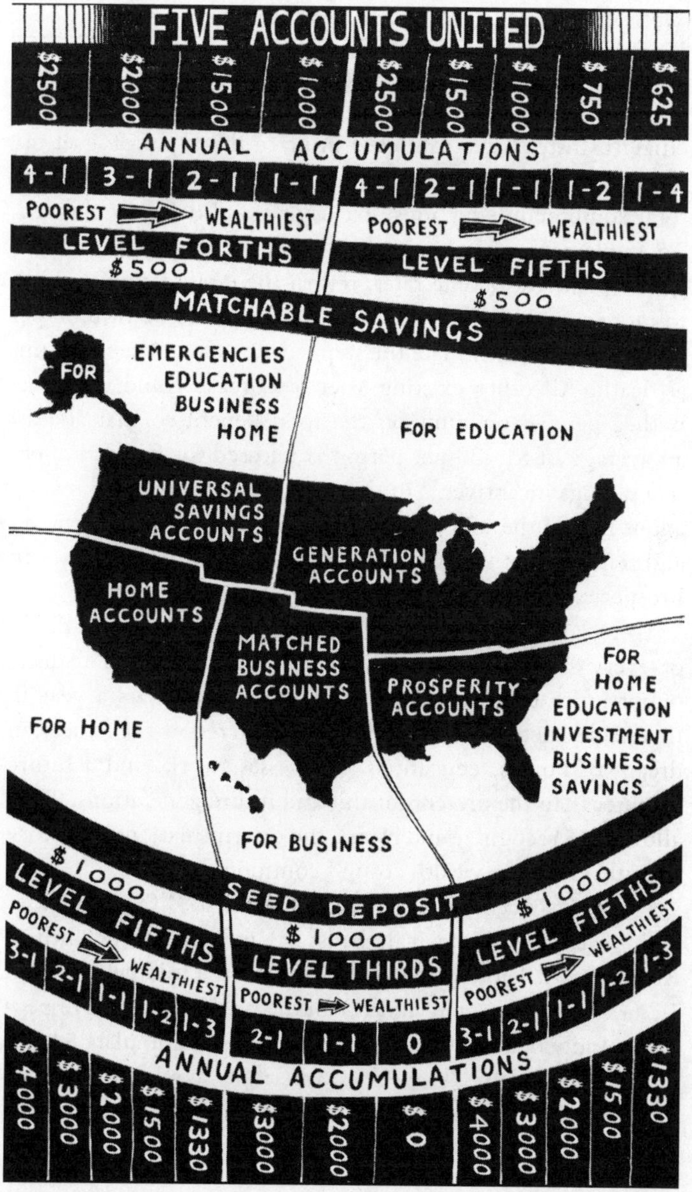

FIVE ACCOUNTS UNITED
$2500
$2000
$1500
$1000
$2500
$1500
$1000
$750
$625
ANNUAL ACCUMULATIONS
4-1
3-1
2-1
1-1
4-1
2-1
1-1
1-2
1-4
POOREST WEALTHIEST
POOREST WEALTHIEST
LEVEL FORTHS
$500
LEVEL FIFTHS
$500
MATCHABLE SAVINGS
FOR
EMERGENCIES
EDUCATION
BUSINESS
HOME
FOR EDUCATION
UNIVERSAL SAVINGS ACCOUNTS
GENERATION ACCOUNTS
HOME ACCOUNTS
MATCHED BUSINESS ACCOUNTS
PROSPERITY ACCOUNTS
FOR
HOME
EDUCATION
INVESTMENT
BUSINESS
SAVINGS
FOR HOME
FOR BUSINESS
$1000
SEED DEPOSIT
$1000
LEVEL FIFTHS
$1000
LEVEL THIRDS
LEVEL FIFTHS
POOREST WEALTHIEST
POOREST WEALTHIEST
POOREST WEALTHIEST
3-1
2-1
1-1
1-2
1-3
2-1
1-1
0
3-1
2-1
1-1
1-2
1-3
ANNUAL ACCUMULATIONS
$4000
$3000
$2000
$1500
$1330
$3000
$2000
$0
$4000
$3000
$2000
$1500
$1330

building tax incentives from scratch, but such an effort may well be a Pyrrhic battle given the vested interests of the wealthiest citizens. Instead, we can leave in place the types of asset tax incentives that already exist, and merely put a limit on the total combined deductions, exclusions, and deferrals allowed. To implement a prosperity economy, we should tax capital gains at earned income rates, return the estate tax exemption to more reasonable estate sizes of $1 million to $2 million per individual, and eliminate the stepped-up value of capital gains at death. All other existing asset tax breaks could continue, with a per-person limit on the total benefit so that at least an average of $1,000 per person is released for fair and effective savings incentives.[74] In this way, we should aim to recoup about half of the $709 billion spent in 2017 on tax incentives and reinvest that in a GI Bill for the twenty-first century—in Prosperity Accounts.

To reclaim prosperity as the rightful expectation and desire of every American, we must offer all Americans a realistic opportunity to accumulate a few thousand dollars a year in investable assets. Prosperity Accounts will renew the American dream of homes, educations, businesses, work, and a future brighter than the present for this and future generations. They allow us to recognize and bridge the discriminations of history to build common wealth around common dreams.

Prosperity Accounts would match the first $1,000 in savings each year on a sliding-scale basis: 3:1 for the poorest fifth of Americans, 2:1 for the next fifth, 1:1 for the middle fifth, and 1:2 (a 50 percent match) and 1:3 for the wealthiest fifths, respectively. Individuals in the poorest fifth could accumulate $4,000 a year, while middle-wealth Americans could accumulate $2,000 and even the wealthiest would be matched 33 percent on their first $1,000 in savings. Over several years, poor families could acquire a down payment on a median-priced house, money to capitalize (or stabilize) a new business, or the savings to go to college without the need to take on crushing debt. These savings could also be used for other life-altering investments, such as applying for citizenship or acquiring assistive technology.

Of course, seed capital alone will not solve all our financial problems, or provide the total restructuring of college finance that we need, or displace all the need for loans. But Prosperity Accounts would build democratic capital, and add investible capital to individual drive, work, talent, and aspiration. They would capitalize an economy of the people, by the people, for the people. They would provide a powerful signal to markets to recognize the effective demand of all would-be homeowners, entrepreneurs, and skilled workers.

Prosperity Accounts would be earned, not given. Savings matches would accrue only to the extent that families save. Extensive experiments over four decades reveal that saving is not easy, but it is possible, even for poor people. Low-income and poor Americans will save if the product of that saving produces stability and hope. That said, saving $1,000 a year is more than most individuals in the bottom half of the income spectrum will be able to manage on their own. Communities, localities, and states, along with the private, nonprofit, and public sectors, must all play a role. If the federal government sets up the basic framework and matches, then states—whose tax systems generally draft off the federal one and provide upside-down subsidies, like the federal tax code—localities, and communities can match and add to the savings of low-income families struggling and saving for a better future. Their investments will be magnified and leveraged by the federal policy. The entrepreneurial and wealth-building energies unleashed will raise all Americans.

Not everyone will be able or willing to save in their accounts. Nor will the down payment alone be sufficient to leverage the full price of the asset; credit will need to be available, as will the affordable house, educational institution, or business. Successful wealth-building depends too on the determination, skills, and dedication of people, the structure of the marketplace, and luck. But enabling all Americans to have a realistic chance to assemble a down payment on their dreams should elevate the rightful expectations of the nation and unleash the productive capacity of the American people, empower the ultimate creators and beneficiaries of an inclusive economy, and put pressure on the institutions of the marketplace—public, private, and nonprofit—to open their doors and find ways of rewarding and profiting by the productivity and dreams of the American people. At the very least, all people will be availed of a key to unlock the doors of economic opportunity.

Sliding-scale matches for Prosperity Accounts take into account the United States' discriminatory history, especially involving people of color and women. By graduating the matches from 3:1 to 1:3 over five quintiles determined by current asset holdings, the playing field will be leveled gradually by lifting the bottom while impelling all ahead.[75] Defining the quintiles by asset holdings rather than income holdings, since wealth disparities are even greater than income disparities, further redresses this history. Recall the current asset stratification: households in the poorest fifth of Americans hold less than $600 in liquid assets. More than a third of African American households find themselves in this poorest quintile—more than four times their presence in the country as a whole. The 3:1 match rate should disproportionately advantage African

Americans, Latinos, and other people of color, a payback for previous exclusions (some might even consider it reparations), while still allowing the displaced white former factory worker in the Midwest without savings to benefit from higher match rates.

Prosperity Accounts incorporate more than incentives—they also establish connection and access to the mainstream financial system. Prosperity Accounts could utilize, democratize, and build upon existing systems of savings accounts, such as state 529 college savings plans, Secure Choice retirement plans, and the federal Thrift Savings Plan. At the same time, new systems are needed. Prosperity Accounts on the model of MyRA retirement savings accounts can serve all uses: business, education, homeownership, retirement, citizenship. Prosperity Accounts should be set up automatically and seeded for all children. Through Prosperity Accounts, all Americans can be connected to the financial system in ways that serve them rather than impoverish them, and allow them to avoid the $2,400 average cost of being unbanked. Blockchain technologies enable a low-cost, secure online system of accounts and transfers.

Through financial education linked with these accounts, financial capability will grow. There is nothing like seeing money in an account grow with each statement to catch the attention of people, especially people accustomed to not having money. Suddenly the financial system and financial knowledge become relevant. Financial coaching and counseling, developed within nonprofits and integrated in public and private systems, can grow to accommodate expanded demand.

What about emergencies? Prosperity Account holders could withdraw their own savings from the accounts for emergencies with a 10 percent penalty.[76] Unlike with existing retirement

Adversity
WORKING FAMILIES
$160190
·1%
$226
$709 BILLION
$354 BILLION
POOREST
$4000
$3000
WEALTHIEST
$1500
$1333
Prosperity
PROSPERITY ACCOUNTS

savings and 529 college savings accounts, however, the penalty would be temporary; when participants repaid the account, the penalty dollars would be restored. Emergency loans can be funded out of longer-term savings if necessary; short- and long-term savings are allies, not competitors, and should be understood as such. Prosperity Accounts should not count toward asset limits in any means-tested program. What I earlier called FutureMoney is key to future prosperity; it should not be frustrated by the current need to get by.

Prosperity Accounts are neither a liberal idea nor a conservative one. These accounts combine key elements of thought and principle across the political spectrum. They are a celebration of individual energy, work, and enterprise; they are an outgrowth of family connection and saving and striving. They are an expression of self-reliance and self-respect. At the same time, they are a recognition of our common history, our inherited inequality, our enduring concern for all, and our respect for the common genius.

Investing in the productive capacity of all Americans, including the bottom 80 percent, and including greater benefits to the long excluded just makes sense. The United States already has a huge budget for family wealth planning. By simply reallocating this money in a way that allows the majority of Americans to benefit commensurately from this national investment in family economic wellness, we would unlock the productive contributions of all 326 million of us without increasing tax rates or spending any more than we are already doing.

Prosperity Accounts are an investment in the future, based on the experience of the past. Prosperity Accounts incorporate the six basic elements that made the GI Bill effective, but this time the policy would include everyone and provide more for those people with the fewest assets—disproportionately people of color and women.

Prosperity Accounts are a hand up, not a handout. They rely on self-directed savings and entrepreneurial and educational efforts. They are oriented toward education, homeownership, and business—investments that generate high returns. They are in the form of liquid capital. Prosperity Accounts would be transformational, inciting and liberating the dreams, talents, and energy of common people.

Instead of the past devouring the future, as Thomas Piketty predicted, democratic capital creates the future. Prosperity Accounts will renew the American dream by renewing American dreams, by unleashing the productive capacity of all Americans to make their futures. Like the GI Bill, Prosperity Accounts would deliver outsized, long-term returns, enabling every American to amass a few thousand dollars of discretionary investment capital a year. A few thousand dollars—a down payment on the American dream of a home, a business, an education, a career, and a nest egg for the next generation—should spark prosperity for all.

Afterword

Cory Booker

In many ways, I am a product of the power of a few thousand dollars that rippled outward through generations.

Both my mom and my dad came from humble beginnings. My mom was the first generation in her family going back to slavery to not grow up in poverty. Her dad worked on a factory assembly line for Ford and was one of the first black members of the United Auto Workers Union.

My dad was born poor in a small North Carolina mountain town to a single mother who was too ill to care for him. A local family took him in, put a roof over his head, and raised him as their own. When the people in his community realized how smart he was, but that he didn't have the money to afford college, his church passed around a collection plate to pay for his first semester.

Once he was at college, my dad worked his way through school to support himself. And when my dad moved to Washington, DC, and couldn't find a job as a black man in the 1960s corporate world, the local Urban League stepped in and helped him get a job at IBM—where he became one of their top salesmen in the country.

In 1969, my dad had received a promotion, which meant he, my pregnant mother, and my brother would move from Washington to a place closer to New York. My mom and dad began looking at homes in Bergen County, New Jersey. Yet on more than one occasion, my parents would express interest in a home and it would be inexplicably pulled off the market.

The Fair Housing Act had been signed into law just the year before, so federal law was on my parents' side, but discrimination persisted. Thankfully, advocates from a group called the Fair Housing Council rose up to help us.

When my parents visited Harrington Park, New Jersey—a mostly white suburban town with great schools—and fell in love with a house there, they were once again told it was no longer for sale. A lawyer from the Fair Housing Council devised a plan: they would conduct a sting operation.

The Fair Housing Council sent a white couple to look at the house posing as my parents. They were able to make an offer to buy it, and the offer was accepted.

But on the day of the closing, instead of the white family showing up, my dad and his lawyer did. A melee ensued: the realtor punched my dad's lawyer, and let a dog loose on my dad. The encounter ended with the realtor begging my father not to go forward with the sale. He said my family would ruin the neighborhood, said my family would affect the housing market, and said my family wouldn't like it there. In hearing my dad describe it years later, the realtor was deeply afraid of my family and what we represented. But the sale went through.

We moved in to our home and my dad liked to joke that our family became "four raisins in a tub of vanilla ice cream."

Our community in Harrington Park embraced my family, my public school teachers empowered me to succeed, and most of my friends went on to college and successful careers. I went on to college, a Rhodes Scholarship, and law school—and, eventually, a career in public service.

My mom is, and my dad was, extraordinary; in so many ways, their success in blazing a trail for my brother and I was a testimony to their work ethic, their rugged individualism, and their ability to overcome and sacrifice greatly. My father worked harder than any person I have ever known—he showed up first at work in the morning and was the last to leave at night. That's the thing about giving a good person a chance: they will work harder than anyone else and make the most of it.

But the story I heard from my parents growing up wasn't about that; it was about the community of people, throughout their lives, who had stepped up for them, fought for them, opened doors for them, created a place at the table for them.

In other words, in a very real way, I am where I am today because of the family that took my dad in. Because of the church that passed a collection plate to pay for my dad's tuition. Because of the activists who helped my dad and my mom break down barriers in employment and in housing. These contributions, modest when taken by themselves, combined and compounded over time to yield a great dividend for me.

My family's story is really an extraordinary testimony to what happens when people invest in one another, and have the freedom to invest in themselves. It's one deeply rooted in the American dream.

Individual excellence can only get us so far. After all, it wasn't rugged individualism alone that got us to the moon, that ushered in the civil rights movement, that organized workers, that developed some of the greatest innovations of our time.

These things were the result of extraordinary coalitions of ordinary Americans working together—committed to one another. My parents taught me that, as an American, I shouldn't expect handouts, but that I had a responsibility to lend a hand when I could.

This is what makes our country great: the choice by the American people to choose one another, to invest in one another. As *A Few Thousand Dollars* explains, this country has repeatedly invested in the common genius of the American people—with universal public education, the Homestead Acts, the GI Bill—and the American people in turn have created the greatest economy on earth.

And the data bears this out—I am one of those people who believes in the power of data—America's greatness really is anchored in our commitment to each other.

Everything from the historic global dominance of our education system, to the strength of our infrastructure, to our advances in technology and medicine, to our economic power, is rooted in the coalitions of Americans who worked together, generation after generation, to invest in each other and in making our country great.

But much of the data we're seeing today is deeply concerning, and points to an America that is falling far short of its potential.

We are failing to reward hard work fairly; we're failing to invest in the health and well-being of the American people; and we're failing to invest in our most precious natural resource: our people.

As a result, divides along economic lines are growing deeper, the hurdles working families have to face have only grown higher, and the gap between those who have much and those who don't is widening precipitously.

I see how our failure to invest in our people is evident in my home of Newark, New Jersey, where I have lived for close to twenty years.

I see how the folks in my community are working harder

than my own parents and yet they're still living in poverty. I see the folks in my corner bodega who work full-time jobs and still have to use food stamps to get by. I know how at the end of the month, when those food stamps are running low, how their kids suffer, they struggle in school.

In response to these challenges, we have seen President Trump and Republican leaders in Congress only compound the problems we face. The 2017 Trump tax plan is a shining example, a law that lavishes tax cuts on those who need them the least—the wealthiest individuals and biggest corporations—on the backs of Americans who could benefit the most from modest but common sense changes in our tax code, like some of the ideas outlined in this book. Instead of lavishing tax incentives only on the wealthy few, we could match the savings of every American who works and dreams and saves so they can go to college, start businesses, create jobs, buy homes.

We are not doing enough to empower Americans to succeed, to make room for American workers to grow, to create an economy that can create both great wealth and great opportunity—and make it available for all.

That is why as mayor of Newark and as senator I championed child savings accounts, so every child would have a reason to dream and the means to achieve. That is why I have worked across the aisle to champion rainy day savings and innovative individual development account programs.

And as my own family's experience demonstrates so well, the limits on Americans' potential are unbounded when people are given just a modest chance to succeed, whether it's a few hundred dollars from a church collection plate, or a barrier broken down.

What we need, as this book recommends, is a renewed commitment to our shared prosperity. So that every family can amass the few thousand dollars they need to realize their dreams. So that everyone has the opportunity to go to college, start a business, create jobs, assemble a down payment on a house—to seek the American Dream. So that, in the words of Langston Hughes, America "can be America again," the America that "never was, yet still must be."

We can be a nation that invests in, empowers, and champions its people—all of its people. We can create millions of new businesses, jobs, homeowners, skilled workers. It's a matter, now, of will.

Acknowledgments

This book would not exist but for the vision, encouragement, guidance, support, faith, editing, and patience over years of Andrea Levere, president of Prosperity Now (formerly the Corporation for Enterprise Development, CFED). As she has built Prosperity Now, Andrea builds communities and fields. Currently, Prosperity Now has eighty-eight employees, is financially transparent and resilient, effective, accountable, with a community of 25,000 friends. Andrea was the first person I went to with the idea for a book and she is its first and most unwavering enthusiast. As she does, Andrea immediately introduced me to her neighbor (everyone is Andrea's neighbor), book agent Lisa Adams, who affirmed its viability and gave the book its title. Early in the development of the book, Andrea referred me to David Erickson, director of Community Development of the San Francisco Federal Reserve Bank, who cultivated this book with the same vision, generosity, and dedication he nurtures the whole community development field.

As she was writing her important book on slavery and motherhood, my older daughter, Alison Kiehl Friedman, connected me to her book agent, the irrepressible Joanne Jarvi, who became the book's biggest advocate and never doubted it would find a publisher.

Joanne found editor Julie Enszer and The New Press. But for Julie, this book would not exist, and would not be what it has come to be. In our first interview she asked, "Do you want a policy book or a popular book?" From there on she championed the book with The New Press, shaped the book with suggestions large and small, profound and practical. She made writing a book not only doable but enjoyable, focusing me on the twenty feet ahead illuminated by the headlights she provided, reassembling the pieces, encouraging me when I lost direction, pruning the prose, mixing fundamental questions and deft edits. Her compatriots at The New Press—Ben Woodward, who redlined several chapters; Maury Botton, who shepherded the book through production; and the marketing team of Brian Ulicky, Bev Rivero, and Jessica Yu—were essential partners. Sue Warga did a marvelous job copy editing the manuscript, and Christopher Moisan provided the book with its wonderful cover.

My colleagues at Prosperity Now were my resources of first resort, each providing the best of very different skills and knowledge generously and wisely. Kasey Weidrich and Lebaron Sims developed the Prosperity Index central to the idea of this book, measuring how many families had the few thousand dollars they need to launch. Diego Quezada provided essential data and insight on entrepreneurship and especially Latino entrepreneurship. David Newville reviewed the policy proposals and brilliantly suggested the Joker Upside Downside treatment for the policy illustrations. Doug Ryan reviewed the Home chapter and schooled me in manufactured housing and home ownership in his wise and understated way. The Leadership Team—Leigh Tivol, Jeremie Greer, Kate Griffin—offered critical reviews, direction and connection. Adnan Bokhari, the rare CFO/COO that understands the value of all things, not just their price, never doubted the value of this venture despite knowing its cost better than anyone, and contributed his own story. Emanuel Nieves provided essential racial wealth divide data and perspective. Dedrick Asante Muhammad and Lillian Singh provided perspective and guidance on closing the Racial Wealth Divide, and Lillian her important story of home loss. The Communications Team of Kristin Lawton and Sean Luechtefeld rebranded Prosperity Now and the book, teaching always how to communicate, nurturing gently. Danielle Fox tried mightily to bring me into the world of social media. Carl Rist's longtime cultivation of the child development account field (after championing what would become SEED and the Prosperity Now Scorecard) extended to providing not only guidance but the underlying story. Parker Cohen, Shira Markoff, and Melissa Grober-Morrow each added their input and wisdom.

Former Prosperity Now intern Xavier Buck provided the background research on the history of American investments in the common genius as well as painstaking assistance cleaning up the references. Someday he will publish the definitive economic history of asset building and racial disparity in America.

Lisa Kawahara stood by me every step of this book, as she has for almost thirty years; she set aside time, unearthed old files, reminded me of old connections, and urged me to apply to Mesa Refuge.

Two weeks at Mesa Refuge—the writers' retreat founded by visionary social entrepreneur Peter Barnes, creator of the new economic commons and mensch, and now run by Susan Tilletts—allowed me to take the book proposal into a first draft. The tides and fogs of Point Reyes still flow through these pages.

Roberto Arjona, Prosperity Now's creative services director, presided over the art in this book and found Rohan Daniel

Eason, who turned the messages of the book into compelling illustrations.

At an early low point, my younger daughter, writer, philosopher, social entrepreneur, and stylist, Anne Kiehl Friedman, reassured me in a time of doubt: "It has beautiful bones."

I realized somewhat late into the writing of the book the great advantage I had was that I could interview the real pioneers in the field, ask them my hardest questions, and they would answer, guide, encourage me: Michael Sherraden, Tom Shapiro, Lisa Mensah, Bill Bynum, Gloria Steinem, Mauricio Lim Miller, David Erickson, Jose Quiñonez, Fred Goldberg, Gene Steuerle, Margaret Clancy, Melinda Kay Lewis, Willie Elliott, Paul Bradley, Ron Grzywinski, Mike Bullard, Bob Haas, Ida Rademacher, Kriss Deiglemeier, Ben Mangan, and Anne Stuhldreher.

Errors and omissions in the book are certainly mine, as Andrea Levere, David Newville, Frank DeGiovanni, Leigh Tivol, Doug Ryan, Margaret Clancy, Melinda Kay Lewis, Fred Goldberg, Gene Steuerle, Noel Poyo, and Anne Kiehl Friedman reviewed various chapters, with eyes that were at once acute and profound.

I need to pay tribute to four books and their authors: *Assets and the Poor* by Michael Sherraden led me to most of the lines of inquiry and practice reflected here. *Toxic Inequality* by Thomas Shapiro is breathtaking in its breadth, depth, and unwavering devotion to recognizing and repairing the racial wealth divide. Peter Barnes and his *With Liberty and Dividends for All* calls attention to the common assets we all share, and the dividends we should, while combatting climate change along the way. Mauricio Lim Miller's *The Alternative* underscores the brilliance of families leading their own lives and the ways to unleash that brilliance. These are works that move history, the contemporaneous products of lifetimes fomenting social change

I want to particularly thank the people whose stories, I hope, bring alive the power and promise of people building wealth and futures for themselves and their communities: Warren Hellman, Grace Capitello, Marguerite Sisson, Michael Sherraden, Juliet Garcia, Mauricio Lim Miller, LC, Darius Atkins, Caheri Gutierrez, Minh Tran, Regina Blackmon, Paty Cruz, Dion King, Harold Alfond, Bill Bynum, Ed Roberts, David and Heather Greer, Mariana, Robin Craig, Natividad Seefeld, Lillian Singh, Wilma Mankiller, Adnan Bokhari, and Donna Brazile.

This book has its feet firmly planted in the growth of at least three fields of economic development—microenterprise and entrepreneurship, asset building, and community economic development—and the social entrepreneurs that created, nurtured, and guided them, among them my friends and guides: Kathy Keeley, Jing Lyman, Sara Gould, Jack Litzenberg, Craig Kennedy, Sharon King, Maryjo Mullen, Bob Woodson, Cicero Wilson, Stuart Butler, Rebecca Adamson, Craig Kennedy, Debby Leff, Paul Pryde, Mark Greenberg, Bob Greenstein, Gene Steuerle, Fred Goldberg, Joyce Klein, Pete Plastrik, Elaine Edgecomb, Peggy Clark, Doug Ross, Benita Melton, and Bob Zdenek. My former colleagues at Prosperity Now/CFED: Bill Schweke, my earliest colleague in thought and deed, so prolific my mother thought he was my pen name; Ray Boshara, who led so much of the policy effort to install a universal progressive asset-building policy; Joyce Klein, Brian Dabson, Ida Rademacher, Joanne Irby, Jocelyn Harmon, Janet Topolsky, Meriwether Jones, Rene Bryce Laporte, and Anita DeFrantz. The Prosperity Now/CFED board, present and past, from whom I always learn: Ellen Lazar, Brandee McHale, Asheesh Advani, Jamie Kalamarides, Ron Grzywinski, Bill Bynum, Gary Cunningham, Victor Reinoso, Judith Bell, Sherry Salway Black, Annie Burns, Naomi Camper,

Martha Kanter, Dan Letendre, Bea Stotzer, Robin McKinney, Angela Blackwell, Don Baylor, Deborah Wild, Steve Damato, Janie Barrera, Elsie Meeks, David Dodson, Mary Mountcastle, Rebecca Adamson, Pete Plastrik, Doug Ross, Paul Pryde, R. Craig Kennedy, Joan Wills, Bob Woodson, Jeff Hallett, and John Naisbitt.

This book grows too from family and lifetime friends whose love and spirit are the surest source of my belief in the potential of people: my mom, Phyllis Koshland Friedman, who, with my father, Howard Abraham Friedman, live a set of values, humor, and generosity I only need try to follow. Kristina Kiehl, my starter wife of forty years, who always supported my devotions with resourcefulness, humor, practicality, and fervor. My daughters, Alison Kiehl Friedman and Anne Kiehl Friedman, who repair the world and teach their parents well, and my granddaughter, Olivia Danger Friedman, who radiates joy, kindness, and creativity. Lifetime friends and guides, Gerald Torres (my closest tie to the spirit of law and justice), Rob Caughlan, Lew Butler, Anita DeFrantz, Steven Damato, Marjorie Classen, Spencer Beebe, Tim Silard, and Fred Blackwell. My aunt and uncle, Sissy and Ted Geballe, encouraged my writing always, and in this case by providing the solitude and views of their Pescadero house.

Which leaves the largest categories—the folks I left out, the resources recognized in the footnotes, the millions of people who could transform a few thousand dollars into full lives and legacies, and the readers of this book who will, I hope, pardon its faults, make its promise their own, and bring a time when this country indeed offers everyone a chance at life, liberty, and the pursuit of happiness.

Life, and bookwriting, are exercises in humility. I am convinced that if we could just spend our wealth-building tax incentives rationally, as investments in the common genius, everybody would be better off. To the extent I did not make that case here, I hope you will improve the proposition and take it forward.

With gratitude for all,
Bob Friedman
June 2018

NOTES

1. Wealth

1. Michael Sherraden, Richard P. Barth, John Brekke, Mark W. Fraser, Ron Manderscheid, and Deborah Padgett, "Social Is Fundamental: Introduction and Context for Grand Challenges in Social Work," working paper, Grand Challenges for Social Work Initiative, 2015.

2. Ibid., 6.

3. I confess that I have a love-hate relationship with experimental randomized control treatment impact studies when they are applied to economic development demonstrations, as we did with the SEID, ADD, and SEED programs. Of course, only studies with randomized control and experimental/treatment groups can establish causation and impact. They are generally accepted to be the best methodology for assessing the difference social programs make in the lives of those given access to them. But that certainty comes at a cost. It is expensive and narrow in examining causes and impacts. I used to describe it as the electron microscope of evaluation technologies—very precise, very expensive, and very narrow. In the SEED demonstration in our Michigan quasi-experimental (comparison rather than control group) demonstration, the requisites of randomization and data collection displaced the program development and technical assistance. It took the credibility of the Manpower Demonstration Research Corporation (MDRC) to give SEID the legitimacy to attract funding and for states to secure the Section 1115 waivers necessary to waive asset limits for participants. MDRC would later write to the Office of Program Evaluation at the U.S. Department of Health,

Education and Welfare, advising that an impact study of SEID was not feasible. Extensive impact evaluations were conducted in the ADD and SEED, with notable outcomes. There is much more to learn than causation, including lessons about how to conduct effective asset development programs, the relative effectiveness of different program elements (e.g., financial education and coaching, self-employment training, account design), the roles of private financial institutions, and recordkeeping and operating systems, to give a few examples.

4. Litzenberg, a winner of the Robert Scrivner Award for Creative Grantmaking from the Council on Foundations, is also known as the father of the U.S. microenterprise field.

5. Alan Okagaki, "Windows on the World: Best Practice in Economic Opportunity Strategy," *Entrepreneurial Economy Review* 7, no. 4 (November 1988). "The long-term solution to poverty lies in transforming these inner-city neighborhoods from 'engines of doom' to 'success machines.' To do so requires understanding the process of individual economic advancement and the ways neighborhoods foster or retard it." And the way neighborhoods could do that was by engendering efficacy, learning, and linkage in residents:

> Efficacy is the belief that one's actions can improve one's life. . . . Efficacy is rooted in self-esteem, a belief in your intrinsic value or worth as a human being. If you look at the very disadvantaged people who do escape poverty, you discover that the first and most important step a person takes is deciding that her present life is not acceptable and that she can do something about it. In doing so, she makes a transition from being fundamentally reactive concerning her life and her future to being proactive. She learns that she can have dreams for herself and that she has the will and ability to make those dreams come true. Developing that sense of personal efficacy is the seed from which all further personal development springs. It precedes further education, skills training or job search. Developing efficacy necessarily involves recognizing and building on strengths and abilities people have. Learning—building on strengths and remedying weaknesses—comes later. Most people think learning is acquiring academic knowledge and job skills, both of which are clearly part of the development process. However, we found that another type of learning—learning about the world-at-large and envisioning where one wants to fit into it—is equally essential to human development. . . . Learning is a matter of sensing one's possibilities, of expanding one's horizons.

If learning requires seeing out into the world, linkage requires developing the connections and paths that overcome isolation. "For residents of low-income neighborhoods, where contacts to the world of employers are sparse, geographic and social isolation translates into economic isolation." Okagaki concludes that "efficacy, learning, and linkage define the personal advancement progress," but notes that in a successful neighborhood, mediating (connecting) organizations work, development happens, talent stays, capacity builds, isolation fades, and citizenship prospers, all in a reinforcing cycle.

6. William E. Nothdurft with Barbara Dyer, "Out from Under: Policy Lessons from a Quarter Century of Wars on Poverty," Council of State Policy and Planning Agencies, Washington, DC, January 1990, 5–18.

7. Robert E. Friedman, *The Safety Net as Ladder: Transfer Payments and Economic Development* (Washington, DC: Council of State Planning Agencies, 1988).

8. Robert E. Friedman and William Schweke, *Expanding the Opportunity to Produce: Revitalizing the American Economy Through New Enterprise Development: A Policy Reader* (Washington, DC: Corporation for Enterprise Development, 1981). With the help of Bill Schweke, my real partner in establishing CFED, who made it his business to know every creative applied economist around, we compiled innovative ideas for building local economies floating around as photocopies into *Expanding the Opportunity to Produce: Revitalizing the American Economy Through New Enterprise Development.* In its pages were seminal works by the likes of David Birch, who would later attract attention to the role of small business in job creation; Derek "Pete" Hansen, then deputy superintendant of banking in California and creator of the loan loss reserve and capital access programs, distinguishing between capitalism and entrepreneurialism; Robert Woodson Sr., then at AEI, who would later found the National Center for Neighborhood Enterprise; Jack Kemp, then a congressman and later HUD secretary; Stuart Butler, of the Heritage Foundation, highlighting the entrepreneurialism of inner cities; Albert Shapero, who tracked new businesses throught the Yellow Pages, extolling the role of entrepreneurship at the less-than-national level; the brilliant Michael Kieschnick, then in the EPA Office of Economic Adjustment, later founder of Working Assets/Credo, drawing the link between environmental quality and economic development and discussing the role of venture capital in development; Stanley Hallett, Calvin Bradford, Leon Finney, and John McKnight, talking about structural disinvestment and the importance of building on the strengths

of disinvested communities; new capitalists Belden Daniels, Beth Seigel, and Paul Pryde; Neal Peirce and Carol Steinbach, journalists of community vitality; Jerry Brown, then in his first term as Governor of California, talking about the role of pension funds in economic development; economist Roger Vaughan, writing freshly about taxes and economic development; Jay Forrester and Roger Sant, writing about the role of technology and innovation; Daniel Zwerdling and Mitch Rofsky, explaining the role of employee ownership and cooperatives; and many more. Here was a blueprint for a resurgent local economy that would be filled in over the coming decades. *Expanding the Opportunity to Produce* and the eponymous conference that followed brought together a growing national network of social entrepreneurs. Their ideas would fill the *Entrepreneurial Economy* newsletter that followed, and they would become the faculty of this emerging field.

9. Board of Governors of the Federal Reserve System, Division of Consumer and Community Affairs, Consumer and Community Development Research Section, *Report on the Economic Well-Being of U.S. Households in 2016* (Washington, DC: Federal Reserve Board, 2017), 25–27.

10. Defined as "having the financial security and financial freedom of choice, in the present and in the future." Consumer Financial Protection Bureau, *Financial Well-Being in America* (Washington, DC: CFPB, 2017).

11. Income volatility is increasing in the United States, and especially in low-income families. See Jonathan Morduch and Rachel Schneider, *The Financial Diaries: How American Families Cope in a World of Uncertainty* (Princeton, NJ: Princeton University Press, 2017), and Federal Reserve Board, *Survey of Household Economics and Decisionmaking* (Washington, DC: Federal Reserve Board, 2016).

12. The poverty line is presently drawn at about $1,700 per month for a family of three. The poverty line was calculated decades ago to estimate the minimum necessary to survive a temporary disruption in income, not an enduring condition. Hence other researchers have developed more realistic levels of sustenance, such as the Self-Sufficiency Standard, established by the Center for Women's Welfare and Wider Opportunities for Women, www.selfsufficiencystandard.org. The official poverty line also fails to take into account cost-of-living differences in different parts of the country. A standard based on real contemporary costs and drawing on Area Median Income (AMI) is probably more accurate and more relevant. See Thomas M. Shapiro, Melvin L. Oliver,

and Tatjana Meschede, "The Asset Security and Opportunity Index," Institute on Assets and Social Policy, Brandeis University, 2009.

13. For adults, this sum could range from $1,000 to $8,000. For children, a few hundred dollars can be transforming, per Willie Elliott's finding, discussed later in this book, that poor children with less than $500 in a savings account in their own name are three times as likely to attend college and four times more likely to complete college as those without.

14. Calculations based on 2014 SIPP data, calculated by Lebaron Sims and Kasey Weidrich, Prosperity Now, November 2017.

15. Shapiro, Oliver, and Meschede, "The Asset Security and Opportunity Index."

16. Calculations based on projected data from the Urban-Brookings Tax Policy Center, 2017. "Working families" are defined as those with $50,000 or less in income. Dollar amounts reflect the average benefit in 2017 from several tax programs for tax units in the two income categories.

2. Saving

1. Michael Sherraden, *Assets and the Poor: A New American Welfare Policy* (Armonk, NY: M.E. Sharpe, Inc., 1991), 231.

2. Ibid.

3. Ibid., 148–68. See also Margaret Sherraden, Amanda Moore McBride, Elizabeth Johnson, Stacie Hanson, Fred M. Ssewamala, and Trina Shanks, "Saving in Low-Income Households: Evidence from Interviews with Participants in the American Dream Demonstration," Center for Social Development, Washington University in St. Louis, 2005.

4. Sixty percent of job losses during the 2008 Great Recession were middle-wage jobs, while only 27 percent of the job gains during the subsequent recovery were. Thomas M. Shapiro, *Toxic Inequality: How America's Wealth Gap Destroys Mobility, Deepens the Racial Divide, & Threatens Our Future* (New York: Basic Books, 2017), 101–2.

5. Melvin L. Oliver and Thomas M. Shapiro, *Black Wealth / White Wealth: A New Perspective on Racial Inequality* (New York: Routledge, 2006). Liquid asset poor, as defined by Oliver and Shapiro, equates to

having insufficient savings or readily accessible money to survive three months at the poverty line without income. It equals about $5,000 to $6,000 in 2017 dollars.

6. Shapiro, 13

7. Ibid.

8. Sherraden, *Assets and the Poor.*

9. Ibid., 297.

10. Bruce Ackerman and Anne Alstott, *The Stakeholder Society* (New Haven, CT: Yale University Press, 1999). Ackerman and Alstott explained the rationale for their proposal for universal stakeholder accounts in resonant ways:

> In contrast to most public programs this one does not restrict the rights of private property on behalf of some collective good. It is based on the opposite premise: property is so important to the free development of individual personality that everybody ought to have some. Without stakeholding, formal freedom easily degenerates into a farce—as Anatole France once jested, the equal right to sleep under the bridges of Paris.
>
> . . . A propertyless person lacks crucial resources needed for self-definition. He can never taste the joys and sorrows of real freedom—and the possibilities of learning from his own successes and mistakes. He is condemned to a life on the margin, where the smallest shocks can send him into a tailspin. He can never enjoy the luxury of asking himself what he really wants out of life, but is constantly responding to the exigent demands of the marketplace.

11. Robert L. Rose, "For Welfare Parents, Scrimping Is Legal, But Saving Is Out," *Wall Street Journal*, February 6, 1990.

12. ADD and the change it created were possible only because of the sizable long-term support of eleven pioneering foundations and their entrepreneurial leadership: Ford Foundation (Susan Berresford, Melvin Oliver, Lisa Mensah, Frank DeGiovanni, Mitty Owens), Charles Stewart Mott Foundation (Bill White, Jack Litzenberg, Benita Melton), John D. and Catherine T. MacArthur Foundation (Kavita Ramdas), Citigroup Foundation (Janet Thompson, Brandee McHale), F.B. Heron Foundation (Sharon King), Ewing Marion Kauffman Foundation (Willis Bright, Andres Dominguez), Fannie Mae Foundation (Andrew Pleppler), Levi Strauss Foundation (Judy Belk), Joyce Foundation (Craig Kennedy, Debby Leff, Unmi Song, Joel Getzen-

danner), Rockefeller Foundation, and Moriah Fund (Maryanne Stein, Christine Robinson).

13. The fourteen programs were: ADVOCAP, Fond du Lac, WI; Alternatives Federal Credit Union, Ithaca, NY; Bay Area IDA Collaborative, San Francisco, CA; Capital Area Asset Building Corporation, Washington, DC; Central Texas Mutual Housing Association, Austin, TX; Central Vermont Community Action Council, Barre, VT; Community Action Project of Tulsa County, Tulsa, OK; Heart of America Family Services, Kansas City, MO; Human Solutions, Portland, OR; Mountain Association for Community Economic Developmetn, Booneville, KY; Near Eastside Community Federal Credit Union, Indianopolis, IN; Shorebank Corpoeration, Chicago, IL; and Women's Self-Employment Program, Chicago, IL.

14. Michael Sherraden, Lissa Johnson, Margaret Clancy, Sondra Beverly, Mark Schreiner, Min Zahn, and Jami Curley, "Savings Patterns in IDA Programs: Downpayments on the American Dream Policy Demonstration: A National Demonstration of Individual Development Accounts," Center for Social Development, Washington University in St. Louis, 2000, 2. Ninety percent of ADD participants had incomes below 200 percent of the poverty line, and 43 percent had incomes below the poverty line (then $19,000 for a family of four); 78 percent were women, and more than half were people of color—41 percent African American, 12 percent Latino, and 2 percent each Native American and Asian American. As compared to the U.S. population as a whole, they were more likely to be female, African American, never married, educated, banked, and employed.

15. There was evidence that ADD savers took the maximum savings matched as a target and raised their savings to meet it. While ADD match rates varied from 1:1 to 7:1, match rates above 3:1 did not change the amount saved or the frequency of saving. Sherraden et al., "Savings Patterns."

16. Ibid., 3. See also "American Dream Demonstration: The First Large Scale Test of Individual Development Accounts," Corporation for Enterprise Development, 2009.

17. "American Dream Demonstration" Ibid.

18. Sherraden et al., "Savings Patterns," 5. See also "American Dream Demonstration."

19. Mark Schreiner and Margaret Clancy, "Saving and Asset Accumulation in the American Dream Demonstration Through June 30, 2001," Center for Social Development, Washington, DC, 2001.

20. Jonathan Morduch and Rachel Schneider, *The Financial Diaries: How American Families Cope in a World of Uncertainty* (Princeton, NJ: Princeton University Press, 2017), 94–96. Detailing increasing income and expense volatility in the lives of low-income Americans, Morduch and Schneider underscore the significant and rising need for short-term and emergency savings. They note that 25 percent of withdrawals from 401(k)s and IRAs are for pre-retirement uses. In the fifteen years since the end of ADD, income has stagnated, debt and volatility have risen, and calls for short-term savings facilitation and support have mounted.

21. Amanda Moore McBride, Margaret Sherraden, Elizabeth Johnson, and Fred Ssewamala, "How Do Poor People Save Money? Implications for Social Work," Center for Social Development, Washington University in St. Louis, 2003.

22. Match rates of 8:1 have been used successfully in homeownership accounts by the Federal Home Loan Bank Board and IDA programs like those operated by CAAB in Washington, DC, which has 2,200 IDAs under its belt.

23. Sherraden et al., "Savings Patterns," 3.

24. Michal Grinstein-Weiss, Michael Sherraden, William Gale, William M. Rohe, Mark Schreiner, and Clinton Key, "Ten-Year Impacts of Individual Devlopment Accounts on Homeownership: Evidence from a Randomized Experiment," Brookings Institution, Washington, DC, 2011.

25. Mark Schreiner, Michael Sherraden, Margaret Clancy, Lissa Johnson, Jami Curley, Michal Grinstein-Weiss, Min Zhan, and Sondra Beverly, "Savings and Asset Accumulation in Individual Development Accounts: Downpayments on the American Dream Policy Demonstration: A National Demonstration of Individual Development Accounts," Center for Social Development, Washington University in St. Louis, 2001, 118. Interestingly, additional hours of financial education reduced savings by 70¢ per hour.

26. Ibid., 119. Additional hours of asset-specific training (up to twelve hours) actually decreased savings by $1.80 per hour.

27. There is little persuasive evidence that financial education without accounts and financial incentives actually increases savings or other financial outcomes.

28. Michelle Miller-Adams, *Owning Up: Poverty, Assets, and the American Dream* (Washington, DC: Brookings Institution Press, 2002), 165–66, 171–72, 180–81, 184, 189, 191.

29. U.S. Senate, "Building Assets for Low-Income Families, Testimony Before Senate Committee on Finance, Subcommittee on Social Security and Family Policy," April 28, 2005; Michael S. Barr and Michael D. Sherraden, "Institutions and Inclusion in Savings Policy," in *Building Assets, Building Wealth: Creating Wealth in Low-Income Communities*, ed. N. Retsinas and E. Belsky (Washington, DC: Brookings Institution Press, 2005).

30. Mauricio Lim Miller, *The Alternative: Most of What You Believe About Poverty Is Wrong* (Morrisville, NC: Lulu, 2017), 34

31. Projected to become 10,000 families and 40,000 people by the end of 2020. See "Trust and Invest in Families: 2016 Annual Report."

32. Ibid., 145.

33. Ibid., 148.

34. Ibid., 180.

35. Ibid., 194.

36. Ibid., 192.

37. Miller, *The Alternative*, 194.

38. Ibid., 186.

39. Ibid., 195.

40. ADD also inspired three much larger initiatives: the Savings for Working Families Act, which would have provided $500 tax credits to financial institutions that matched the savings of low-income Americans, and the Clinton administration's $750 million Universal Savings Account and $500 million Retirement Savings Account initiatives. While they received bipartisan interest and support, these initiatives did not pass.

41. Based on 2014 AFI data, 50 percent of account holders choose homeownership, 20 percent business, and 25 percent postsecondary education and training.

42. Signe-Mary McKernan, Caroline Ratcliffe, Gregory B. Mills, Michael Pergamit, and Breno Braga, "Family Savings Policy: Matched Savings Programs Show Promise for Financial Security and Upward Mobility," Urban Institute, Washington, DC, 2017.

43. Gregory Mills, Signe-Mary McKernan, Caroline Ratcliffe, Sara Edelstein, Michael Pergamit, Breno Braga, Heather Hahn, and Sam Elkin, "Building Savings for Success: Early Impacts from the Assets for Independence Program Randomized Evaluation," U.S. Department of Health and Human Services, Administration for Children and Families, Office of Policy, Research and Evaluation, 2016.

44. The Office of Refugee Resettlement (ORR) IDA program was created free from legislative constraint and was informed and guided by best practices. Automobiles were accepted as assets and became the most popular use, underscoring the key role vehicles play as instruments of economic mobility and access to jobs, schools, and a larger world. Similarly, ORR raised asset limits and allowed IDA programs to become enfolded in established comprehensive refugee resettlement programming. "IDA Program Report," Office of Refugee Resettlement, Administration for Children and Families, U.S. Department of Health and Human Services, 2010.

45. Reid Cramer and Jeff Lubell, "The Family Self-Sufficiency Program: A Promising Low-Cost Vehicle to Promote Savings and Asset-Building for Recipients of Federal Housing Assistance," New America Foundation, Washington, DC, 2005. Amounts saved in escrow could be much higher, as much as $7,000: Barbara Said, "The Family Self-Sufficiency Program: HUD's Best Kept Secret for Promoting Assets, Employment and Asset Growth," Center on Budget and Policy Priorities, Washington, DC, 2001. The FSS program, established in 1990, was open to individuals eligible for Section 8 housing choice vouchers in participating public housing authorities. Under the program, which provided case management, employment search, training, education, financial literacy lessons, and assistance with child care and transportation, rent and utility payments above 30 percent AGI were diverted to an interest-bearing escrow account and were available to participants as long as they remained employed, were free of welfare receipt for twelve months or so, and achieved the goals of the self-sufficiency plan.

46. While the ADD, AFIA, ORR, and FSS IDA demonstrations suggest the potential of IDAs and matched savings, it is important to recognize the limitations of these versions of matched accounts as demonstrated. The demonstrations were temporary and time-limited, and thus saving periods in ADD averaged 1.5 years. The matched savings opportunity should be ongoing. Demonstration programs were mounted as stand-alone nonprofit community-based programs, which required lots of labor-intensive

and expensive implementation; a system of accounts should resemble Social Security, 401(k)s, or 529 programs, with centralized administration, low-cost investment options, and financial institution management of accounts. Financial education should be integrated into school systems, social service programs, and housing administrations, where they can be delivered wholesale and more efficiently.

47. EARN, based in San Francisco, has started SaverLife, an online platform linking to nine thousand financial institutions nationwide, which helps would-be savers assemble $500 in six months with small incentives ($10 to $20) for monthly deposits and steady savings. It employs the latest findings in behavioral economics to design essential saver prompts and promotion. EARN claims that 80 percent of its low-income savers continue saving after the six-month period, even without incentives. See the organizations website, EARN.org.

48. The Growing Wealth Working Group, the SEED Policy Council, CSD, and others have outlined the core principles of such a system.

49. Author interview with Kriss Deiglemeier. See Kriss Deiglemeier, "Scaling Social Innovation: Gaps and Opportunities," in Jurgen Howaldt, Christoph Kaletka, Antonius Schroder, Marte Zirngiebl, *Atlas of Social Innovation: New Practices for a Better Future* (Dortmund: Cozialforschungsstelle, 2018), 198–201.

50. The EITC, a refundable tax credit for low-income working families, has arguably been the greatest anti-poverty innovation of the last forty years, drawing rare bipartisan support and growing accordingly.

51. "Prosperity Now's Framework for Increasing Household Financial Security," Prosperity Now, Washington, DC, July 2017.

52. "Financial Well-Being: The Goal of Financial Information," Consumer Financial Protection Bureau, Washington, DC, 2016.

53. Perer Georgescu and David Dorsey, *Capitalists Arise! End Economic Inequaltiy, Grow the Middle Class, Heal the Nation* (Oakland, CA: Berrett-Koehler, 2017), 17–18.

54. Andy Stern and Lee Kravitz, *Raising the Floor: How a Universal Basic Income Can Renew Our Economy and Rebuild the American Dream* (New York: Public Affairs, 2016), 171.

55. Ioana Marinescu, "No Strings Attached: The Behavioral Effects of U.S. Unconditional Cash Transfer Programs," Roosevelt Institute, New York, 2017, 7.

56. Stern and Kravitz, *Raising the Floor*, 212–15.

57. There are at least three versions of UBI proposals that merit attention. One is Peter Barnes's proposal for the creation of an American Permanent Fund, based on the Alaska Permanent Fund, which would claim ownership of common assets such as the carbon-absorptive capacity of the atmosphere and the liquidity of the stock market in the name of all citizens and pay dividends to all. Such common assets, he argues, are best understood not as belonging to government or private individuals but instead as representing a common patrimony. The Alaska Permanent Fund last year paid nearly $2,000 to every Alaskan as their share of the oil wealth beneath them. It stands to reason that if the underlying asset belongs to all, dividends should accrue to all equally as an extension of their common ownership. See Peter Barnes, *Who Owns the Sky? Our Common Assets and the Future of Capitalism* (Washington, DC: Island Press, 2001) and Peter Barnes, *With Liberty and Dividends for All: How to Save Our Middle Class When Jobs Don't Pay Enough* (San Francisco: Berrett-Koehler Publishers, 2014). Another, more progressive version that may appear as a proposition on the 2018 California ballot would impose a wealth tax to increase the California Earned Income Tax Credit and include domestic workers and caregivers as beneficiaries. Chris Hughes, co-founder of Facebook, proposes a third version also based on an extension of the Earned Income Tax Credit that is employment-based, targeted, and progressive. Chris Hughes, *Fair Shot: Rethinking Inequality and How We Earn* (New York: St. Martin's Press, 2018).

58. Daniel Kurtzleben, "While Trump Touts Stock Market, Many Americans Are Left Out of the Conversation," National Public Radio, March 1, 2017.

59. Urban-Brookings Tax Policy Center, 2017.

60. Current data on the net worth/wealth of Americans is of uncertain quality, and income could be used as a rough proxy, but, in fact African Americans and other people of color own less wealth than their white counterparts, even at the same income level. For example, among families with children living below the poverty line, African American and Latino families owned half the assets their white counterparts did.

61. Citizenship, assistive technology, and cars should also be considered.

62. The Rainy Day EITC: A Reform to Boost Financial Security by Helping Low-Wage Workers Build Emergency Savings, Washington, DC: Prosperity Now, April 2015.

63. Accounts and saving should occur within plan structures such as 401(k)s, 529 accounts, or the federal Thrift Savings Plan, which ensures low costs, a simplified (limited) choice of sound investment options maximizing appreciation opportunities, and other appropriate supervision.

64. Shapiro, Oliver, and Meschede, "The Asset Security and Opportunity Index." Also based on research by Kasey Weidrich and Lebaron Sims for Prosperity Now, 2017. I use the term *Americans* as inclusively as possible.

3. Education

1. The wonderful phrase "hope in concrete form" is from Michael Sherraden, *Assets and the Poor.* Child Development Accounts (CDAs) are also referred to as child savings accounts, educational savings accounts, SEED accounts, kids' accounts, lifetime savings accounts, universal savings accounts, Individual Development Accounts (IDAs), I Have a Dream Accounts, and more. In their forthcoming book, Willie Elliott and Melinda Lewis refer to them as Opportunity Investment Accounts. See Michael Sherraden and Julia Stevens, "Lessons from SEED: A National Demonstration of Child Development Accounts," Center for Social Development, Washington University in St. Louis, 2010, 1. In this chapter we refer to them as Generation Accounts. Features may differ along with the name, but they generally are universal, lifelong, progressive, and asset-building, as discussed.

2. Peter D. Hart Research Associates, Inc., "Public Opinion Focus Group Findings on Children's Savings Accounts," Corporation for Enterprise Development, Washington, DC, 2006.

3. Sherraden and Stevens, "Lessons from SEED," 9.

4. Income is a rough proxy for assets, though asset inequity is greater in magnitude and significance.

5. Thomas M. Shapiro, *Toxic Inequality: How America's Wealth Gap Destroys Mobility, Deepens the Racial Divide, and Threatens Our Future* (New York: Basic Books, 2017), 26.

6. Ibid., 139. And white parents will give their children an average of $74,000 in college support, while black parents who do can give only $16,000—less than one-quarter of the amount.

7. William Elliott III and Melinda K. Lewis, *The Real College Debt Crisis: How Student Borrowing Threatens Financial Well-Being and Erodes the American Dream* (Santa Barbara, CA: Praeger, 2015).

8. William Elliott and Melinda Kay Lewis, *Making Education Work for the Poor: The Potential of Children's Savings Accounts* (New York: Oxford University Press, 2018). This work includes a comprehensive overview of findings from the extensive research on and relevant to child accounts.

9. Ibid.

10. Shapiro, *Toxic Inequality*, 107. The sevenfold differential is due to a multiplicity of factors, including different levels of debt, interest, unemployment, pension coverage, family support—people of color tend to support their parents and extended families, while white parents tend to support the educations and houses of their children—value of housing, etc.

11. Ibid., 138.

12. Ray Boshara, "Black College Graduates Are Losing Wealth," *Washington Post*, April 12, 2017.

13. Shapiro, *Toxic Inequality*, 106.

14. William Elliott, Hyun-a Song, and Ilsung Nam, "Small-Dollar Children's Savings Accounts and Children's College Outcomes by Income Level," *Children and Youth Services Review* 35 (2013): 560–71.

15. Ibid. William Elliott and his colleagues at Kansas University and now the University of Michigan have explored the impact of assets on educational expectations and success, demonstrating a profound connection between assets and educational outcomes.

16. Elliott and Lewis, *Making Education Work for the Poor.*

17. Ibid., 183.

18. Ibid., 192.

19. Ibid. 273.

20. Thomas Paine, "Agrarian Justice" (1795), quoted in Reid Cramer, "Net Worth at Birth: Creating a National System for Savings and Asset Building with American Stakeholder Accounts," New America Foundation, Washington, DC, 2004, 9–10.

21. Ibid.

22. Ibid.

23. Tobin, quoted in Duncan Lindsey, *The Welfare of Children* (Oxford: Oxford University Press, 2004), 360. See also James Tobin, "Raising the Incomes of the Poor," in *Agenda for the Nation: Papers on*

Diplomatic and Foreign Policy Issues, ed. K. Gordon (Washington, DC: Brookings Institution, 1968).

24. Robert Haveman, *Starting Even: An Equal Opportunity Program to Combat the Nation's New Poverty* (New York: Simon & Schuster, 1988); Lester Thurow, *Head to Head: The Coming Economic Battle Among Japan, Europe and America* (San Francisco: William Morrow, 1992); Bruce Ackerman and Anne Alstott, *The Stakeholder Society* (New Haven, CT: Yale University Press, 1999).

25. Ray Boshara and Michael Sherraden, "For Every Child, a Stake in America," *New York Times*, July 23, 2003. Even as they issued that call, their institutions, the Center for Social Development and the New America Foundation, were working with the Corporation for Enterprise Development (now Prosperity Now), the Aspen Institute Initiative for Financial Security, and the Kansas University School of Social Work in launching the Saving for Education, Enterprise and Downpayment (SEED) Initiative, the first systematic and comprehensive demonstration of the design, implementation, effects and impacts of child accounts in the United States.

26. Dozens of papers and studies by the Center for Social Development, Kansas University School of Social Work, Research Triangle Institute, Corporation for Enterprise Development, New America Foundation, and other contain various lessons. The most comprehensive overview is Sherraden and Stevens, "Lessons from SEED."

27. Ford Foundation (Frank DeGiovanni, Mitty Owens, Kilolo Kijakazi), Charles Stewart Mott Foundation (Bill White, Jack A. Litzenberg, Benita Melton), Lumina Foundation for Education, Charles and Helen Schwab Family Foundation (Rick Williams), Jim Casey Youth Opportunity Initiative (Gary Stangler, Leonard Burton), Citi Foundation (Brandee McHale), Ewing Marion Kauffman Foundation (Andres Dominguez), Richard and Rhoda Goldman Foundation (Eric Sloan), MetLife Foundation, Evelyn and Walter Haas Jr. Foundation (Ira Hirschfield), Edwin Gould Foundation for Children (Helen Alessi), and W.K. Kellogg Foundation.

28. Sherraden and Stevens, "Lessons from SEED," 1–3, 9–19.

29. Ibid., 16.

30. Yunju Nam, Youngmi Kim, Margaret Clancy, Robert Zager, and Michael Sherraden, "Do Child Development Accounts Promote Account Holding, Saving, and Asset Accumulation for Children's

Future? Evidence from a Statewide Randomized Experiment," *Journal of Policy Analysis and Management* 32, no. 1 (2013): 6–33. See also Robert Zager, Youngmi Kim, Yunju Nam, Margaret Clancy, and Michael Sherraden, "The SEED for Oklahoma Kids Experiment: Initial Account Opening and Savings," Center for Social Development, Washington University in St. Louis, 2010.

31. Sondra G. Beverly, Youngmi Kim, Michael Sherraden, Yunju Nam, and Margaret Clancy, "Can Child Development Accounts Be Inclusive? Early Evidence from a Statewide Experiment," *Children and Youth Services Review* 53 (2015): 92–104. See also Nam et al., "Do Child Development Accounts Promote."

32. Margaret M. Clancy, Michael Sherraden, and Sondra G. Beverly, "College Savings Plans: A Platform for Inclusive and Progressive Child Development Accounts," Center for Social Development, Washington University in St. Louis, 2015.

33. Margaret M. Clancy and Sondra G. Beverly, "529 Plan Investment Growth and a Quasi-Default Investment for Child Development Accounts," Center for Social Development, 2017.

34. Nam et al., "Do Child Development Accounts Promote"; Clancy, Sherraden, and Beverly, "College Savings Plans."

35. Youngmi Kim, Michael Sherraden, Jin Huang, and Margaret Clancy, "Child Development Accounts and Parental Educational Expectations for Young Children: Early Evidence from a Statewide Social Experiment," *Social Service Review* 89, no. 1 (2015).

36. Jin Huang, Michael Sherraden, Youngmi Kim, and Margaret Clancy, "Effects of Child Development Accounts on Early Social-Emotional Development: An Experimental Test," *JAMA Pediatrics* 168, no. 3 (2014): 265–271.

37. Margaret M. Clancy and Sondra G. Beverly, "Statewide Child Development Account Policies: Key Design Elements," Center for Social Development, Washington University in St. Louis, 2017.

38. Universal inclusion is crucial so that all kids and the larger community see accounts as a basic investment and foundation for all rather than as a handout for some (as welfare is sometimes perceived).

39. The automatic initial deposit serves to jump-start accumulation.

40. People freeze at too many choices. A few, usually three—including a conservative option that preserves principal, a more aggressive growth option, and a mixed fixed-income option based on appreciating stock indexes—are ideal.

41. This is intended to protect current benefits for poor and disabled children and their families.

42. Clancy, Sherraden, and Beverly, "College Savings Plans."

43. $1.75 billion in 2013, out of $30 billion in federal tax incentives. Ezra Levin, Jeremie Greer, and Ida Rademacher, "From Upside Down to Right-Side Up," Corporation for Enterprise Development, Washington University in St. Louis, 2014, 41.

44. Ibid., 44. In 2013, 80 percent of the state 529 credit accrued to the wealthiest 11 percent of households. In Louisiana, households earning over $100,000 claimed 70 percent of the benefits.

45. Clancy and Beverly, "529 Plan Investment Growth." With decreased costs, families get more from MOST 529 college savings plan.

46. Margaret Clancy and Michael Sherraden, "Automatic Deposits for All at Birth: Maine's Harold Alfond College Challenge," Center for Social Development, Washington University in St. Louis, 2014, 8. The tax incentive for 529s is a federal and sometimes state income tax deduction, only available to taxpayers itemizing and not taking the standard deduction, and worth more to wealthier taxpayers contributing higher amounts (the current limit is $150,000 per year, well beyond the capability of most families) and in higher tax brackets.

47. Margaret Clancy and Terry Lassar, "College Savings Plan Accounts at Birth: Maine's Statewide Program," Center for Social Development (2010).

48. Ibid.

49. Margaret Clancy and Michael Sherraden, "Automatic Deposits for All at Birth: Maine's Harold Alfond College Challenge," Center for Social Development, Washington University in St. Louis, 2014.

50. Among the recommendations are automatic enrollment, default investment (if none selected), streamlined enrollment, greatly simplified enrollment form, a single account for all savings and deposits, and financial education in every quarterly statements. Clancy and Lassar, "College Savings Plan Accounts at Birth," 4.

51. Clancy and Sherraden, "Automatic Deposits for All at Birth," 1.

52. William Elliott, Melinda Lewis, Megan O'Brien, Christina LiCalsi, Leah Brown, Natalie Tucker, and Nicholas Sorensen, "Contribution Activity and Asset Accumulation in a Universal Children's Savings Account Program," Center on Assets, Education, and Inclusion, University of Michigan, 2017.

53. Martha Shirk and Gary Stangler, *On Their Own: What Happens to Kids When They Age Out of the Foster Care System* (New York: Basic Books, 2004), 1–2.

54. Ibid.

55. "National Youth in Transition Database: Lessons Learned from the Jim Casey Youth Opportunities Initiative," Annie E. Casey Foundation, Baltimore, 2010.

56. In Creole, a *nanan* is an unrelated woman who housed the kids in return for help on the plantation.

57. "2017 State of the Children's Savings Field Survey," Prosperity Now, Washington, DC, 2018.

58. By 2017 those numbers had grown to 200 community organizations, 1,000 endorsers, 60 community ambassadors, and 29 college partners.

59. Generation Accounts are a form of child development accounts, college savings accounts, most similar to Willie Elliott's and Melinda Kay Lewis's Opportunity Investment Accounts and Darrick Hamilton's and William "Sandy" Darity's Baby Bonds. Just as there are many variations of the proposals and many names, the core concept is shared—large, at birth, progressive, and designed to help close the racial wealth divide. The title Generation Accounts is designed to emphasize that these accounts are about more than education (though education is a key focus), multigenerational and productivity expanding.

60. The cost of the 2017 expansion of the estate tax exclusion was unavailable at time of this writing.

61. These are not the only two inheritance tax preferences—gift tax provisions and generation-skipping tax preferences are others.

62. Shapiro, *Toxic Inequality*, 134–35.

63. Ibid.

64. Ibid., 132.

65. Ibid.

66. Levin, Greer, and Rademacher, "From Upside Down to Right-Side Up," 23–24.

67. Doris Kearns Goodwin, *Team of Rivals: The Political Genius of Abraham Lincoln* (New York: Simon & Schuster, 2005), 367.

68. Sherraden and Stevens, "Lessons from SEED."

69. Existing 529 tax deductions could be considered the match for the wealthier two quintiles, eliminating the need for savings matches for families who can already benefit from deductions.

70. Lynn Parramore, "Baby Bonds: A Plan for Black/White Wealth Equality Conservatives Could Love?," Institute for New Economic Thinking, New York, 2016; Elliott and Lewis, *Making Education Work for the Poor.*

71. Jonathan Morduch and Rachel Schneider, *The Financial Diaries: How American Families Cope in a World of Uncertainty* (Princeton, NJ: Princeton University Press, 2017).

72. *Mishkan HaNeFesh*, Yom Kippur Edition (New York: CCAR Press, 2015), 585.

4. Home

1. William J. Collins and Robert A. Margo, "Race and Home Ownership from the Civil War to the Present," *American Economic Review* 101, no. 3 (2011): 355–359.

2. The 2017 rates: all, 63.9 percent; white, 72.5 percent; black, 42 percent; Hispanic, 46.1 percent. U.S. Census, "Quarterly Residential Vacancies and Homeownership, Fourth Quarter 2017," CB18-08, January 30, 2018.

3. "Post-Miller Center Poll: American Dream and Economic Struggles," *Washington Post*, November 25, 2013.

4. Bruce Katz, "Foreword," in *Low-Income Homeownership: Examining the Unexamined Goal*, ed. Nicolas P. Retsinas and Eric S. Belsky (Washington, DC: Brookings Institution Press, 2002).

5. Matthew Desmond, *Evicted: Poverty and Profit in the American City* (New York: Broadway Books, 2016), 300.

6. William M. Rohe and Mark Lindblad, "Reexamining the Social Benefits of Homeownership After the Housing Crisis," presentation at the conference Homeownership Built to Last: Lessons from the Housing Crisis on Sustaining Homeownership for Low-Income and Minority Families, Boston, April 1–2, 2013.

7. Desmond, *Evicted*, 295.

8. Thomas Shapiro, *Toxic Inequality: How America's Wealth Gap Destroys Mobility, Deepens the Racial Divide, and Threatens Our Future* (New York: Basic Books, 2017), 55.

9. William M. Rohe, Shannon Van Zandt, and George McCarthy, "Social Benefits and Costs of Homeownership," in *Low-Income Homeownership: Examining the Unexamined Goal*, ed. Nicolas P. Retsinas and Eric S. Belsky (Washington, DC: Brookings Institution Press, 2002), 400.

10. Donald R. Haurin, Toby L. Parcel, and R. Jean Haurin, "Impact of Homeownership on Child Outcomes," in *Low-Income Homeownership: Examining the Unexamined Goal*, ed. Nicolas P. Retsinas and Eric S. Belsky (Washington, DC: Brookings Institution Press, 2002), 439–40.

11. Svenja Gudell, "Down Payment the Top Hurdle Holding Back Would-Be Home Buyers," Zillow, April 12, 2017.

12. Desmond, *Evicted*, 4.

13. Ibid.

14. Ibid., 5.

15. Shapiro, *Toxic Inequality*; Michal Grinstein-Weiss, Clinton Key, and Shannon Carrillo, "Homeownership, the Great Recession, and Wealth: Evidence from the Survey of Consumer Finance," *Housing Policy Debate* 25, no. 13 (2013): 419–45.

16. Shapiro, *Toxic Inequality*.

17. U.S. Census, "Quarterly Residential Vacancies and Homeownership, Fourth Quarter 2017," CB18-08, January 30, 2018.

18. White home values increased 54 percent and 34 percent more than for Hispanic and black owners, respectively, from 2004 to 2014. Thomas Shapiro, Tatjana Meschede, and Sam Orso, "The Roots of the Widening Racial Wealth Gap: Explaining the Black-White Economic Divide," Institute on Assets and Social Policy, Brandeis University, 2013; Anju Chopra, Dedrick Asante-Muhammad, David Newville, and Doug Ryan, "A Downpayment on the Divide: Steps to Ease the Racial Inequality in Homeownership," Prosperity Now, Washington, DC, 2017, 8.

19. Laura Sullivan, Tatjana Meschede, Lars Dietrich, and Thomas Shapiro, "The Racial Wealth Gap: Why Policy Matters," Institute on Assets and Social Policy, Brandeis University, 2015.

20. Richard Rothstein, *The Color of Law: A Forgotten History of How Our Government Segregated America* (New York: Liveright, 2017).

21. Richard Rothstein, *The Color of Law: A Forgotten History of How Our Government Segregated America* (New York: Liveright Publishing Corporation, 2017).

22. Henry Cisneros et al., *The Future of Fair Housing: Report of the National Commission on Fair Housing and Equal Opportunity* (Washington, DC: Leadership Conference on Civil Rights Education Fund, 2008), 21.

23. The homeownership rate for whites is 72 percent versus 43 percent for blacks and 45 percent for Hispanic Americans. Chopra et al., "A Downpayment on the Divide," citing Drew DeSilver and Kristen Bialik, "Blacks and Hispanics Face Extra Challenges in Getting Home Loans," Pew Research Center, Washington, DC, 2017.

24. Debbie Gruenstein Bocian, Wei Li, and Keith S. Ernst, "Foreclosures by Race and Ethnicity: The Demographics of a Crisis," Center for Responsible Lending, Durham, NC, 2010.

25. "The State of the Nation's Housing 2016," Joint Center for Housing Studies, Harvard University, 2016, citing data from CoreLogic on the 2007–2015 period.

26. There were some efforts to help owners, such as HAMP, but too late and too few.

27. Rising credit standards have cut mortgage loans to once-qualifying borrowers with credit scores below 660 by 65 percent. The Urban Institute estimates that, compared with the perfectly adequate credit standards of 2001, Procrustean credit criteria applied from 2009 through 2016 resulted in 7 million fewer sales. Laurie Goodman, Jun Zhu, and Bing Bai, "Overly Tight Credit Killed 1.1 Million Mortgages in 2015," Urban Institute, Washington, DC, 2016.

28. Levin, Greer, and Rademacher, "From Upside-Down to Right-Side Up," 12–21.

29. Ibid., 14.

30. Ibid.

31. PL 115–97.

32. Levin, Greer, and Rademacher, "From Upside-Down to Right-Side Up," updated with data from OMB's President's FY 2018 Budget Documents, Analytical Perspectives, Tax Expenditures, 127–67, https://www.whitehouse.gov/omb/analytical-perspectives.

33. Levin, Greer, and Rademacher, "From Upside-Down to Right-Side Up," 15.

34. Thus, while only the interest on the first $1 million of mortgage debt are deductible, all state and local real estate taxes on a $25 million mansion are deductible. Ibid, 14.

35. Ibid., 15, updated with data from OMB's President's FY 2018 Budget Documents, Analytical Perspectives, Tax Expenditures, 127–67.

36. Levin, Greer, and Rademacher, "From Upside-Down to Right-Side Up," 13.

37. $72.4 billion in 2013; ibid.

38. Ibid.

39. Names here have been changed at the request of the subjects; the essential facts of the story have not been.

40. Alison Freeman and Roberto G. Quercia, "Low and Moderate Income Home Ownership and Wealth Creation," University of North Carolina at Chapel Hill Center for Community Capital, 2014.

41. "Regaining the Dream: Case Studies in Sustainable Low-Income Mortgage Lending," University of North Carolina at Chapel Hill Center for Community Capital, 2014.

42. Freeman and Quercia, "Low and Moderate Income Home Ownership."

43. "Making Resident Ownership a Reality Nationwide 2008–2014 Report," Resident Owned Communities USA, Concord, NH.

44. Typical chattel loan rates are 6–12 percent, two to three times the rates on a typical mortgage loan.

45. In addition to New Hampshire, Vermont, Massachusetts, Rhode Island, and Oregon have adopted opportunity-to-purchase statutes, and Minnesota is considering it as of this writing.

46. Andrea Levere is president of Prosperity Now, founder of I'M HOME, and chair of ROC USA; George McCarthy was affordable housing program director of the Ford Foundation and venture funder of the three organizations and the national strategy; Paul Bradley is president and founder of ROC USA; Stacey Epperson is founder, president and CEO of Next Step; and Doug Ryan is director of affordable housing at Prosperity Now and I'M HOME.

47. Tracy Jan, "America's Affordable-Housing Stock Dropped by 60 Percent from 2010 to 2016," *Washington Post*, October 23, 2017.

48. Information here was gleaned from interviews with Paul Bradley, Michael Sloss, and Mike Bullard of ROC USA, Natividad Seefeld, and

Andrea Levere of Prosperity Now. It also draws from Daniel Zwerdling, "When Residents Take Ownership, a Mobile Home Community Thrives," NPR, December 27, 2016.

49. Tracy Mumford, "The Last Week in Lowry Grove: Another Mobile Home Park Shutters." Minnesota Public Radio, June 28, 2017.

50. Tracy Mumford, "The Park Closed, the Land's Empty—Now What?," Minnesota Public Radio, October 11, 2017.

51. Ida Rademacher, Kasey Wiedrich, Signe-Mary McKernan, Caroline Ratcliffe, and Megan Gallagher, "Weathering the Storm: Have IDAs Helped Low-Income Homebuyers Avoid Foreclosure?" Corporation for Enterprise Development and the Urban Institute, 2010.

52. George C. Galster and Anna M. Santiago, "Low Income Homeownership as an Asset-Building Tool: What Can We Tell Policymakers?," in *Urban and Regional Policy and Its Effects*, ed. Margery Austin Turner, Howard Wial, and Harold Wolman (Washington, DC: Brookings Institution Press, 2008); Raphael Bostic and Kwan Ok Lee, "Assets and Credit Among Low-Income Households," *American Economic Review* 98, no. 2 (2008): 310–14.

53. Rademacher et al., "Weathering the Storm."

54. Abdighani Hirad and Peter Zorn, "Prepurchase Homeownership Counseling: A Little Knowledge Is a Good Thing," in *Low-Income Homeownership: Examining the Unexamined Goal*, ed. Nicholas P. Retsinas and Eric S. Belsky (Washington, DC: Brookings Institution Press, 2002).

55. "SNAP Stat: Sizing Up Certified CDFIs," CDFI Fund, U.S. Department of the Treasury, Washington, DC, 2016.

56. "20 Years of Opportunity Finance 1994–2013: An Analysis of Trends and Growth," BBC Research and Consulting, Denver, CO, 2015.

57. Instead of the single Home Credit recommended here, Prosperity Now has proposed a Housing Pathways Credit, which would provide four different refundable credits—a Low-Income Renters Credit, a Down Payment Builder Credit, a First Time Homebuyers Credit, and a Homeowners Mortgage Interest and Property Tax Credit—covering the same ground. The last of these would substitute a flat 15 percent refundable credit on mortgages up to $500,000. See Housing Pathways Credit Proposal Overview, Prosperity Now, Washington, DC, December 2017.

58. Thomas Shapiro, applying the Brandeis Institute for Assets and Social Policy Racial Wealth Audit, modeled accounts like this that

closed the racial wealth divide as much as 30 percent Shapiro, *Toxic Inequality*.

59. Ellen Seidman, "Urban Wire: Housing and Housing Finance," Urban Institute, New York, 2017. She notes that there are as many as 7.6 million consumers without credit scores who might become scoreable with resulting scores above 620 should rent, utility, and telecommunications records become available, and that 3 million of these would have income and credit sufficient to qualify them for a mortgage on a median-priced home in their zip code.

60. Or other proven asset-building purposes.

5. Business

1. William J. Clinton, "Remarks on Presenting the Presidential Awards for Excellence in Microenterprise Development," January 30, 1997.

2. John Haltiwanger, Ron S. Jarmin, and Javier Miranda, "Who Creates Jobs? Small vs. Large vs. Young," US Census Bureau, Washington, DC, August 2011.

3. Ibid.

4. Ibid.

5. Ben Casselman, "St. Louis Is the New Startup Frontier," FiveThirtyEight, September 12, 2016.

6. John Haltiwanger, Ron Jarmin, and Javier Miranda, "Business Dynamics Statistics Briefing: Where Have All the Young Firms Gone?," Kauffman Foundation, Kansas City, MO, 2012. See also Jessica Stillman, "Start-up Fever? Actually, We're in a New-Business Drought," *Inc.*, May 9, 2012.

7. Haltiwanger, Jarmin and Miranda, ibid.

8. Haltiwanger, Jarmin, and Miranda, "Business Dynamics Statistics Briefing."

9. This is all the more crucial since it is likely the economy will be losing jobs in many traditional occupations and businesses due to technology and global competition. See Andy Stern, *Raising the Floor: How a Universal Basic Income Can Renew Our Economy and Rebuild the American Dream* (New York: Public Affairs, 2016).

10. "The State of Women-Owned Businesses, 2014," Womenable, 2014.

11. Adam Bluestein, "The Most Entrepreneurial Group in America Wasn't Born in America," *Inc.*, February 2015.

12. Alberto Dávila, Marie T. Mora, and Angela Marek Zeitlin, "Better Business: How Hispanic Entrepreneurs Are Beating Expectations and Bolstering the U.S. Economy," Partnership for a New American Economy and the Latino Donor Collaborative, April 2014.

13. Sarah Alvarez, "Unleashing Latino-Owned Business Potential: A Report on the Aspen Institute Forum on Latino Business Growth," Aspen Institute Latinos and Society Program, 2017.

14. Ibid.

15. Mauricio Lim Miller, *The Alternative: Most of What You Know About Poverty Is Wrong* (Morrisville, NC: Lulu, 2017), 145.

16. Alicia M. Robb and David T. Robinson, "The Capital Structure Decisions of New Firms," working paper, National Bureau of Economic Research, 2010.

17. Ibid., 18, 32. While the authors make a point that debt is crucial, they note that the three-quarters of firms that have owner's equity have an average of more than $40,000. Ibid., 9.

18. Lauren Williams and Kasey Wiedrich, "In Search of Solid Ground: Understanding the Financial Vulnerabilities of Microbusiness Owners," Prosperity Now, Washington, DC, April 2014.

19. "The Power of One in Three: Creating Opportunities for All Americans to Bounce Back," Association for Enterprise Opportunity, Washington, DC, 2011.

20. Peter Georgescu and David Dorsey, *Capitalists Arise! End Economic Inequality, Grow the Middle Class, Heal the Nation* (Oakland, CA: Berrett-Koehler, 2017), 60, 61.

21. Georgescu cites William Lazonick's "seminal" *Harvard Business Review* article, "Profits Without Prosperity," 57–59. Georgescu goes on to ascribe this devotion to shareholder enrichment to the detriment of other traditional stakeholders, notably customers, employees, and the larger community, to Milton Friedman's championing the pursuit of shareholder value and steadily increasing quarterly profits as the only legitimate goal of business.

22. Ibid. Race-car driver, industrial engineer, architect, car enthusiast, bowtie wearer, Richard championed the development of flexible networks in the United States, citing cooperative advantages in sharing mounting R&D costs, melding capabilities to produce new goods

and services, aggregating production to serve larger markets, reducing costs through joint purchases of raw materials and management services, acquiring expensive technologies, and increasing market share and export earnings.

23. Corporation for Enterprise Development, Institute on Taxation and Economic Policy, Mt. Auburn Associates, "Taken for Granted: How Grant Thornton's Business Climate Index Leads States Astray," Corporation for Enterprise Development, Washington, DC, 1986.

24. Ibid., 1.

25. Every state had provisions dealing with self-employment income, seen essentially as a source of welfare fraud, not as a strength worthy of nurture.

26. Improve household stability, create an orientation to the future, stimulate development of other assets, enable focus and specialization, provide a foundation for risk-taking, increase personal efficacy, increase social influence, increase political participation, and enhance welfare of offspring. "Lessons from the Self-Employment Investment Demonstration," Corporation for Enterprise Development, Washington, DC, 1990. See also Michael Sherraden, *Assets and the Poor: A New American Welfare Policy* (New York: M.E. Sharpe, 1991).

27. "Lessons from the Self-Employment Investment Demonstration," 34.

28. Robert E. Friedman, Brian Grossman, and Puchka Sahay, "Building Assets: Self-Employment for Welfare Recipients—Overview of the Findings from the Self Employment Investment Demonstration (SEID)," Corporation for Enterprise Development, Washington, DC, 1995.

29. "Lessons from the Self-Employment Investment Demonstration."

30. Marguerite's story here is taken from Michelle Miller Adams's excellent review of asset-building programs and policies, including the Self-Employment Investment Demonstration and the American Dream Demonstration. See Michelle Miller-Adams, *Owning Up: Poverty, Assets, and the American Dream* (Washington, DC: Brookings Institution Press, 2002), 18, 119–22, 132–39, 146–50, 192–93.

31. Ibid., 150.

32. Ibid., 149.

33. Ibid., 147.

34. "Answers to Common Questions about the Self-Employment Investment Demonstration (SEID)," Corporation for Enterprise Development, Washington, DC, 1990, 3–4.

35. Among my guides in recognizing the power of women's economic leadership were Jing Lyman and Sara Gould, who established the HUB Program on Women's Enterprise at CFED.

36. By 1991, there were one hundred women's self-employment programs operating in the United States, which, along with Shorebank and Self-Help, pioneering community development banks, led to Bill Clinton's promise to create "100 community development banks and 1,000 microenterprise programs," which would later emerge in the form of the Community Development Financial Institutions fund. In 1991 we organized a national trade association—the Association for Enterprise Opportunity—to allow diverse communities to do together what they couldn't alone. Microenterprise development organizations and support continues to mature, endure and spread in the United States as well as the larger world, as documented and nurtured by Peggy Clark, Elaine Edgecomb, Joyce Klein, and FIELD (Fund for Innovation, Effectiveness, Learning and Demonstration). In its first twenty years, the microenterprise field grew to encompass more than five hundred programs in virtually every state, serving a quarter of a million entrepreneurs a year. In their 2005 review, Edgecomb and Klein conclude that the experience proves that "there is a segment of the population for whom self-employment is a necessary—and in some cases the best—source of employment and income," and that by assisting individuals to build businesses and assets, "microenterprise can open wealth and ownership opportunities to individuals who have been excluded from our economy . . . and play a role in the revitalization of local economies." They also identify the challenges—growing to scale, finding less expensive and labor-intensive ways of providing business assistance, and supporting the necessary infrastructure in the market.

37. International programs specialized in small repeat microloans operated at a much larger scale and at a hundredth the cost of U.S. efforts, often using peer-group guarantees, and involving much less business and financial education. Other countries, ironically, where entrepreneurship was less touted and evident, found new ways to foster grassroots

entrepreneurship. Great Britain and France offered unemployed workers the benefits they would otherwise receive as a self-employment incentive, in the French case paying future benefits in a lump sum that could be used as seed capital. In their first couple of years, these programs launched 63,000 entrepreneurs. Freshman congressman Ron Wyden read an article on the programs in *Inc.* magazine, and a year later introduced the Self-Employment Assistance Act, which authorized states to provide unemployment compensation to eligible claimants choosing self-employment. Rigorous evaluations established beyond reasonable doubt that the self-employment assistance generated more employment, more businesses, and more positive economic outcomes than traditional assistance and penalties. U.S. Department of Labor, Employment and Training Administration, "Self-Employment Programs for Unemployed Workers," Washington, DC, 1992.

38. By collecting and disseminating county-by-county comparative data, he created a dynamic where state legislators extended themselves to ensure microenterprise starts in their jurisdiction.

39. "The Self-Employment Tax Initiative," Corporation for Enterprise Development, Washington, DC, 2012.

40. Tim Kane, "The Importance of Startups in Job Creation and Destruction," Kauffman Foundation, Kansas City, MO, 2010.

41. Adam Looney and Kathryn Martin, "One in Five 2014 Marketplace Consumers Was a Small Business Owner or Self-Employed," U.S. Department of the Treasury, Washington, DC, 2017. This study also found that independent workers were three times more likely to rely on marketplace coverage than other workers.

42. Richard C. Hatch, Flexible Manufacturing Networks: Cooperation for Competitiveness in Global Economy, Corporation for Enterprise Development, Washington, DC, 1988.

43. Freelancers Union and Upwork, "Freelancing in America: A National Survey of the New Workforce," Freelancers Union, 2017.

44. Centro Community Partners' online business planning guide, for example, enables aspiring entrepreneurs to create a solid business plan online simply by answering basic questions. See www.centrocommunity.org.

45. C. Richard Hatch, "Flexible Manufacturing Networks:. Cooperation for Competitiveness in a Global Economy," Corporation for Enterprise Development, Washington, DC, 1988.

6. Prosperity

1. "Financial Well-Being: The Goal of Financial Education," Consumer Financial Protection Bureau, Washington, DC, 2016.

2. Thomas Piketty, *Capital in the Twenty-First Century*, trans. Arthur Goldhammer (Cambridge, MA: Belknap Press of Harvard University Press, 2014), 571.

3. Ibid.

4. Ibid., 572.

5. John P. Caskey, "HOPE: The Evolution of a Community Development Organization," Swarthmore College, Swarthmore, PA, October 2013.

6. Retirement accounts, share certificates, money market accounts, non-predatory loans (vehicle loans, home equity loans, signature loans, credit builder loans, borrow and save loans, savings/share certificate loans), credit cards (Platinum Visa, Secured Platinum Visa), home and insurance products (home loans, TruStage Insurance), convenience services (HOPENet Online Banking, HOPE Mobile Banking, HOPE E-Statements, HOPE24, Direct Deposit), and more.

7. Isabel V. Sawhill, Jeffrey Tebbs, and William T. Dickens, "The Effects of Investing in Early Education on Economic Growth," Brookings Institution, Washington, DC, 2006.

8. Ibid. See also Edward Denison, *Trends in American Economic Growth, 1929–1982* (Washington, DC: Brookings Institution Press, 1985).

9. Sawhill, Tebbs and Dickens, ibid.

10. Trina R. Williams Shanks, "The Homestead Act of the Nineteenth Century and its Influence on Rural Lands," Center for Social Development, Washington University in St. Louis, 2005, 3. The Southern Homestead Act of 1866 opened southern lands to freed slaves. The Timber Culture Act of 1873 granted lands for forestry. The Kinkaid Amendment of 1904 gave 640-acre parcels to homesteaders to settle in western Nebraska. The Enlarged Homestead Act of 1909 and Raising Homestead Act of 1916 increased the allotted acreage to 320 and 640 acres, respectively.

11. Ibid.

12. Paul W. Gates, *The Jeffersonian Dream: Studies in the History of American Land Policy and Development*, ed. Allan G. Bogue and Margaret Beattie Bogue (Albuquerque, NM: University of New Mexico Press, 1996), 11–12.

13. Claude Oubre, *Forty Acres and a Mule: The Freedmen's Bureau and Black Land Ownership* (Baton Rouge: Louisiana State University Press, 1978).

14. Reginald Washington, "The Freedman's Savings and Trust Company and African American Genealogical Research," *Federal Records and African American History* 29, no. 2 (1997).

15. Shanks, "The Homestead Act," 8.

16. Steve Newcomb, "Five Hundred Years of Injustice: The Legacy of Fifteenth Century Religious Prejudice," *Shaman's Drum*, 1992, 18–20.

17. Wilma Mankiller and Michael Wallis, *Mankiller: A Chief and Her People* (New York: St. Martin's Press, 1993), 135.

18. Ibid., 93–95.

19. Ibid., 133.

20. Ibid.

21. Ibid., 133–34.

22. Ibid., 135.

23. As Trina Shanks notes, as compared to nations in Latin America that also distributed land, but under tenancy and peonage systems more onerous to homesteaders, the U.S. Homestead Acts, by providing free or almost free land, led to higher standards of living, development of a middle class, and the attraction of larger number of immigrants. See S.A. Mosk, "Latin America Versus the United States," *American Economic Review* 41, no. 2 (1951): 367–83.

24. Shanks, "The Homestead Act," 7. Settlers established agricultural societies, cooperatives, banks, and other community institutions.

25. Richard H. Keehn and Gene Smiley, "Mortgage Lending by National Banks," *Business History Review* 51, no. 4 (1977): 474–91.

26. Kenneth A. Snowden, "Mortgage Rates and American Capital Market Development in the Late Nineteenth Century," *Journal of Economic History* 47, no. 3 (1987): 671–91.

27. Wilma Mankiller and Michael Wallis, *Mankiller: A Chief and Her People* (New York: St. Martin's Press, 1993), xix. Sometimes when confronted by a particularly rude comment on her name, Wilma would reply, "It's a nickname, and I earned it."

28. Ibid., 66.

29. There were several different routes for the forced marches of nearly some 15-16,000 Cherokees. 3-4,000 died along the way.

30. Mankiller and Wallis, *Mankiller*, xix.

31. My daughter, having been enticed to read *Mankiller* at an early age in order to learn about her friend, commented that she had been tricked: every other chapter was about the history of the Cherokee Nation and not Wilma.

32. Wilma Mankiller, speech before the Assets Learning Conference, September 19–21, 2006.

33. Ibid.

34. Ibid.

35. The reestablished Cherokee Nation established a court system and the first college west of the Mississippi. Cherokees were far more literate in their first decades in Oklahoma than their white counterparts.

36. Snowden, "Mortgage Rates."

37. Richard K. Green and Susan M. Wachter, "The American Mortgage in Historical and International Context," *Journal of Economic Perspectives* 19, no. 4 (2005): 93–114. See also William J. Collins and Robert A. Margo, "Race and Home Ownership from the End of the Civil War to the Present," Boston University, 2010, 27. Other races also undoubtedly experienced housing downturns as well, but we don't have this data.

38. Green and Wachter, "The American Mortgage," 95–96.

39. Ibid., 96. Other entities—Ginnie Mac, Freddie Mac, FSLIC, and others—were added in subsequent decades, but the general blueprint for America's new housing market was set.

40. Ibid., 97.

41. Christine Berwick, "Patterns of Discrimination Against Blacks and Hispanics in the US Mortgage Market," *Journal of Housing and the Built Environment* 25, no. 1 (2010): 117–24.

42. Ibid., 119.

43. Ibid.

44. Edward Humes, *Over Here: How the GI Bill Transformed the American Dream* (Orlando, FL: Harcourt Books, 2006), 5–6.

45. Of course, the GI Bill coincided with the rebuilding of the country (and world) after the war, and much of the gains were also a result of rebuilding the infrastructure of the country depleted by the war.

46. Humes, *Over Here*, 94.

47. Ibid., 307.

48. Ibid., 52.

49. Ibid.

50. Ibid., 6.

51. Ibid., 120.

52. Ibid., 189.

53. Ibid., 205.

54. Ibid., 199.

55. Ibid.

56. Ibid., 227.

57. Ira Katznelson, *When Affirmative Action Was White: An Untold History of Racial Inequality in Twentieth-Century America* (New York: W.W. Norton, 2005), 140.

58. Humes, *Over Here*, 227.

59. Gavin Wright, *Sharing the Prize: The Economics of the Civil Rights Revolution in the American South* (Cambridge, MA: Belknap Press of Harvard University Press, 2013), 72.

60. Humes, *Over Here*, 220.

61. Ibid., 221.

62. Katznelson, *When Affirmative Action Was White*, 140.

63. Ibid.

64. Humes, *Over Here*, 291.

65. Ibid., 304.

66. Ibid.

67. U.S. 265 (1978).

68. Dedrick Asante-Muhammad, Emanuel Nieves, Chuck Collins, and Josh Hoxie, "The Road to Zero Wealth: How the Racial Wealth Divide Is Hollowing Out America's Middle Class," Prosperity Now, Washington, DC, 2017.

69. Ibid. Data updated with information from OMB's President's FY 2018 Budget Documents, Analytical Perspectives, Tax Expenditures, 127–67, https://www.whitehouse.gov/omb/analytical-perspectives.

70. The Tax Cuts and Jobs Act of 2017 reduced the cap for the home mortgage interest deduction from $1 million to $750,000 for new mortgages in 2018 and beyond.

71. John N. Friedman, "Building on What Works: A Proposal to Modernize Retirement Savings" (Washington, DC: Brookings Institution, June 2015), 7.

72. I would be remiss if I did not give credit to Ray Boshara, Reid Cramer, Justin King, and their colleagues at the New America Foundation for leading this effort at bipartisan consensus-building, and for the partners in this effort, including the Center for Social Development, the Aspen Initiative on Financial Security, University of Kansas School of Social Work, and my colleagues at Prosperity Now, for developing this rare convergence in a non-partisan, evidence-based way.

73. Jeff Sessions, "A Bipartisan Fix for Retirees," *Washington Post*, December 26, 2006. Fred Goldberg, IRS commissioner and assistant secretary for tax policy in the Reagan and George H.W. Bush administrations, has been a continuing and guiding force in this effort.

74. Stephen Moore of the Club for Growth has suggested we do this at $150,000; we would suggest $25,000 to $50,000, enough to free up half the wealth tax budget for fair and progressive incentives.

75. If it is impossible to assess net worth annually and centrally, then income quintiles are the next best test.

76. Emergency savings accounts could also be set up separately from Prosperity Accounts using the model of rainy-day or side-car savings accounts, as have been proposed by bipartisan teams, even in this divided Congress.

Photography Credits

Index

About the Author

Robert E. Friedman is founder and chair emeritus of Prosperity Now, formerly the Corporation for Enterprise Development (CFED), a national economic development nonprofit founded in 1979. He helped create the U.S. microenterprise savings and asset-building fields and the international enterprise development and child savings fields. He lives in San Mateo, California.

Publishing in the Public Interest

Thank you for reading this book published by The New Press. The New Press is a nonprofit, public interest publisher. New Press books and authors play a crucial role in sparking conversations about the key political and social issues of our day.

We hope you enjoyed this book and that you will stay in touch with The New Press. Here are a few ways to stay up to date with our books, events, and the issues we cover:

- Sign up at www.thenewpress.com/subscribe to receive updates on New Press authors and issues and to be notified about local events
- Like us on Facebook: www.facebook.com/newpressbooks
- Follow us on Twitter: www.twitter.com/thenewpress

Please consider buying New Press books for yourself; for friends and family; or to donate to schools, libraries, community centers, prison libraries, and other organizations involved with the issues our authors write about.

The New Press is a 501(c)(3) nonprofit organization. You can also support our work with a tax-deductible gift by visiting www.thenewpress.com/donate.